STEVE BIRNBAUM

BRINGS YOU THE BEST OF

Walt Disney World ®

STEPHEN BIRNBAUM
EDITOR

PAUL POSNICK
DESIGN DIRECTOR

KAREN CURE
EXECUTIVE EDITOR

ASSOCIATE EDITORS
Edward H. Fitzelle
Jessie Hunter
Sandra Miller
David Walker

HOUGHTON MIFFLIN COMPANY & DIVERSION COMMUNICATIONS, INC.

CONTENTS

need to organize your WDW visit right down to the smallest detail: When To Go; Reservations; How To Get There; Answers To The Tough Questions On Budgets and Packages; Hints On Traveling With Children; Hints For The Handicapped, For Singles, and For Older Visitors; plus lots of other useful information.

AND ACCOMMODATIONS

Similarly, the complex transportation system within the World moves millions of visitors by monorail, bus, and various waterborne vehicles. It's organized to provide swift, efficient access to all facilities, but it is complicated. Here are all the details.

THE MAGIC KINGDOM

Here is a land-by-land guide to all that there is to see and do, where to shop, and how to avoid the crowds, plus lots of other special tips to make your visit most pleasant and most rewarding.

ELSE IN THE WORLD

Whether you want to ride down high watery slides, shop at elegant boutiques, wander among exotic birds, or "go to school" behind the scenes, here's all the information you need.

It's very easy to combine all these athletic endeavors with all the rest of the fun that Walt Disney World offers, and lots of sports activities are available to turn your visit into the best sort of well-rounded holiday.

AND GREAT TIMES

rea-by-area directories that let you know which restaurants are where and what pecialties they offer. From fried ice cream to special French toast, we put all the dining hoices right on your plate.

CONVENTIONS

ogether. Here's all the information you need to help plan a perfect onference or seminar, plus all the opportunities for nearby accommo- ations and the best possible after-hours diversions.

omplement to the World's own attractions, with all sorts of restaurants, hops, and other sights to see. Here is comprehensive data on the world urrounding Walt Disney World, with emphasis on its major urban center.

For Alex, who went on all the rides.

ISBN: 0-395-31792-4

Printed in the United States of America

A WORD FROM THE EDITOR

I suspect that my wife may be the most blasé traveler I know. I've actually come home and asked if she'd like to go to Paris for the weekend, only to have her answer that she was planning to wash her hair.

So you can understand why I was a little apprehensive the first time I asked her if she'd like to spend a few days at Walt Disney World. It is perhaps the ultimate tribute to the appeal of this extraordinary place that my otherwise demure and dignified spouse immediately began jumping up and down, screaming, "Can we go on all the rides?"

My wife's reaction was clearly not very unusual, since Walt Disney World occupies the unique position of being the most popular man-made attraction on this planet. On a slow day (admittedly a relative term, and usually the by-product of unseasonable cold, wind, or rain), more than 15,000 visitors still find their way onto the grounds, while a really busy day in the Magic Kingdom can mean as many as 90,000 souls streaming onto the premises. As a matter of fact, as we went to press, the record for a single day's attendance was nearly 93,000 visitors, all of whom visited the Magic Kingdom on December 31, 1980—without the park ever having to close because of overcrowding. It was a memorable day.

Because I first experienced Walt Disney World as an unescorted raw tourist, I feel eminently qualified to edit this new guide. I feel I'm able to lead readers to Walt Disney World because I personally made just about every possible error an unknowing guest could make. Like many other uninitiated visitors before me, I wasted enormous amounts of time by queuing up for attractions I should have left for another time during the day, and finally missed a lot of things I really wanted to see because time ran short. I didn't allow enough days to do even a large fraction of all that was available, and I even chose the wrong time of the year to come to the park as a first-timer. I picked one of the most crowded times, when the mass of other visitors made orientation difficult and exaggerated every problem that one encounters at any truly popular destination.

I also committed the ultimate sin where Walt Disney World is concerned: I believed that the Magic Kingdom amusement area was all that Walt Disney World included. So the pleasures of places like River Country, Discovery Island, and the trio of first-class golf courses were never encountered by me until far later in the course of the research for this guide.

So what we've tried to do in designing this book is

to keep you and yours from making the same mistakes that dogged my own early encounters with Walt Disney World. Even the most willing vacation planner needs adequate information in order to prepare an intelligent itinerary and daily plan, and what we hope we've done is to organize all the information necessary for a productive visit into as accessible and comprehensible a context as possible. Anyone who will take the time to read even the outlines of the chapters that follow will find an emerging pattern that fits his or her special tastes; for those unwilling to exert even that much effort, we've compiled specific prospective day-by-day itineraries for several lengths of visits in order to protect you from yourself.

Travel guides of any sort are, of course, ultimately reflections of personal taste, and putting one's name on a title page obviously places one's preferences on the line. But I think I ought to amplify exactly what "personal" means with reference to this book. Literally dozens of very talented people have worked on preparing this guide, and what you will read on the pages that follow is the collected wisdom of myself and Karen Cure, amplified and expanded by comments from other knowledgeable editors, friends, and Disney World staff members whose tastes most closely approximate our own. We've tried to avoid doggedly alliterative or oppressively onomatopoetic text in favor of simple, straightforward descriptions of what we think is good and bad.

So despite the considerable numbers of contributors, what follows is as close to the gospel according to Birnbaum as you're likely to find. It represents as much of my own taste and preferences as possible, and it's likely, therefore, that if you like your steak medium rare, your ice cream served only in a sugar cone, and can't tolerate fish that's been frozen or overcooked, we'll probably have a long and meaningful relationship. Readers with dissimilar tastes conceivably may be less enchanted.

This guidebook also owes an enormous debt to one of the most extraordinary groups of executives and operations people ever assembled—the ladies and gentlemen who manage and run Walt Disney World. Despite the designation of *Official Guide*, I must hasten to add that the Walt Disney World staff has exercised no veto power whatever over the contents of this book. Quite the contrary, they have opened their files and explained operations to us in the most generous way imaginable, so that we could prepare the comprehensive appraisals, charts, and schedules that were necessary to help visitors understand the very complex workings of a very complex enterprise.

I daresay there were times when Disney folk were less than delighted at some of our opinions or conclusions, yet these analyses all stayed in. Furthermore, we've been flattered again and again by Disney staff members who've commented about how much they've learned about some unfamiliar aspects of Walt Disney World from the material in this guide.

But the fact remains that this guide could never have been created without the extremely forthcoming cooperation of Walt Disney World personnel on every level. Both in the park and behind the scenes, they've been the source of the most critical factual data. I can only hope that I'm not omitting any name in thanking Jim Bertoluzzi (Foods); Sara Beverly and Larry Brooks (Wardrobe); Dave Pritchett, Linda Hallman, Clay Collier, and Dawn Condlin (Marketing); Ralph Mitchell and Dale Thornton (Casting); Bill Dennis (Disney University); Deede Sharpe (Wonders Program); Gary Hallman, Jim Beckwith, Gene Terrico, and Judy Daley (Operations); Spencer Craig and Jerry Szenfeld (Merchandise); Tom Rother and Ben Rossi (Entertainment); Bob MacKinnon (Resorts); John Dreyer and Bob Mervine (Publicity); Ed Beaver (Walt Disney Travel); Jean Besterman and Jim Rye (WDW Sales); Jim James (WDW Village Training); Danni Mikler (Guest Relations); Lee Blankenship and Marianne Raver (Central Reservations); Phil Ritson and Eric Frederickson (Golf Resort); Steve Babb (Tennis); Charlie Cook (Discovery Island); Phil Holmes (Transportation); Jill Krotky (Employee Relations); and Bob Obenour and Spencer Oberle (Fort Wilderness).

In addition, Joice Veselka of the Florida Division of Tourism, Bonnie Manjura of the Orlando Area Chamber of Commerce, and Norman Glass of the Greater Orlando Aviation Authority deserve a tip of the editor's pen for assistance well beyond the call of duty.

Most of all, we owe a debt of gratitude larger than we can say to those Walt Disney World executives and their staffs who believed in and nurtured this project, and who allowed us to do it—often against their basic instincts and better judgments. To Vince Jefferds, Bo Boyd, and Tom Elrod, there are no words to say thanks in quite the way we mean it. To Don MacLaughlin, Charlie Ridgway, Kathy Bruce, and Roni Wieners, who did so much to make our job easier (and often possible), more thanks for their extraordinary help.

Lastly, I should also point out that every worthwhile travel guide is a living enterprise; that is, this book may be our best effort at explaining how best to enjoy Walt Disney World at this moment, but its text is in no way cast in bronze. In our anticipated annual revisions, we expect to refine and expand our material to serve our readers' needs even better. To this end, no contribution is of greater value to us than *your* personal reaction to what we have written, as well as information about *your* own experiences while you were trying our suggestions. We eagerly and enthusiastically solicit your comments about this guide, and your opinions and perceptions based on your own visit. In this way, we are able to provide the best and most current information—including the actual experiences of individual travelers—and make it more readily available to others. So please write me at 60 East 42nd Street, New York, New York 10165.

I sincerely hope to hear from you.

GETTING READY TO GO

The key to a successful visit to Walt Disney World is advance planning. In the most simple terms, this vast attraction is just too complex and too varied to allow a spontaneous visit to be accomplished with notable success. That doesn't mean that even the most casual visitor can't have a fair amount of fun, but rather that such a visitor is likely to discover a host of opportunities that were missed because of the pressure of time or the absence of knowledge.

What follows, then, is intended to provide a sensible scheme for organizing a prospective visit to Walt Disney World, one that will allow the maximum amount of enjoyment and produce the minimum level of frustration.

WHEN TO GO

When talk finally turns to the best time to make a trip to Walt Disney World, Christmas and Easter are often mentioned, as well as summer vacation—especially if there are children in the family. But there are good reasons to avoid these periods, chief among them that almost everybody else goes then, and when Walt Disney World is crowded, it can be very crowded indeed. On the busiest days, visitors may wait more than an hour for admission to some particularly popular attraction—at least twice as long as at less crowded times of year.

Considering both the weather and crowd patterns described in the charts below, optimal times to visit WDW are September, October, and early November, the six weeks before and after spring school vacations, and the early part of June. Room reservations in the area are easiest to obtain from September through November. Youngsters who need to be taken out of school to visit at these times can enroll in WDW's new and innovative Wonders of Walt Disney World, a day-long educational program that uses the World as a classroom.

WDW WEATHER

	Average high	Average low	Mean	Average Rainfall
	Temperature			
January	70	50	60	2.28
February	72	51	62	2.95
March	76	56	66	3.46
April	82	61	71	2.72
May	87	66	76	2.94
June	89	71	80	7.11
July	90	73	81	8.29
August	90	74	82	6.73
September	88	72	80	7.20
October	82	76	74	4.07
November	76	57	67	1.56
December	72	52	62	1.90

SPECIAL EVENTS

INSIDE WALT DISNEY WORLD: Special festivities are staged to celebrate holidays throughout the year both in Walt Disney World Village and in the Magic Kingdom, where frequent special entertainment evenings are also held. For these, the park closes early, then reopens from 9 P.M. to 1:30 A.M., with top-name entertainment in the park's theaters. Part of a World Series of Entertainment (called the Tencennial Series of Entertainment in 1981–1982 in honor of WDW's tenth-birthday celebration), these are usually held around Valentine's Day, Halloween, and back-to-school time, as well as on scattered weekends throughout the year. Sales of tickets, while running into the thousands, are usually of a sufficiently small total that the park remains remarkably uncrowded. And since many visitors have come primarily to watch the performers, the rides and attractions remain remarkably uncongested, and any one of these special entertainment nights is an excellent time for a park visit—even if the entertainment doesn't particularly appeal to you.

Frequently throughout the year, WDW stages special promotions in the Magic Kingdom that salute Canadians, members of the Armed Forces, local residents, and Floridians by offering discounted Magic Kingdom passports. Dates for these can be obtained by calling 305-824-4321.

JANUARY: Walt Disney World New Year's Eve Celebration (Dec. 31). There are parties in all the hotels, and an extra-large fireworks display over the Magic Kingdom, which is open until 2 A.M. for the occasion. The celebration at the Top of the World, the stand-out, sells out a year in advance, despite the fact that it costs guests more than almost any other Disney wingding: not one but two top-name performers are on hand, and the glass-walled room gives a fantastic view of the pyrotechnics.

FEBRUARY: Valentine's Day festivities. On February 14, all the wonderful female Disney characters put in appearances in that day's parade. The weekend nearest the holiday is traditionally the occasion for a special evening opening of the Magic Kingdom, featuring rides and attractions and top-name performers; this year's Tencennial Series of Entertainment Valentine's Day event is scheduled for February 12 and 13.

MARCH 26: Tencennial Series of Entertainment.

EASTER SUNDAY: The Easter Parade. Comedians, antique-automobile club members and their vehicles, and the Easter Bunny all join in the act annually on Easter Sunday (this year, April 11) along with assorted other participants—usually carrying parasols and wearing ruffly finery and fancy hats. In the Magic Kingdom, during a very busy time of year.

JUNE 5: Tencennial Series of Entertainment.

JULY 4: Fourth of July Celebration. Fireworks are set off in the evening above the Cinderella Castle—

as is usual when the park is open until midnight—and over the Seven Seas Lagoon as well. Very busy.

SEPTEMBER 10–11: Tencennial Series of Entertainment.

OCTOBER: Walt Disney World National Team Championship Pro-Am. Top PGA tour players compete alongside amateurs in this big tourney, one of the most important events on the WDW calendar.

OCTOBER 31: Halloween. The most devilish of Disney characters—among them, Cruella de Ville from *101 Dalmations*, the Wicked Witch from *Snow White and the Seven Dwarfs*, and the magnificent Maleficent from *Sleeping Beauty*—participate in a special daytime parade in the Magic Kingdom; after dark, on a weekend night close to the holiday, the park is reopened for a special evening of top-name entertainment and rides and attractions. After dark on the holiday itself, youngsters can get dressed up and join Disney villains in another Halloween parade, this one at Walt Disney World Shopping Village.

NOVEMBER: Festival of Masters at Walt Disney World Shopping Village. One of the best of the area's art shows, this event draws exhibitors from all around the country. Only a small percentage of those who apply are chosen to show their work by the festival's jury, so the quality is high.

DECEMBER: Christmas celebrations. Nightly at Walt Disney World Shopping Village, from mid-month until the eve of the holiday, some 40 players present a nativity pageant. In the Magic Kingdom, a large, perfect Christmas tree is erected in Town Square; Main Street is decorated to the nines and patrolled by groups of carolers; a special Christmas parade is staged; and the park stays open late throughout the season.

OUTSIDE WALT DISNEY WORLD: A handful of major events in the Central Florida communities around Walt Disney World are also worth a visit.

JANUARY: Orlando; Scottish Highland Games. The sizable Scottish population of the area turns out in force for Highland dancing and bagpipe competitions, as well as such traditional field events as tossing of the caber. Scottish shops are also set up. Details: Scottish-American Society of Central Florida; Box 2948; Orlando, FL 32802; 305-277-5744.
Sarasota; Medieval Fair. A medieval town square is recreated on the grounds of the Ringling Museum complex. Costumed Sarasotans portray kings, queens, rooks, pawns, knights, and bishops as part of a living chess match, and there's singing and dancing, a royal procession, music, medieval morality plays, fire eating, and even belly dancing. Details: Ringling Museums; Box 1838; Sarasota, FL 33578; 813-355-5101.

Sarasota; International Kite Flying Contest. Prizes go to the largest, the most original, and the highest-flying at this competition staged at a large beachfront hotel. Details: Sheraton Sandcastle Hotel; 1540 Ben Franklin Dr.; Lido Beach, FL 33580; 813-388-2181.

FEBRUARY: Tampa; Gasparilla Pirate Invasion. Costumed as renegades of the pirate band led by the legendary José Gaspar, members of a local club sail into Tampa Harbor in a full-sized buccaneer ship (accompanied by a flotilla of local boats), claim the city as their own, and then parade through the streets. Among the activities during the subsequent two weeks are another raid, this one on Ybor City—Tampa's Latin quarter—and a Spanish bean soup day during which this thick, delectable broth is served free (along with Cuban bread and Cuban coffee). A torchlight parade to the fairgrounds, where the Florida State Fair is in progress, winds up the event. Details: Ye Mystic Krewe of Gasparilla; Box 1514; Tampa, FL 33601; 813-228-7338.

Daytona; Speed Weeks. All the top names in stock-car racing are on hand at the Daytona International Speedway for two weeks of almost-daily competitions, culminating in the Daytona 500. Details: Daytona Beach Area Chamber of Commerce; Box 2775; Daytona Beach, FL 32015; 904-255-0981.

Grant; Grant Seafood Festival. Some 50,000 visitors show up to eat fresh Indian River seafood at this huge affair staged by a small community just south of Titusville on Florida's east coast. Details: Seafood Festival; U.S. Highway 1; Grant, FL 32949; 305-389-5052.

Kissimmee; Silver Spurs Rodeo. This three-day event, held annually since 1944, draws professional cowboys from all over the United States and Canada to compete for thousands of dollars in prizes. Details: Kissimmee–St. Cloud Convention and Visitors Bureau; Box 2007; Kissimmee, FL 32741; 305-847-5000.

Orlando; Minnesota Twins Spring Training. The season at Tinker Field begins during the last week in February and runs through early March, with exhibition games nightly thereafter until the first week in April. The Orlando Twins, a farm team, play a full schedule during the summer months. Details: Orlando Office of Public Facilities; 400 W. Livingston St.; Orlando, FL 32801; 305-849-2185.

MARCH: Orlando; Bay Hill Classic. Held annually during the first week in March; Arnold Palmer hosts this $250,000 PGA Tour event, one of five in the state of Florida, at the Bay Hill Club. Details: Bay Hill Club; 9000 Bay Hill Blvd.; Orlando, FL 32811; 305-876-2888.

Winter Park; Winter Park Sidewalk Art Festival. Held annually during the third weekend of the month, this display of macrame, etchings, pottery, paintings, sculpture, and other crafts and artwork also features concerts, strolling musicians, and a folk sing; it's one of the most prestigious events of its type in the Southeast. The backdrop is a small municipal park full of ancient trees draped with Spanish moss; the town itself is as toney as they come in Central Florida, with its array of chic boutiques and elegant French restaurants. Details: Chamber of Commerce; Box 280; Winter Park, FL 32790; 305-644-8281.

APRIL: Titusville; Great Indian River Festival. This community near the Kennedy Space Center makes an annual tribute to the celebrated Indian River with a weekend of arts and crafts, carnival rides, food, and the Great Indian River Raft Race, in which any kind of craft that floats can participate. Details: Titusville Area Chamber of Commerce; Box 880; Titusville, FL 32780; 305-267-3036.

MAY: Sarasota; International Sandcastle Contest. Creative sand sculptors build whales, mermaids, poodles, sheep, and even an occasional castle on the beach in front of a local hotel. Details: Sheraton Sandcastle Hotel; 1540 Ben Franklin Dr.; Lido Beach, FL 33580; 813-388-2181.

Zellwood; Zellwood Sweet Corn Festival. The Zellwood area, about 20 miles northwest of Orlando, is famous for its production of sweet corn, and it celebrates its bounty every year at the end of May with this festival. There's a corn-eating contest and entertainment by bluegrass bands; corn is sold by the crate; and hundreds upon hundreds of ears are devoured at stands on the spot. Details: Carol Adkins; Box 628; Zellwood, FL 32798; 305-886-6987 or 305-886-0014.

JUNE: Kissimmee; Boat-A-Cade. *Reader's Digest* called this affair "the world's greatest outdoor event," for it brings Florida boat owners out in droves for a six-day cruise that begins on Lake Tohopekaliga and winds through state waters. Barbecues, banquets, and other land activities are staged at docking points en route. Details: Kissimmee Boat-A-Cade; Box 1855; Kissimmee, FL 32741; 305-847-5662.

OCTOBER: Kissimmee; Florida State Air Fair. The U.S. Navy's Blue Angels and the U.S. Air Force's Thunderbirds headline (in alternating years) a roster of activities that also includes aerial acrobatic demonstrations and aeronautical displays. Details: Kissimmee–St. Cloud Convention and Visitors Bureau; Box 2007; Kissimmee, FL 32741; 305-847-5000.

NOVEMBER: Orlando; Pioneer Day. Two days of folk music, square dancing, and other old-fashioned good times. Details: Pioneer Day; 5903 Randolph St.; Orlando, FL 32809; 305-855-7461.

DECEMBER: St. Petersburg; Florida Tournament of Bands. Marching bands from all over the state get together to compete for top honors in a series of concerts that will send shivers up and down the spines of anybody who ever loved a parade. Details: Florida Tournament of Bands; Box 1731; St. Petersburg, FL 33731; 813-898-3654.

MAGIC KINGDOM HOURS: Hours of operation in the theme park—which may also figure in decisions on when to go—vary from season to season. For about a third of the year—in September, October, parts of November and December, and all of January—the park is usually open from about 9 A.M. to 7

P.M. Hours are extended to 10 P.M. during Washington's Birthday week and during college spring breaks; and to midnight for summer and certain holiday periods (Thanksgiving weekend, Christmas, and the two weeks straddling Easter). On New Year's Eve, an additional couple of hours is added to the nighttime schedule.

Occasionally, during busy periods, the park may open earlier or close later. Call 305-824-4321 for up-to-the-minute details.

WHICH DAYS TO VISIT: Most visitors to Walt Disney World routinely assume that weekends are by far the busiest days on the property, but Saturday is busiest *only in the fall, not during the summer.* In the summertime, *the biggest crowds are usually found on Tuesdays*, with Wednesdays and Mondays just about as busy. Saturdays and Thursdays rank next. So it's a wise visitor who knows that Fridays are usually the quietest days of the week, with Sunday (particularly Sunday morning) the least crowded time in the Magic Kingdom.

HOW BIG ARE THE CROWDS?

The following statistics on the average number of people in the Magic Kingdom on any given day amply illustrate the optimal times for a visit.

January through the first week in February	20,000 to 28,000
Second week of February to beginning of Washington's Birthday week	30,000 to 40,000
Washington's Birthday week	40,000 to 55,000
The period from the end of Washington's Birthday week until college Spring Break week	30,000 to 40,000
College Spring Break week	40,000 to 55,000
The two weeks around Easter Sunday	45,000 to 65,000
Easter to early June	25,000 to 35,000
June through August	45,000 to 65,000
September through November	15,000 to 25,000
EXCEPTION: Thanksgiving weekend	45,000 to 60,000
Thanksgiving to Christmas (the slowest time of year)	12,000 to 18,000
Christmas Day through New Year's Day	60,000 to 80,000

What the Statistics Mean

10,000	.... Exclusive	50,000	.... Getting busy
20,000	.... Semi-private	60,000	.... Highly active
30,000	.... Festive but not jammed	70,000	.... Crowded
40,000	.... Longer lines but still comfortable	80,000 and up	... Body to body

PLANNING AHEAD

Mapping a trip takes time, but most travelers find that the increased enjoyment that comes from custom-tailoring a vacation to the family's individual tastes is well worth the effort.

This goes most smoothly when it's done in an organized fashion, and kids will enjoy WDW all the more if they're involved in the planning process, too. First, collect details about all the options from the various sources of travel information that are listed below. Then peruse these materials and begin to make specific decisions. Allow plenty of time for sightseeing and sports, and don't try to see and do too much.

SAMPLE SCHEDULES: The abundance of things to see and do around Orlando is such that it's no exaggeration to say that a visitor could stay in Central Florida for three weeks and not see everything. And no matter how well the pretrip research is done, it's hard to estimate just how long to spend where. As for Walt Disney World, it requires every bit of three days—two of them in the Magic Kingdom alone. Tackling the myriad attractions in less than that— say, a single day, as many vacationers do—is bound to be discouraging. The pressure of having so limited a number of hours to see so much will make even the least ominous line seem interminable, and short tempers born of frustration are bound to result. So travelers in a big hurry should either skip Walt Disney World altogether (and return to Central Florida when more time is available), or pass up all the other area attractions and concentrate exclusively on the Magic Kingdom. The suggested schedules described here provide some sense of the options that are available:

Two-Day Visit: Spend a full day and a half in the Magic Kingdom. On the second day, lunch in the Magic Kingdom and then head for River Country in the late afternoon (operating hours permitting). Enjoy one evening at an early performance of the Luau or the Hoop-Dee-Doo Revue, and afterward

head for the nearest beach to watch the Electrical Water Pageant. Be sure to check show times in advance. On your other night, go back to the Magic Kingdom (when it's open late) for dinner and the Main Street Electrical Parade, the fireworks, and (in certain seasons) another installment of the Electrical Water Pageant.

Nonswimmers may want to substitute a shopping excursion at Walt Disney World Shopping Village for the time suggested at River Country.

Three-Day Visit: Follow the same program outlined above for the first two days. On the third day, spend the morning in the Magic Kingdom, then head for Discovery Island around lunchtime, to spend the afternoon. Sandwiches are available aboard the narrated World Cruise, which goes to Discovery Island, or at the Snack Shop on the island itself. Start the evening early with drinks in the Baton Rouge Lounge aboard the riverboat restaurant *Empress Lilly* while waiting for dinner in the Steerman's Quarters or the Fisherman's Deck, two of the shipboard choices. Afterward, do some shopping in adjacent Walt Disney World Shopping Village. If you've still got energy left, stop at the Village Lounge to listen to some live jazz, or stroll back to the *Empress Lilly* and up to the elegant Empress Lounge, where a harpist entertains. (Jackets are required for men in the Empress Lounge.)

Four-Day Visit: Add some sports to the activities noted above. Spend a morning playing tennis or golf at the Golf Resort, and at lunchtime enjoy the salad bar and French fried ice cream at the Trophy Room there. Or go boating at the Polynesian Village and have lunch afterward at its Papeete Bay Verandah buffet. In the afternoon, try another sport—fishing or boating, perhaps—or go shopping at Walt Disney World Shopping Village and have a drink afterward at Cap'n Jack's there. Then take in one of the dinner shows you haven't seen. If no reservations are available, try the Village Restaurant at Walt Disney World Shopping Village, or have dinner and French fried ice cream in the Trophy Room at the Golf Resort, or, for an elegant treat, have dinner in the Gulf Coast Room on the second floor of the Contemporary Resort, and after-dinner drinks on the 15th-floor Top of the World Lounge—which offers a fine view of the fireworks over the Magic Kingdom.

Five- and Six-Day Visits: Spend a day at Sea World, the other at Cypress Gardens, lunching at restaurants in those areas. Late in the afternoon, you'll have time for more tennis, golf, or other sporting activities inside Walt Disney World. On the fifth day, spend the evening at a dinner show you've missed, and on the sixth, try one of the restaurants suggested above.

Seven-Day Visit: Head for Busch Gardens in Tampa (on Florida's west coast) for the day, or drive to Cape Canaveral and the Atlantic beaches to the east.

DO YOU NEED A CAR? Not if you're staying at a Walt Disney World resort. Public transportation within the World gets guests from point to point almost as quickly as a private car, and sometimes more so. And there's no parking problem. Those lodging outside the World can usually get to and from the Magic Kingdom by public transportation, or via their own hotels' bus service (which most hotels offer). Limos and cabs are also available, but a car is a must for taking in Orlando area restaurants and attractions.

INFORMATION SOURCES: For details about other things to see and do in Central Florida, contact the Florida Division of Tourism; 107 W. Gaines St.; Tallahassee, FL 32301; 904-487-1462. To find out about the area directly around Orlando, contact the Orlando Area Chamber of Commerce, Tourism Development/Visitor Inquiries; Box 1234; Orlando, FL 32802; 305-425-1234. And for general information about Walt Disney World, write the Walt Disney World Co.; Box 40; Lake Buena Vista, FL 32830; 305-824-4321.

Upon arrival at Walt Disney World, a variety of other information sources are available.

First, tune into the WDW radio station after entering the grounds—640 on the AM dial from inbound lanes. (Helpful information is broadcast to departing guests on 1200.)

At check-in, guests at all WDW-owned resorts—that is, the Contemporary Resort, the Golf Resort, the Polynesian Village, Fort Wilderness, and the Walt Disney World Village–area villas–are given copies of the *Magic Kingdom Guide* at no charge, plus the latest *Walt Disney World Vacation Guide*, detailing a variety of activities inside the World. In addition, all guests except those camping out at Fort Wilderness can tune to Channel 5 on their hotel-room television sets to see a filmed overview of all WDW attractions—a complete orientation tour of the property which is essential viewing for all first-time visitors. It's broadcast continuously. Guests at Walt Disney World Village Hotel Plaza establishments will see a similar program on Channel 7. (The latter gives somewhat more emphasis to the dining rooms and lounges at these lodging places, which, though located on WDW property, are neither Disney-owned nor Disney-operated.) For further information, guests at WDW properties can watch the daily program *Around the World Today*, which provides operating hours, name entertainers that are currently performing, special events, weather forecasts, and other useful information, on Channel 10. (This program is not shown outside WDW-owned lodging places.) For additional information, guests at WDW resorts should contact Guest Services. To do this, those staying at the Contemporary Resort, the Polynesian Village, and the Golf Resort should touch "1" on their room phones or house phones; Fort Wilderness campers should stop at the Pioneer Hall Information and Ticket Window or call extension 2788 from the

phones at the comfort stations located at the center of each campground loop area; and guests at Walt Disney World Village–area villas should call 828-2382. After 11 P.M., guests at all these WDW resort properties should call their respective front desks.

Day visitors: All day visitors—that is, those staying off the property, as well as those living in the Orlando area—receive a card detailing ticket prices and other useful information at the Toll Plaza at the entrance to the parking lots. City Hall distributes copies of the useful *Magic Kingdom Guide* at no charge, and this is the best source of practical information produced by the Disney organization. From off the property, day visitors should phone 824-4500.

Some hotels off the property—but not all of them—show their own version of the WDW resorts' Channel 5 orientation film; this attempts to give visitors an overview of all Central Florida attractions (WDW among them), rather than concentrating on the World.

For further information, phone WDW Guest Relations at 824-4321.

WHAT TO PACK: Walt Disney World is not so casual that all you need to bring is a bathing suit, but except for the dinner show at the Top of the World and dinner at the Empress Room aboard the *Empress Lilly* riverboat restaurant in Walt Disney World Village, where jackets are necessary for men, casual clothing is the rule. That means anything from T-shirts and cutoffs in the daytime to slacks or dresses in the evening. Men commonly wear sport jackets for dinner in fancier restaurants, but seldom ties. Bathing suits are a must, and a spare one is useful, as are the right togs for any other sports you might want to pursue. On the tennis courts, tennis whites are appropriate, though not required. Guests should bring lightweight sweaters even in summer—to wear indoors when the air conditioning gets too frigid. From November through March, warmer clothing is a must for evening wear. Always pack something to keep you comfortable should the weather turn unseasonably warm or cool. Especially in summer, lightweight rain gear and a folding umbrella come in handy.

And the most important item of clothing of all? Well broken-in walking shoes.

RESERVATIONS

Walt Disney World vacations go most smoothly when details are planned well ahead of time. Procrastinators may find no room at the inn, or no space left for a show that they wanted to see. Golf starting times, tennis courts, and other sporting activities, as well as dinner reservations and other special affairs, also should be reserved in advance.

Central Reservations Office: Many arrangements are handled by the Central Reservations Office (CRO); the phone number is 305-824-8000 or, for speakers of French, Spanish, German or Italian, 305-824-7900.

When calling, expect the phone to ring for a couple of minutes (up to five or even ten minutes during some very busy periods) before being answered. This is to avoid putting callers, most of whom are phoning long distance, on hold. The telephone system is handled by a computer that automatically puts calls in order, so don't hang up.

Have a pencil and paper close at hand when calling, to jot down dates and the number of your reservation.

Room Reservations: It is especially important to book accommodations in advance—up to two years in order to have your first choice of dates for visits during holiday periods, and 12 to 18 months ahead to get your pick of dates for a mid-summer visit. Even during other times of year, it's necessary to call six to nine months before arrival, and even then it may not be possible to get space in the precise resort you've selected, or the exact number of nights you wanted.

When Central Reservations can't accommodate your first preference, don't despair. Cancellations do come up. There are waiting lists for guests who have managed to reserve at least one evening of the multinight stay that they had originally requested. Visitors who were not able to arrange for a room at all may sometimes get one by calling later on. There is also a very slim chance of snagging space, left vacant by the occasional early departure, on the day of arrival; you can contact Central Reservations or get help from Guest Relations (at City Hall, the Transportation and Ticket Center, or at the individual hotel's front desk.)

Eastern Airlines: As the "Official Airline of Walt Disney World," Eastern Airlines has a substantial number of rooms specifically allocated for its use. Eastern is, therefore, a very good means of access to hard-to-book Walt Disney World-owned hotel rooms. These rooms are available as part of Eastern packages, which also have the added attraction of saving visitors some money on air fares as well.

Reservations for supper seatings, dinner shows, and sporting activities: Some of these are handled by Central Reservations, while others are handled by the individual restaurants and sporting centers. It's always wise to make your plans and reserve your place as far in advance as WDW policy will allow. Just how far in advance may vary, depending on where you lodge. (See chart below.)

Package vacationers take note: Your packages cover only the *cost* of dinner shows and activities, *not the reservations that may be necessary to enjoy them: It's up to the individual traveler to make all the specific bookings.* (Eastern Airlines can, however, confirm reservations for the Luau at the Polynesian Village for purchasers of its on-site packages.)

RESERVATION GUIDE

ACTIVITY	Phone for reservations (area code 305)	Advisability of reservations	Guests in WDW hotels/villas	Guests at WDW Village Hotel Plaza establishments	Guests at off-property hotels
How far in advance can reservations be made?					
Sports					
Golf starting times— all courses	824-3625	Necessary from February through April; a good idea at other times	As far ahead as desired, the year round	Ditto, except for play between January 1 and April 30; maximum five days ahead	
Walt Disney World Golf Studio, Golf Resort	824-3625	Necessary	.... No limit for any guest		
Private golf lessons, Golf Resort	824-3628	Necessary	.... No limit for any guest		
Private golf lessons, Lake Buena Vista course	828-3748	Necessary	.... No limit for any guest		
Tennis courts, Contemporary Resort Hotel	824-1000, ext. 3578	Suggested	.... 24 hours in advance		
Tennis courts, Golf Resort	824-2200	Suggested	.... 24 hours in advance		

ACTIVITY	Phone for reservations (area code 305)	Advisability of reservations	How far in advance can reservations be made?		
			Guests in WDW hotels/villas	Guests at WDW Village Hotel Plaza establishments	Guests at off-property hotels
Tennis courts, Lake Buena Vista Club	828-3741	Suggested	. . . . 24 hours in advance		
Tennis lessons, private and group, at all locations	824-1000, ext. 3578	Necessary	Up to three months in advance; most guests reserve a week or two ahead		
Trail rides, Fort Wilderness	828-2734	Necessary	. . . . Two days in advance		One week in advance
Fishing trips, Fort Wilderness	828-2757	Necessary	No more than five days; at least one day	. . . . Resort guests only	
Massages, Olympia Health Spa, Contemporary Resort Hotel	824-1000, ext. 3410	Necessary	Up to three months, but a day or two is sufficient	. . . . Resort guests only	
Good Meals					
Empress Room, *Empress Lilly* Riverboat, Walt Disney World Shopping Village	828-3900	Necessary	. . . . 30 days		
Lake Buena Vista Club	828-3735	Requested	Upon receipt of confirmed reservations	45 days	30 days
Gulf Coast Room, Contemporary Resort Hotel	824-1000, ext. 3684	Suggested	Upon receipt of confirmed reservations	45 days	30 days
Papeete Bay Verandah, Polynesian Village Resort Hotel	824-5494	Suggested	Upon receipt of confirmed reservations	45 days	30 days
Tangaroa Terrace, Polynesian Village Resort Hotel	824-2000	Suggested; available for dinner only	Upon receipt of confirmed reservations	45 days	30 days
Trophy Room, Golf Resort Hotel	824-2200, ext. 1484	Suggested; available for dinner only	Upon receipt of confirmed reservations	45 days	30 days
Great Times					
Top of the World Dinner Show, Contemporary Resort Hotel	824-8000	Necessary	. . . . 21 days for all		
Hoop-Dee-Doo Musical Revue, Pioneer Hall, Fort Wilderness	824-8000	Necessary	Upon receipt of confirmed reservations	45 days	30 days
Polynesian Revue, Polynesian Village Resort Hotel	824-8000	Necessary	Upon receipt of confirmed reservations	45 days	30 days
Breakfast a la Disney, *Empress Lilly* Riverboat	824-8000	Necessary	Upon receipt of confirmed reservations	45 days	30 days
Moonlight Cruise	824-1000	Requested	. . . . Up to 30 days for all		
Night of Wine and Roses, Lake Buena Vista Club; offered May through September only	828-3735	Necessary	. . . . Up to 30 days for all		
Marshmallow Marsh Excursion, Fort Wilderness	828-2788	Necessary	Four days	. . . . Resort guests only	
Sunday Brunches					
Top of the World, Contemporary Resort Hotel	824-1000	Recommended	Upon receipt of confirmed reservations	45 days	30 days
Papeete Bay, Polynesian Village Resort Hotel	824-2000	Recommended	Upon receipt of confirmed reservations	45 days	30 days
Trophy Room, Golf Resort Hotel	824-2200, ext. 1484	Recommended	Upon receipt of confirmed reservations	45 days	30 days
Lake Buena Vista Club	828-3735	Recommended	Upon receipt of confirmed reservations	45 days	30 days

HOW TO GET THERE

The preponderance of visitors who come to Walt Disney World arrive by car. This is a by-product of perceived economy—though this is not always the case—and also because a Walt Disney World holiday is usually part of a somewhat broader tour around Central Florida.

BY CAR

Here are some suggested routes to WDW from the downtown areas of several major metropolitan areas, as recommended by the American Automobile Association.

Figure on driving 350 to 400 miles a day—a reasonable distance that won't wear you down so much that you can't enjoy your stay.

Atlanta: I-75 south, Florida Turnpike south, U.S. 27 south, Rte. 192 east. Total mileage: 438.

Baltimore: I-95 south, I-4 west, Rte. 192 west. Total mileage: 929.

Boston: Massachusetts Turnpike, I-86 south to Hartford, I-84 west, I-684 south, 287 west, Garden State Parkway south, New Jersey Turnpike south to the Delaware Memorial Bridge, I-95 south (through the Harbor Tunnel), I-4 west, Rte. 192 west. Total mileage: 1,352.

Buffalo: I-90, I-79, Rte. 19, West Virginia Turnpike, I-77 south, I-20 west, I-26 south, I-95 south, I-4 west, Rte. 192 west. Total mileage: 1,320.

Chicago: I-65 to Nashville, I-24 to Chattanooga, I-75 south, Florida Turnpike south, U.S.-27 south, Rte. 192 east. Total mileage: 1,190.

Cincinnati: I-75 south, Florida Turnpike south, U.S.-27 south, Rte. 192 east. Total mileage: 949.

Cleveland: I-71 south, I-76 east, I-77 south, I-20 west, I-26 south, I-95 south, I-4 west, Rte. 192 west. Total mileage: 1,166.

Dallas: I-20 east to Shreveport, Rte. 1 to Alexandria, U.S.-71 south, U.S.-190 east, U.S.-1 south, I-10 east, I-12 east, I-10 east, I-75 south, Florida Turnpike east, U.S.-27 south, Rte. 192 east. Total mileage: 1,076.

Detroit: I-75 south, Florida Turnpike south, U.S.-27 south, Rte. 192 east. Total mileage: 1,225.

Indianapolis: I-65 south to Nashville, I-24 to Chattanooga, I-75 south, Florida Turnpike south, Rte. 192 east. Total mileage: 1,008.

Louisville: I-64 east to Lexington, I-75 south, Florida Turnpike south, U.S.-27 south, Rte. 192 east. Total mileage: 717.

Minneapolis: I-94 east, I-90 south, I-294 south, I-90 east, I-65 south to Indianapolis, I-465 south, I-65 south to Nashville, I-24 south to Chattanooga, I-75 south, Florida Turnpike south, U.S.-27 south, Rte. 192 east. Total mileage: 1,524.

New York City: Lincoln Tunnel to New Jersey Turnpike, south to Delaware Memorial Bridge, I-95 south (through Harbor Tunnel), I-4 west, Rte. 192 west. Total mileage: 1,126.

Pittsburgh: I-79 south, U.S.-19 south, West Virginia Turnpike south, I-77 south to Columbia (S.C.), I-20 west, I-26 south, I-95 south, I-4 west, Rte. 192 west. Total mileage: 1,093.

Philadelphia: I-95 south (through Harbor Tunnel), I-4 west, Rte. 192 west. Total mileage: 1,027.

Richmond: I-95 south, I-4 west, Rte. 192 west. Total mileage: 776.

Toronto: Queen Elizabeth Way south, I-90 south, I-290 south, I-79 south, U.S.-19 south, West Virginia Turnpike south, I-77 south to Columbia (S.C.), I-20 west, I-26 south, I-95 south, I-4 west, Rte. 192 west. Total mileage: 1,307.

AUTOMOBILE CLUBS: Reputable national automobile clubs can offer help with en route breakdowns; insurance that covers personal injury, accidents, arrest, bail bond, and lawyers' fees for defense of contested traffic cases; and travel planning services—not only advice, but also free maps and route-mapping. Programs vary from one club to the next; fees range from about $25 to $50 a year.

Among the leading clubs are the following:

Allstate Motor Club; 3701 West Lake; Glenview, IL 60025; 312-291-5461.

American Automobile Association; 8111 Gatehouse Rd.; Falls Church, VA 22047; 703-222-6000.

Amoco Motor Club; 3700 Wake Forest Rd.; Raleigh, NC 27609; 919-876-7500.

Ford Auto Club; PO Box 4219; South Bend, IN 46634; 800-348-5220.

Gulf Auto Club; PO Box 4189; South Bend, IN 46634; 800-348-5126 outside Indiana; 800-342-5666 in Indiana.

JTX Club Inc.; PO Box 13901; Philadelphia, PA 19101; 800-523-1965 outside Pennsylvania; 215-241-3223 in Pennsylvania.

Montgomery Ward Auto Club; 1400 W. Greenleaf Ave.; Chicago, IL 60626; 800-621-5151 outside Illinois; 800-572-5577 in Illinois; 312-973-7305 in Alaska.

Motor Club of America; 484 Central Ave.; Newark, NJ 07107; 201-733-1234.

United States Auto Club Motoring Division; 1720 Ruskin St.; South Bend, IN 46624; 219-236-3700.

FREE MAPS AND ROUTINGS: Those who don't belong to an automobile or travel club can get free maps from state tourist boards or from:

The Exxon Touring Service; 1251 Avenue of the Americas; New York, NY 10010.

The Mobil Travel Service; Box 25; Versailles, KY 40383.

The Texaco Touring Service; Box 1459; Houston, TX 77001.

Also excellent for main roads and routes is *Rand McNally's Road Atlas* (about $5.95 in bookstores).

BY BUS

Relatively few vacationers come to Walt Disney World by bus. But it makes sense to consider this means of transportation if you're traveling just a short distance or have plenty of time, if there are only two or three in your party, or if cost is a major consideration: bus travel is extremely economical.

Both Greyhound and Trailways provide frequent direct service into Orlando; some buses deposit their passengers on the very threshold of the Magic Kingdom, at the Transportation and Ticket Center (where there are lockers in which luggage can be stored until the end of the day). From there, taxis and limousines provided by the various area hotels and motels provide transportation to the lodging place that you have selected. For further information, phone Greyhound at 305-843-7720, or Trailways at 305-472-7107.

Sample Travel Times
Jacksonville, Florida . . . 2 to 2½ hours
Tallahassee, Florida . . . about 9 hours
Atlanta, Georgia . . . . about 11 hours
Charleston,
  South Carolina . . . . . . about 10 hours

BY TRAIN

Auto-Train, which once transported vacationers and their cars to Central Florida, is no more. But Amtrak still serves the Orlando area twice daily from New York City. The trip takes about 24 hours and costs in the neighborhood of $240, round-trip. Special discounted fares are sometimes available; it's a good idea to check.

Stops are made en route in Washington, D.C., Virginia, North Carolina, South Carolina, and Georgia.

BY AIR

The Orlando airport that arriving travelers encountered in the early 1970s is a far cry from the sleek, brand-new, multimillion-dollar international facility that greets vacationers today. Back then, only four airlines served the city; now, there are more than a dozen offering direct flights from all parts of the country. Eastern Airlines alone—the "Official Airline of Walt Disney World"—carries more than a million passengers into Orlando annually, on nonstop flights from more than 20 cities, direct flights (not including a change of planes) and connecting flights from 67 more—so many that more than 30 ticketing positions, 10 gates, its own baggage claim area, and a special desk to serve Eastern's tour-package purchasers are required to handle them all. Over the years, Eastern's special style of service, with special meals and "Fun Flight" gift kits for youngsters, has grown up around the flourishing Walt Disney World/ Central Florida trade.

The airline you decide to fly will depend in large part on where you live, when you'll be traveling, and which airline can get you there when you want to go, for the price you want to pay. Remember, direct flights—those whose lure is that they do not include a change of planes—are not always the swiftest way to get from point to point. If your itinerary requires several stops, it might be wise to investigate all of the possible connection alternatives.

THE WINGS OF THE WORLD

As the "Official Airline of Walt Disney World," Eastern Airlines not only has its own attraction, If You Had Wings, in the Magic Kingdom, but also its own ticket offices right on the property—one right inside its Magic Kingdom attraction, the other on the first-floor lobby of the Contemporary Resort Hotel. The close Disney-Eastern relationship also means that when guests make a reservation at a Walt Disney World hotel, the Central Reservations Office also can arrange for an Eastern representative to call and help with flight arrangements. It couldn't be easier. Eastern's passengers also benefit from the tie by being able to fly on the only airline that is able to offer packages that include lodgings at the Contemporary Resort, the Polynesian Village, and the Golf Resort. It is not an insignificant advantage.

DISCOVERING THE LOWEST AIR FARE

Gone are the days when it always cost a finite number of dollars to get from point A to point B, so it's more important than ever before to shop around.

Find out the names of all the airlines that serve your destination, then call them all—more than once if your route is complex. Tell the agent how many people there are in your party, and emphasize that you're interested in economy. The more flexible you can be in your dates and duration of stay, the more money you're likely to save. Fares are usually lowest on highly competitive, heavily traveled routes; if you live halfway between two airports—one a major city, the other relatively untraveled—you may do better from one than from the other. Check both.

- Watch the newspapers for ads announcing new promotional fares.

- When it's necessary to change planes en route, it's best to stick with one airline; the agent will know his or her own company's routing—and its discounted fares—better than those offered by other carriers. (For the same reason, smart travelers book all of a trip through the carrier they'll be using most.)

- Fly when other people don't—at night; on weekends on routes that usually serve business travelers; or midweek to and from vacation destinations.

- Plan ahead. Most carriers guarantee their fares—which means that you won't have to pay extra to use a valid ticket even if fares go up after you buy it. (But if your ticket has to be rewritten due to a change in dates or times of flights, you'll probably have to pay any new fare.) So pick up and pay for your ticket as soon as possible—before fares go up.

WHICH AIRLINE
FLIES FROM YOUR CITY?

You can fly directly to Orlando—that is, without changing planes—from about 50 different cities, on more than a dozen airlines. Schedules do change from time to time, and flights occasionally are dropped or new ones added. This was the operative direct and same-airline connecting service at press time:

NONSTOP/DIRECT/
CONNECTING SERVICE

Akron/Canton, OH	UA
Albany, NY	US
Albuquerque, NM	EA, AA
Alexandria, LA	DL
Allentown, PA	EA, US
Amarillo, TX	AA, BN
Asheville, NC	PI
Atlanta, GA	EA, DL, NW, RC
Atlantic City, NJ	US
Augusta, GA	DL
Austin, TX	EA, AA, DL, BN
Baltimore, MD	EA, US, PI, DL
Bangor, ME	DL
Baton Rouge, LA	RC, DL, AA
Birmingham, AL	EA, RC, DL
Boise, ID	UA
Boston, MA	EA, NW, DL, US
Brainerd, MN	RC
Brownsville, TX	BN
Buffalo, NY	EA, US, UA
Burlington, VT	DL
Cape Girardeau, MO	OZ
Cedar Rapids/ Iowa City, IA	UA, OZ
Champaign, IL	OZ
Charleston, SC	EA, DL
Charleston, WV	PI, US
Charlotte, NC	EA, PI, DL
Chattanooga, TN	DL
Chicago, IL	EA, UA, DL, OZ
Cincinnati, OH	DL
Cleveland, OH	EA, UA, RC, DL, US
Columbia, MO	OZ
Columbia, SC	EA, DL
Columbus, GA	DL
Columbus, MS	RC
Columbus, OH	EA, US, DL
Corpus Christi, TX	AA, BN
Dallas/ Fort Worth, TX	EA, AA, BN, DL, QH, PI
Dayton, OH	DL
Decatur, IL	OZ
Denver, CO	EA, UA, DL, BN, RC
Des Moines, IA	OZ, UA, TW
Detroit, MI	EA, DL, RC, TW, US
Duluth, MN	RC
Eau Claire, WI	RC
El Paso, TX	EA, AA
Evansville, IN	EA, DL
Fargo, ND	RC

Fayetteville, NC .... PI
Ft. Lauderdale, FL .... RC, DL, QH
Ft. Wayne, IN .... DL
Fresno, CA .... UA
Grand Forks, ND................... RC
Grand Rapids, MI .... UA, US, RC
Greensboro/High Point/....... EA, PI, DL
  Winston-Salem, NC
Greenville/ .... EA
  Spartanburg, SC
Hartford, CT/ .... EA, DL, US
  Springfield, MA
Houston, TX .... EA, PA, DL, QH, BN,
                              PI, AA
Huntsville/Decatur, AL .... RC
Indianapolis, IN .... EA, OZ, DL
Iron Mountain, MI .... RC
Jackson, MI .... RC
Jackson/Vicksburg, MS .... DL
Jefferson City, MO .... OZ
Kalamazoo, MI .... RC
Kansas City, MO.... BN, DL, OZ, TW, UA
Kinston, NC .... PI, DL
Knoxville, TN .... DL
Lansing, MI .... RC
Las Vegas, NV ..EA, BN, AA, DL, UA, PA
Lexington/Frankfort, KY.............. DL
Little Rock, AR .... TW, DL
Los Angeles, CA .... EA, DL, PA, AA,
                              BN, UA
Louisville, KY.................... EA, DL
Lubbock, TX .... AA, BN
Madison, WI .... NW
Marion, IL .... OZ
Memphis, TN.................. RC, DL
Miami,FL .. EA, RC, PA, DL, QH, OZ, NW
Midland/ .... AA, BN
  Odessa, TX
Milwaukee, WI......... EA, NW, OZ, RC
Minneapolis/... EA, RC, NW, OZ, UA, US,
  St. Paul, MN   BN, AA
Mobile, AL/................. EA, PA, RC
  Pascagoula, MS
Moline, IL .... OZ, UA
Monroe, LA .... RC
Monterey, CA .... UA
Montgomery, AL................ RC, DL
Montreal, Que .... RC, DL
Muscle Shoals, AL .... RC
Muskegon, MI .... RC
Myrtle Beach, SC .... PI
Nashville, TN .... EA, RC, DL, PI
New Orleans, LA........ EA, PA, DL, RC
New York/...... EA, TW, PA, DL, US, QH
  Newark
Norfolk/..................... EA, PI, US
  Virginia Beach, VA
Oklahoma City, OK .... EA, TW, BN
Omaha, NE .... EA, TW, UA, BN

Ontario, CA .... AA, UA
Panama City, FL.................... RC
Pensacola, FL................. EA, PA
Peoria, IL .... OZ, TW
Philadelphia, PA/........... EA, US, DL
  Wilmington, DE
Phoenix, AZ .... EA, UA, TW, AA, DL,
                              BN, PA
Pittsburgh, PA.............. EA, US, UA
Portland, ME...................... DL
Portland, OR .... UA, AA
Providence, RI .... EA, US
Quincy, IL .... OZ
Raleigh/Durham, NC .... EA, PI, DL
Reno, NV................. UA, BN, AA
Richmond, VA................... EA, PI
Roanoke, VA .... PI
Rochester, MN .... NW
Rochester, NY .... EA, US, UA
Sacramento, CA................. UA, AA
Saginaw, MI .... RC
St. Louis, MO ...... EA, OZ, TW, DL, RC
Salt Lake City, UT....... EA, DL, AA, UA
San Antonio, TX .... EA, AA, BN, DL
San Diego, CA .... PA, DL, UA, AA
San Francisco/ ......EA, DL, UA, PA, AA
  Oakland, CA
San Jose, CA .... UA, AA
San Juan, PR .... EA, DL, PA
Santa Barbara, CA.................. UA
Savannah, GA .... EA, DL
Seattle/......... EA, UA, AA, PA, DL, BN
  Tacoma, WA
Shreveport, LA .... DL, AA
Sioux City, IA .... OZ
Sioux Falls, SD.................... RC
South Bend, IN .... RC
Spokane, WA .... UA
Springfield, IL .... OZ
Springfield, MO.................... OZ
Syracuse, NY .... EA, US
Tallahassee, FL .... EA, RC, QH
Toledo, OH .... QH, DL, US
Toronto, Ont................ EA, US, RC
Traverse City, MI .... RC
Tri-City Airport, TN .... PI
Tucson, AZ .... UA, AA
Tulsa, OK.......... BN, AA, OZ, TW, DL
Vancouver, B.C..................... UA
Washington, DC ..... EA, PA, US, PI, DL
Waterloo, IA....................... OZ
Wichita, KS .... TW, RC, BN
Wilmington, NC...................... PI

ABBREVIATIONS—AA: American Airlines.
BN: Braniff. DL: Delta. EA: Eastern.
NW: Northwest. OZ: Ozark. PA: Pan Am.
PI: Piedmont. QH: Air Florida.
RC: Republic. TW: TWA. UA: United.
US: US Air.

TOUGH QUESTIONS

SHOULD YOU BUY A PACKAGE?

The vast array of Central Florida vacation packages can bewilder even the savviest traveler. In some cases, the chief advantage of buying a package is the convenience of having a vacation already planned in detail. In others, the package offers a savings over the total cost of its various elements if these items were purchased separately. (Eastern Airlines' Super 7 packages, for example, cost lots less than conventional round trip coach airfare from most cities, though they also include accommodations, a rental car with unlimited mileage for a week, and two days' admission to the Magic Kingdom and unlimited use of its attractions.)

Some Central Florida packages include off-site accommodations in a variety of price ranges, while some of those put together as a convenience by Walt Disney World, Eastern Airlines, and American Express can be purchased with lodgings in WDW's own properties. Some packages don't include hotel rooms at all. Some provide purchasers with admission to the Magic Kingdom, rental cars, local bus transportation, coupons for dinner or sporting activities, or other goodies; some do not. Be sure you know precisely what you are buying.

To find the package that's right for you, it's first necessary to decide just what sort of vacation you want. The various sections of this book describe the activities and attractions available in and around Walt Disney World in some detail. Know what's available, and then, by calling airlines that fly between your city and Orlando or by working with your hometown travel agent, find the package that comes closest to the vacation you've envisioned.

Don't pick a package that includes elements that you don't want or won't use, because you're paying for them. And remember that while offerings like welcome cocktails sound attractive, their cash value is negligible. Also note that some packages announce as selling points certain services that are actually available to every Magic Kingdom guest. (For instance, monorail transportation, boasted of in some package brochures, *never* costs extra to holders of any Magic Kingdom admission media.)

On the other hand, there is real value in certain other features. Purchasers of Eastern's tour packages may, for example, opt for a three-day passport ordinarily available only to guests at WDW resorts; the additional cost, about $7, represents a small savings over the price of this same passport if purchased at the WDW hotels. Some of Eastern's packages also include a breakfast with the Walt Disney World characters; other packages include golf or tennis lessons, green fees or court charges, half-hour boat rentals, and the like.

SHOULD YOU USE A TRAVEL AGENT?

Our answer has to be an unqualified "maybe." There have been some complaints from travelers who've found their travel agents less than eager to book Walt Disney World accommodations. The reason is not terribly obscure: No direct commissions are paid to travel agents by Walt Disney World for bookings in the Walt Disney-owned hotels—the Contemporary Resort, Polynesian Village, and Golf Resort. So there's little financial incentive to motivate agents to try to help fill these properties. Travel agents

do, however, receive commissions from the four hotels in the Walt Disney World Village Hotel Plaza—Travelodge, Howard Johnson's, the Royal Plaza, and the Dutch Inn—and several airlines also pay commissions on package arrangements. (Eastern's packages even include on-site accommodations.) Our suggestion, therefore, is that you call Central Reservations yourself (305-824-8000) if you get a vague answer from your travel agent on availabilities in the Walt Disney World hotels.

HOW TO CUT TRAVEL COSTS

Between general inflation and the rising cost of gasoline, vacations are not getting any less expensive. Yet scrapping the annual family getaway is no answer. It's better to simply prune the vacation budget in three main areas:

Food: Get hot meals in cafeterias instead of waitress-service restaurants. Visit fancier establishments at lunchtime rather than dinner. (The very same entrees usually cost less then.) Carry sandwich fixings and have lunches alfresco when possible. Look for lodging places with kitchen facilities: The savings on food, especially for families, may be more than the extra accommodations expense.

Lodging: The chief rule of thumb here is not to pay for more than you need. Budget chains such as Days Inns and Days Lodges, Suisse Chalet Motor Lodges and Inns, Imperial 400 Motor Inns, Passport Inns and Downtowners, Red Roof Inns, Family Inns of America, and Motel 6's can prove economical, though they may not offer many frills. (The best single guide to their whereabouts from coast to coast is the *National Directory of Budget Motels*, revised annually and available for $3.50 from Pilot Books; 347 Fifth Ave.; New York, NY 10016; 212-685-0736.)

If swimming pools and other amenities matter, consider the nonbudget chain establishments that have them—but remember that cutoff ages (above which there is a charge for children sharing parents' room) do vary. At Holiday Inns, children over 13 count as extra adults, while Quality Inns charge for youngsters over 17—and Sheratons, Rodeways, and Howard Johnson's charge for young people over 18. Ramada Inns and Marriotts don't charge until offspring reach 19. Get prices for Orlando area hostelries in advance, then calculate the exact costs for your whole family.

Depending on the number of people in your party, guest houses and tourist homes may or may not be a good buy. Since these establishments usually levy substantial extra charges for more than two people, regardless of their ages, rooms that are inexpensive for two can prove costly for a family. Consult the small guidebook ($5) published by Tourist Home Associates Inc. (RD 2; Box 355A; Greentown, PA 18426) for locations and prices. Also look into the Bed and Breakfast League of America (2855 29th St. N.W.; Washington, DC 20008); the membership fee (around $35) entitles members to lodge in a number of establishments with prices pegged around $15 to $30 a night (including breakfast) for two.

Also consider traveling with another family. At Walt Disney World, for instance, the cost for a three-bedroom villa that sleeps eight is only about $40 more than for a one-bedroom apartment that accommodates just four. That can mean a savings of about $20 per night per family.

Transportation: Comparative shopping is vital. Consider transportation needs at your destination, then figure the total transportation cost. Calculate the cost of driving based on your car's mileage, current gasoline prices, the distance you expect to cover, and the cost of accommodations and food en route; then figure what you'll pay by bus, plane, or train. Don't fail to add in the cost of getting to and from the airport or terminal, and the cost of renting a car (if necessary) in Orlando. And remember that special low fares that are economical for couples can sometimes prove less advantageous for families.

Remember too, that the lowest air fares to Orlando at press time were those called "tour basing." This is a technical term connoting an air fare that is part of a package that includes land arrangements as well.

During the designing of the Magic Kingdom, one of the most important steps was the making of a scale model. Then, using a small periscope-like device with a rectangular viewing screen, they looked at the model from the same viewpoint that today's visitors see the finished product through their cameras. So if the scenery hereabouts makes you instinctively want to reach for your camera, it's because it was laid out to do so. In fact, some 150,000,000 photos are snapped here every year.

Of course, there are limitations to what any camera can do. No camera can capture all the charm and the life of the Magic Kingdom in quite the same way that it's perceived when the colors crowd your peripheral vision and the boom-boom-boom of the drums of an approaching marching band assails your ears.

Nonetheless, there are so many other wonderful images to be snatched in the Magic Kingdom, that just about any camera in good working order can get them for you, so long as you use the right techniques. Here are some hints:

- Don't shoot from closer than 4 feet from your subject, and don't try for a flash picture more than 12 feet away. The former will probably turn out fuzzy, and the latter likely will prove dark. Note that flash attachments can't illuminate a subject more than a dozen feet distant. (Important: Flash photography is prohibited inside the Magic Kingdom's attractions.)

- Fill the frame with as much of the subject as possible. Especially when shooting people, remember that the larger the subject appears in the picture, the more interesting it will be.

- Hold the camera steady as you *gently* squeeze the shutter.

- Don't shoot into the sun. The camera's electric eye will assume that there's more light on the subject than there actually is, and the image will turn out too dark in the snapshot. Instead, position yourself so that light is falling directly on your subject—coming from behind you or from the side.

- Check the camera's batteries and battery contacts regularly.

- Use film that is fresh. When purchasing film, check the expiration date stamped on the bottom of the box. Keep the film as cool as possible; don't leave it in a hot car for long periods of time.

- Keep the camera clean. Blow dust off the lens and then wipe it with a soft tissue. Blow dust out of the inside of the camera.

- When taking movies or using videotape cameras, note that they'll be more effective if you pick a theme such as "A Walk Down Main Street," or the like. Don't shoot into the sun, and make sure that all subject matter is evenly lighted. Pan very slowly and smoothly, and give every scene plenty of time—at least five seconds. Don't use the zoom lens too often; it can be distracting.

- If you suspect that your camera isn't functioning correctly, visit the Polaroid Camera Center on the east side of Main Street near Town Square.

Rental cameras: One of the best deals in the Magic Kingdom is the free camera rental offered at the Polaroid Camera Center. You must leave a deposit (cash or MasterCard): $50 for a Sonar One-Step or $100 for a Polaroid Polavision instant movie camera. All you pay for is the film.

A variety of other cameras is also available: Vivitar 110s, Kodak 110 Pocket Instamatics, Kodak 126 Instamatics, and Kodak 110s with built-in flash. Deposits of up to $25 or so are required; the modest rental fee (about $5) includes the price of a 20-exposure roll of film.

Camera repairs: Those of a minor nature can be handled by the Camera Center.

Film processing: Exposed film can be left for processing at Mickey's Film Express, at the Camera Center in the Magic Kingdom, or at Fort Wilderness or the hotels. Processing takes seven to ten days.

THE BEST PHOTOS

WHERE TO BUY FILM

Walt Disney World is one of the largest retail outlets in the world for postcards and film.

Magic Kingdom

Main Street—Camera Center, Emporium
Adventureland—Tropic Toppers
Frontierland—Frontier Trading Post
Liberty Square—Heritage House
Fantasyland—Castle Camera, Royal Candy Shoppe

In the Hotels

Contemporary Resort—Plaza Gifts & Sundries
Golf Resort—Golf Gifts and Sundries
Polynesian Village—News from Civilization

At Walt Disney World Shopping Village

Village Gifts and Sundries

THE MAGIC KINGDOM'S BLUE RIBBON PHOTO SPOTS. Certain locations in the Magic Kingdom seem made for family photos:

- The bridge by the Crystal Palace, with Cinderella Castle in the background.
- Anywhere right in front of the Castle.
- The Milk Cart in Town Square, at the top of Main Street.
- Fuente de la Fortuna, the fountain opposite Pirates of the Caribbean, next to the stage where the steel drum band usually plays, in Adventureland.
- In front of the Singing Drums, opposite the Enchanted Tiki Birds pavilion, in Adventureland. The drums start beating every four or five minutes.
- The stocks in Liberty Square.
- On the Barrel Bridge at Tom Sawyer Island.
- With the characters when they make their daily appearances in the Castle Forecourt or in front of City Hall. The character breakfasts or dinners are also good bets.
- Outside the Magic Kingdom, near the topiaries on the main entrance road.

HOW TO PHOTOGRAPH FIREWORKS: You need a camera with a manually adjustable aperture and shutter speed. Set your camera on a tripod, or arrange to brace it in some other way; set the aperture at f8 and the shutter speed at B; and hold the lens open for three to five seconds at each burst. (Cover the lens with your hand between explosions.)

HOW TO PHOTOGRAPH THE MAIN STREET ELECTRICAL PARADE: Using an adjustable camera with a normal or wide-angle lens, open the aperture as wide as possible to f1.4 or 4/2.8, and shoot at around 1/15 or 1/30 second, using fast films such as Kodacolor 400 (for prints), Ektachrome 160 Tungsten, or Ektachrome 400 Daylight (faster, though it yellows colors slightly). To get an artistic blur, slowly pan with the camera as the float moves past. No tripod is necessary, though a steady hand assures best results.

HINTS ON TRAVELING

Tell youngsters that a Walt Disney World vacation is in the works and the response is apt to be nothing less than overwhelming—and the journey to the park is likely to be fraught with "Are-we-there-yets?" recurring like a stuck record.

En Route: Certain ploys can quiet this refrain. Get older children involved in planning every leg of the trip, and set up a series of intermediate goals to which they can look forward. Younger children can anticipate discovering the contents of a pint-sized suitcase packed with familiar games and toys, plus a few surprises.

In addition, it's smart to take along snacks to keep things peaceful when stomachs start rumbling and food is miles away. Above all, and especially if the trip is by car, take it easy, and allow time for plenty of breaks en route.

Those who fly should schedule travel for off-peak hours, when the chances are better that extra seats will be available. When the plane is taking off and

landing, babies should be given bottles, pacifiers, or even thumbs to promote swallowing and clear ears; a piece of gum or hard candy will provide the same relief for a small child. Newborn babies (those only a couple of weeks old) should not be taken aloft, since their lungs may not be able to adjust to the altitude. For finicky young eaters, request special meals when reserving seats. Eastern Airlines offers a kiddie repast called a Fun Flight Meal—fruit, juice, and cereal for breakfast; and an all-beef hot dog, potato chips, milkshake, chocolate chip cookies, a banana, raisins, and a special Walt Disney World lollipop for lunch or dinner. The meal comes in a box decorated with Disney characters, and is a special treat for kids. Remember, these meals must be ordered when your plane reservations are made. In addition, many airlines offer baby food; some—Eastern again stands out—have terrific packages of goodies for young travelers (ask for Eastern's Fun Flight Bag of diversions, like masks and coloring books).

Budget watchers should pay careful attention to motel rate structures (see page 23 for ideas) when reserving accommodations. Also, some charge for cots, which other motels might bring in at no charge. Note that some hostelries outside the World *seem* a lot less expensive than the WDW resorts—until the actual costs for everything for a whole family are computed. Sometimes airfares that sound inexpensive actually cost more for a family; sometimes air packages cut costs. So check carefully.

At Walt Disney World: This vacationland ranks among the easiest spots on earth for traveling families with children. Older youngsters don't need to be driven around, and the general supervision is such that kids are hard pressed to get into trouble. All the resorts, plus Fort Wilderness and the Pool Pavilion in the Walt Disney World Village villa area have at least a small room full of pinball machines and video games, much to the satisfaction of kids of all ages; the one at the Contemporary Resort Hotel is positively vast. And all the hotels have playgrounds; the one at the Polynesian Village is particularly nifty, with its thatched-roof treehouse, climbing rings, and offbeat slide.

And both the Polynesian Village and the Contemporary Resort (but not the Golf Resort) have child-care facilities. In-room babysitters can be summoned to all resort hotels and villas; contact the Guest Services desk. And there is also a day-care center known as Kindercare, suitable for youngsters aged 2 through 12; parents may drop off their children or call to have them picked up. For details, phone 827-KIDS.

WITH CHILDREN

Nor is there any cause for excessive hand-holding inside the Magic Kingdom: with older youngsters, it's enough to establish a specific meeting place and a meeting time (allowing a little latitude, just in case). If there are younger children along, it's not a bad idea to stop at City Hall or the Baby Center next to the Crystal Palace to pick up a special name tag to facilitate a reunion in case the family gets separated. Aunt Polly's on Tom Sawyer Island is a good bet for lunch; while adults in the party are sipping lemonade, the kids can be bouncing across the Barrel Bridge and exploring every nook and cranny on the island.

Strollers are available for rent for a nominal fee (small deposit required) at the Stroller Shop on the east side of Main Street at the entrance to the Magic Kingdom. If your stroller disappears, as often happens while you're inside an attraction, a replacement may be obtained at Circle-Vision 360 and Space Port (the shop of contemporary decorative gifts) in Tomorrowland; at the Trading Post in Frontierland; and at Tinkerbell's Toy Shop in Fantasyland.

The Magic Kingdom Baby Care Center at the end of Main Street can be helpful in many ways to mothers with young children. It has an old-fashioned–looking, low-lighted room with a couple of comfortable rocking chairs and velvet-upholstered Victorian love seats for nursing mothers; plus a play area for their older children, and a cheerful feeding room decked out with murals of Disney characters. There are highchairs here, and bibs and plastic spoons are also available. The Baby Center also has facilities for changing infants, preparing formulas, and warming bottles. Disposable diapers and nurser bags, pull-on rubber pants, baby bottles with nipples, formula (*Similac*, *Isomil*, and *Infamil*), teethers, pacifiers, prepared cereal, juices, and strained and junior baby food in a limited selection, are available for sale on the spot at a nominal cost. The decor of the whole place is soothing, the atmosphere is such that it seems a million miles away from the Magic Kingdom's hubbub, and the guest book lists more wonderful children's names than many a baby name book—as more than one expectant mother has noted. A stop here for diaper changing makes a good break for child and mother alike, though changing areas are available in most ladies' rest-rooms as well.

A variety of other baby care supplies can be purchased at the Stroller Shop on Main Street. Pampers are sold, though not displayed, in the Children's Books section of the Emporium, on Main Street at Town Square.

Lost Children: That the security force inside the Magic Kingdom is far more careful than the happy appearance of things indicates is a welcome thought on those rare instances when a child suddenly disappears, or fails to show up on schedule. If this happens to you, check the lost children's log books in the Baby Center and at City Hall. Every Disney employee knows where they are—and what to do if a lost-looking child suddenly starts to call for his or her mommy. There are no paging systems in the Magic Kingdom, but in very serious emergencies an all-points-bulletin can be put out among employees.

HELPFUL HINTS

HINTS FOR OLDER TRAVELERS

Walt Disney World can overwhelm an elderly traveler not accustomed to unfamiliar places; the Magic Kingdom can be even more disorienting because of the profusion of sights and sounds, nooks and crannies; and the heat, particularly in summer, can be hard to take. Yet with the proper planning and precautions, the Magic Kingdom can be just as delightful for older visitors as for kids. Here are a few suggestions:

• Join a tour. Of the several organizations that specialize in group trips for older travelers, only one—the National Council of Senior Citizens (1511 K St. N.W.; Washington, DC 20005)—offers a tour to WDW often enough to mention (and even these are arranged only when interest warrants). Note that visitors who do come with a group bus tour should be sure to allow plenty of time to take the monorail or the ferry back to the bus parking area at the Transportation and Ticket Center—usually about half an hour—and should avoid queuing up when time begins to grow short.

Inside the Magic Kingdom, group tours—among the best buys in the World—are offered by Guest Relations. These three-hour guided walks take in the whole park; the price, which is about $15 ($13 for children 3 through 11) includes admission to the Magic Kingdom, the services of the guide, visits to four attractions, and a special ticket good for admission during the rest of the day to all others except the shooting gallery. For details phone 824-4631.

• Schedule visits for off-peak seasons and hours when the crowds will not be discouraging.

• Read all Walt Disney World literature carefully before arrival, so that things are familiar.

• In the park, don't be timid about asking for directions or advice. Disney employees are always happy to help out.

• Eat early or late, to avoid mealtime crowds. Or stop in more sedate restaurants such as the Crystal Palace, the Town Square Cafe, or King Stefan's in Cinderella Castle. Or take the monorail to the still calmer Polynesian Village or the Contemporary Resort, to lunch in one of the waitress-service restaurants there, or make a trip through one of the buffet lines.

• Don't try to save money by scrimping on food. Traveling takes energy, and only a good meal can provide it.

• Protect yourself from the sun. Wear a hat, and slather on the sunscreen. (And don't forget to cover legs, which are easily sunburned by light rays reflected from pavements.)

• Don't become overheated. Take frequent rest stops in the shade, and get out of the mid-afternoon heat by stopping for a snack in an air-conditioned restaurant. Avoid standing in line at Frontierland's Big Thunder and at Fantasyland's 20,000 Leagues in midafternoon; parts of these queues are unprotected from the sun, and can be very hot. If you feel faint or light-headed, visit the First Aid Center.

• Above all, don't push yourself. Half the fun of the Magic Kingdom—the part that younger travelers often miss—is just sitting under a shade tree on a park bench, admiring the scenery, and watching the people go by.

LOST ADULTS

Occasionally, traveling companions do get separated in the press of the crowds, or someone fails to show up at an appointed meeting spot. So it's good to know that Guest Relations maintains a message book in City Hall for just such occasions. Make sure that your whole party knows about it and uses it as necessary.

FOR THE HANDICAPPED

Walt Disney World gets high marks among handicapped travelers because of the attention that has been paid to their special needs. Special parking is available next to the Transportation and Ticket Center (TTC); get directions at the Auto Plaza. From there, the Magic Kingdom is accessible either by ferry or by monorail (though the former is preferable, since the slant of the ramp to the monorails makes holding a wheelchair a bit taxing when there are any waiting lines at all). All monorail stations are accessible to wheelchairs except the one at the Contemporary Resort, which can be reached only by escalator. Special "handicap vans," with motorized platforms that lift wheelchairs inside, are available, too. To request one, day guests should inquire at the Guest Relations Window at the TTC or in City Hall, and resort guests should call Guest Services in their hotel. Count on at least 20 minutes between the request and pick up.

In the Magic Kingdom, wheelchairs are available for rent at the Stroller Shop, on the right-hand side of the souvenir area, just past the turnstiles. Most restrooms in the park have extra-wide cubicles with wall bars for people in wheelchairs (locations are marked on the Magic Kingdom map that's passed out when tickets are purchased); and there are extra-low telephones at the TTC and underneath the Main Street Train Station, and ramps at each street corner along Main Street, the only area in the Magic Kingdom with sidewalks and curbs. Furthermore, most attractions are accessible to guests who can be lifted to and from their chairs. Only the Swiss Family Island Treehouse in Adventureland, the Skyway, Peter Pan's Flight in Fantasyland, and Space Mountain and the WEDway PeopleMover in Tomorrowland cannot accommodate these guests. Certain attractions—the

HINTS FOR SINGLE TRAVELERS

Walt Disney World does not exactly attract the young swinging singles crowd, so those on the lookout for romantic encounters probably would do better elsewhere. But solo travelers who travel alone for the freedom and the fun of it can have as enjoyable a time at Walt Disney World as they would anywhere else.

WDW employees are generally a friendly lot, and entertaining to talk to; chatting with a painter about the perpetual repainting of Main Street woodwork, or talking to the animal keepers on Discovery Island, a single traveler usually learns more about the ways of the World than any group member. Other visitors that might be encountered in the course of a day are away from their own home base as well, and are apt to be just that much less standoffish.

Single women will not find the bars and lounges in WDW hotels off-limits (as they might in their real world counterparts). Sitting at the U-shaped bar at the Baton Rouge Lounge can be particular fun. Another good way to meet people (albeit a somewhat older crowd) is to sign up for one of Guest Relations' Guided Walking Tours of the Magic Kingdom; call 824-4631 for details. River Country, the hotel swimming pools and beaches, and (for those with the inclination), the Giraffe disco at the Royal Plaza Hotel at Walt Disney World Village Hotel Plaza, are also good bets for meeting people.

A note for budget watchers: Rates at all WDW resort hotels and those at Walt Disney World Village Hotel Plaza, and at some others in the Orlando area, are the same whether one or two persons occupy a room.

Similarly, the Walt Disney World Village villas are priced per unit, regardless of the number of people who sleep there. This fact makes sharing accommodations an especially economical idea.

Main Street Cinema and the Walt Disney Story on Main Street; the Tropical Serenade in Adventureland; the Country Bear Jamboree and the Diamond Horseshoe in Frontierland; the Hall of Presidents and the Liberty Square Riverboats in Liberty Square; Mission to Mars; and pre- and post-show sections of Space Mountain, the Carousel of Progress, and CircleVision 360—can be enjoyed without ever leaving a wheelchair.

Outside the Magic Kingdom, all WDW resort hotels are easily explored by wheelchair. The Polynesian Village is the most convenient for vacationers in wheelchairs. The monorail is easy to get to, and there are 48 special first-floor units with grab rails next to the bathtubs and wider automatic entrance doors. In that building, the Oahu, there are even Braille characters on the elevators.

In the Walt Disney World Village villa area, some units are accessible to wheelchairs and some are not; the best bets are the planned-for-the-purpose units in the Fairway Villas. The Fleetwood Trailers at Fort Wilderness would be difficult to manage because of stairway access and narrow interior spaces.

In River Country, life jackets are available for the handicapped. (No other flotation devices are permitted here.)

For blind guests, a tape recorder and cassette that describes the Magic Kingdom in terms of smells and sounds is available at City Hall; the cassette players have Braille keys. A small, refundable deposit (about $5) is required for cassette use. Seeing eye dogs are permitted in the Magic Kingdom.

Getting around Orlando: Handicapped guests who do not have their own cars can phone Handi-Cab of Florida, Inc., at 305-298-1111, a special cab service for the handicapped.

Tours: Several organizations sponsor trips for the handicapped and offer tours to WDW. Among them are:

- Flying Wheel Tours; Box 382; 143 W. Bridge St.; Owatonna, MI 55060; 507-451-5005.
- Evergreen Travel Service; 19505 L 44th Ave. W.; Lynwood, WA 98036; 206-776-1184.
- Powers Travel Agency; 23901 Michigan Ave.; Dearborn, MI 48124; 313-562-1700.
- Monte Tours; 347 Fifth Ave., Ste. 607; New York, NY 10016; 212-679-9179.

All of these organizations can also arrange trips for individuals.

Books: The following are the two best books we know for general hints on travel by the handicapped:

Access to the World by Louise Weiss (Chatham Square Press; $9.95).

Travel Ability by Lois Reamy (Macmillan; $9.95).

Traveling by car: Hertz, Avis, and National all have a limited quantity of hand-control cars for rent in the Orlando area; call well in advance to reserve them.

Traveling by plane: Airlines have not always been as helpful in dealing with handicapped travelers as they are now. Occasionally, vacationers can go into the aircraft in their own chair—providing the chair is narrow and the plane's aisles are wide; more often, travelers transfer to a narrower airline chair at the door of the aircraft, while their own chair is sent down to the luggage compartment. Wheelchair passengers are usually pre-boarded and then deplaned after other passengers. If you are not taking your own wheelchair along and have a tight connection to make, be sure to advise the airlines' attendants well in advance. Similarly, if a passenger wishes to utilize an airline's wheelchair at a connecting point or destination, that wheelchair service should be ordered at the time that flight reservations are being made.

Allow plenty of time to make all your arrangements, and don't fail to alert all airline personnel to your special needs.

Policies on motorized wheelchairs vary, depending on the airline and the type of chair; check with carriers in advance. Seeing eye dogs are always allowed aboard aircraft (though some carriers may require them to be muzzled), but arrangements should be made at the time reservations are made so that a bulkhead seat may be requested.

For general information on traveling by air, get copies of "Air Travelers' Fly Rights" (available free from the Office of Consumer Affairs; CAB; Washington, DC 20428); "Air Transportation of Handicapped Persons" (free, from the Department of Transportation Distribution Unit; TAD-443.1; Washington, DC 20590); and "Air Travel Tips for the Handicapped" (free from the Consumer Information Center; Pueblo, CO 81009).

Traveling by train: Whether riding with or without reservations, it's wise to phone in advance to arrange for one of the special seats that Amtrak maintains for handicapped travelers. Wheelchairs are available at major stations, some 400 in all, including Orlando. New cars have special seats, specially equipped bathrooms, and purposely designed sleeping compartments; older equipment presents enough additional barriers that a traveling companion is a necessity. The Silver Meteor, the afternoon train from New York to Orlando, is a new train; the morning train is an old one. Blind and disabled passengers get a 25 percent discount on normal economy fares, though companions must pay full fare. Seeing eye and hearing ear dogs may ride with passengers at no extra charge.

Motorized wheelchairs are not allowed on passenger cars, but may be transported in baggage cars. The free booklet "Access Amtrak" details services for elderly and handicapped travelers. To get a copy, write the Amtrak Distribution Center; Box 311; Addison, IL 60101.

Traveling by bus: Both Greyhound and Trailways have implemented plans that allow a handicapped vacationer and a companion (to help with boarding and disembarking) to travel together on a single adult ticket; all that's required is a doctor's written statement of the necessity of such aid. Both bus companies carry nonmotorized folding wheelchairs at no additional charge; among motorized chairs, those powered by dry-cell batteries will be accepted as baggage, while those powered by wet-cell batteries must be left behind.

And remember to plan in advance. Allow plenty of time, and at each step of the way, inform air, bus, train, and hotel personnel of your special needs.

OTHER INFORMATION

BARBERS: The most amusing place to get a haircut is the old-fashioned Harmony Barber Shop (824-4550), tucked away at the end of the flower-filled cul-de-sac just off the west side of Main Street in the Magic Kingdom; the Disney books on hand are terrific, and the "Dapper Dans," the park's own barbershop quartet, can often be heard here. Moustache cups and other nostalgic shaving items are for sale.

Outside the Magic Kingdom, visit the Captain's Chair on the third floor of the Contemporary Resort (824-1000, ext. 3411) or the Alii Nui Barber Shop on the first floor of the Great Ceremonial House at the Polynesian Village (824-2000, ext. 1400).

BEAUTY SHOPS: Shampoos, sets, coloring, waving, manicuring, and wig-setting are available at the Pretty Wahine Beauty Shop in the Polynesian Village (824-2000, ext. 1377) and the American Beauty Shoppe on the third floor of the Contemporary Resort (824-1000, ext. 3412); the manicurist at the Contemporary Resort's shop has held the hands of many a Walt Disney World executive, and can provide some fascinating insights into the workings of the park.

CAR CARE: Auto and travel club members probably will want to call their local club-sponsored towing service in the event of problems; anyone else can phone the Disney Car Care Center (824-4813), located on Asian Way near the Main Entrance Toll Plaza as you exit. Though routine maintenance work is probably best done by mechanics who know your car well—before leaving home—the Disney Car Care Center is a good place for gas and repairs in a pinch. Disney personnel here will chauffeur guests to their day's WDW destination, and arrange for later pickup when requested.

It's also reassuring to know that WDW breakdowns don't mean disaster. All WDW roads are patrolled constantly by security cars that can radio for help if needed, and all parking lots are patrolled by tow trucks with jumper cables.

CHURCH SERVICES: Vacations are a good time to broaden the family's religious experience. A variety of services are held around Walt Disney World on weekends.

Protestant: 9 A.M. on Sunday at Luau Cove at the Polynesian Village; and at the Royal Plaza in Walt Disney World Village Hotel Plaza.

Catholic: 8 and 10:15 A.M. on Sunday at Luau Cove at the Polynesian Village; 6 P.M. on Saturday and 8 A.M. on Sunday at the Royal Plaza in Walt Disney World Village Hotel Plaza.

In Orlando, there are services at St. James Catholic Church (215 N. Orange Ave.) at 4 and 6 P.M. on Saturday, and, on Sunday, at 7:30, 9, 10:30 A.M. and noon, and, in Spanish, at 7:30 P.M. Phone 422-2005 for details.

In Kissimmee, there are services at the Holy Redeemer Catholic Church (1603 N. Thacker Ave.) on Saturday at 6 P.M. and on Sunday at 7:30, 9, 10:30 A.M., and noon. Daily masses are said at 7:30 and 9 A.M. Phone 846-3700 for details.

Jewish: There are services at 8:15 P.M. on Friday and at 9 A.M. on Saturday at the Congregation Ohev Sholom (5015 Goddard Ave.) in Orlando. Phone 298-4650 for details.

Kosher dinners are available at any time at the Contemporary Resort Hotel, the Polynesian Village, the Golf Resort, Fort Wilderness, and Walt Disney World Shopping Village—area restaurants. Given two weeks' notice (or sometimes less), it's possible to order veal, roast chicken, Salisbury steak, turkey, or roasted or broiled beef to eat at any location in the World, except the Magic Kingdom. Cost is around $10.

Note also that most airlines also offer special meals conforming to dietary codes. Order them when making reservations.

MAIL: Postcards are for sale at many spots in the resorts and around the Magic Kingdom, among them at the Card Shop on the west side of Main Street. Postage stamps can be purchased from a vending machine at the Card Shop's entrance to the adjacent Penny Arcade and in the book department of the Emporium nearby. The old-fashioned olive-drab mailboxes that punctuate Main Street are no longer official U.S. post boxes, but letters can be mailed there for later pickup by Disney employees and subsequent transportation to the Lake Buena Vista post office. Postmarks read "Lake Buena Vista," *not* "Walt Disney World." All window services are available at the Lake Buena Vista post office, including postal money order and stamp sale, registry, and certification. The post office is located in the mirror-faced Sun Bank Building.

Read'n and Rite'n in Walt Disney World Shopping Village sells attractive stationery and note pads. Postage stamps also are available here.

Mail may be addressed to guests c/o their hotel at Walt Disney World; Box 40; Lake Buena Vista, FL 32830.

Don't forget to arrange for mail at home to be held by the post office or picked up by neighbors while you're at WDW.

LOST AND FOUND: The extensive indexing system maintained by Walt Disney World's Lost and Found department is impressive, especially when a prize possession turns up missing, whether it's false teeth or a camera. (Both have been lost in the past; the dentures were never claimed.) To see just how it works, the first thing to do is to report the loss on the proper forms at City Hall or at the Guest Relations Window on the east end of the Transportation and Ticket Center or the Guest Services desks in the first floor lobby at the Contemporary Resort or the main lobbies at the Polynesian Village and the Golf Resort; at Fort Wilderness, phone ext. 4198 from a comfort station telephone.

Found items lost in the Magic Kingdom can be claimed on the day of the loss at City Hall, and thereafter at the main Lost and Found station at the Transportation and Ticket Center. Items lost in the hotels and at Walt Disney World Shopping Village are kept in those locations for three months before being sent to the Transportation and Ticket Center station. Keep checking; the phone number is 824-4245.

After six months, articles are returned to the finder—an added incentive for visitors to turn over valuable items to Lost and Found.

the larger ones. Items too big to fit into the latter can be checked at the Guest Relations window at the TTC or at City Hall inside the Magic Kingdom.

DRINKING LAWS: In Florida, drinking is legal at 19. There are many bars and lounges all over the World; minors are permitted to accompany their parents, but are prohibited from sitting or standing at the bar. There's no drinking in the Magic Kingdom, where even the piña coladas are nonalcoholic.

By the bottle: Liquor is sold in full-size and mini bottles at Village Spirits at Walt Disney World Shopping Village, the Trading Posts in Fort Wilderness, at Trader Jack's on the second floor of the Great Ceremonial House at the Polynesian Village, at Golf Gifts and Sundries in the lobby at the Golf Resort, and at Spirit World on the Grand Canyon Concourse in the Contemporary Resort. Liquor also may be purchased from Room Service at the resorts.

PLANT-SITTING: Plants do not fare well in the heat of a closed-up car for a day. Those who have purchased greenery at Walt Disney World Shopping Village, or brought a favorite fern from home, will be grateful to know that their horticultural wonders can be accommodated by the kennels at Fort Wilderness or at the Transportation and Ticket Center. There's no charge.

LOCKERS: There are coin-operated lockers underneath the Main Street Railroad Station in the Magic Kingdom and at two locations at the Transportation and Ticket Center—next to Lost and Found on the west end and beside the bus parking lot on the east side. Cost is 25¢ per day for the regular size, 50¢ for

MEDICAL MATTERS: For travelers with chronic health problems, it's a good idea to carry copies of all prescriptions and to get names of local doctors from hometown physicians. However, Walt Disney World is equipped to deal with many types of medical emergencies. In the Magic Kingdom, next to the Crystal Palace, there's a **First Aid Center**, staffed by a registered nurse. Others are located at the Transportation and Ticket Center and in each hotel. Serious emergencies can be reported to WDW's own Orange Vista Hospital on the edge of the property.

The most common malady? Not sensitive stomachs upset by rides, but simple *sunburn.* So be forewarned. Wear a hat, and slather on sufficient sunblock or sunscreen, especially during the spring and summer.

For diabetics: Walt Disney World resorts provide refrigeration services for insulin; the villas and the Fleetwood Trailers at Fort Wilderness have their own refrigerators.

Prescriptions: These cannot be filled on the property. The closest pharmacies are located in Kissimmee on Route 192, about 10 miles from the WDW Auto Plaza.

MONEY: You may not use credit cards to pay for Magic Kingdom admissions. For that purpose, only cash, traveler's checks, and personal checks are accepted. Checks must bear the guest's name and address, be drawn on a U.S. bank, and be accompanied by the proper identification—a valid driver's license and a current major credit card such as American Express, Visa, MasterCard, Diner's Club, or Carte Blanche. Fast food restaurants in the Magic Kingdom operate on a cash-only basis.

For charges at sit-down restaurants and shops inside the theme park, however, and for all other charges throughout Walt Disney World, American Express and Master-Card credit cards are accepted. WDW resort guests may use the WDW resort IDs that each member of a party receives upon check-in to cover purchases in shops, lounge and restaurant charges, and recreational fees incurred inside WDW (but outside the Magic Kingdom). These cards are not valid for charges made past check-out time on the last day of a guest's stay.

Wiring money: Friends and relatives at home can send money to WDW guests through Western Union offices at WDW in the Contemporary Resort (824-1000, ext. 3456), in Kissimmee (847-4838), and in Orlando (841-4733).

The Sun Bank: This institution, which has an old-fashioned branch on Main Street inside the Magic Kingdom and another in Walt Disney World Shopping Village in the same striking contemporary structure that houses the post office, can:

• Give cash advances on MasterCard and Visa credit cards, with a $50 minimum, in amounts as large as a guest's credit limit permits.

• Cash and sell traveler's checks and provide refunds for lost American Express and Bank of America traveler's checks.

• Cash personal checks of up to $1,000 for American Express cardholders upon presentation of their cards (part payable in cash and the rest in American Express traveler's checks).

• Cash personal checks for up to $25 upon presentation of a driver's license and a major credit card for other guests.

• Help with wire transfers of money from a guest's own bank to the Sun Bank.

• Exchange most foreign currency for dollars.

The Sun Bank branch in the Magic Kingdom is open from 9 A.M. to 4 P.M. daily; phone 824-5767 for further information. The Sun Bank in Walt Disney World Village at Lake Buena Vista is open from 9 A.M. to 4 P.M. on weekdays (until 6 P.M. on Thursday); phone 828-6100.

Traveler's checks: Even the most careful of vacationers occasionally loses a wallet, and traveler's checks can take the sting out of that loss. Which type a traveler should buy is not so much a function of which is most easily refunded (because in the U.S., and at Walt Disney World in particular, all the major traveler's check offerers can come through with emergency refunds in a pinch), as of which costs less. It's a good idea, therefore, to look for special promotions by banks at home in the months preceding a vacation, and check to see which of the six major brands—American Express, MasterCard, Visa, Thomas Cook, Citicorp, and Bank of America—are available free.

While at WDW, American Express checks can be purchased at the Sun Bank and at American Express cardmembers' check dispensers, machines that automatically vend traveler's checks when you feed them an American Express card and punch in an identification number that has been obtained from the company in advance. These machines are located in the Fiesta Fun Center at the Contemporary Resort and at the Sun Bank opposite Walt Disney World Shopping Village.

Don't fail to sign checks in the proper place as soon as they are purchased. And stash the receipt bearing the check numbers in a separate place from the checks themselves, along with one piece of identification, such as a duplicate driver's license or spare credit card. These will speed the refund process should your checks get lost.

Foreign currency exchange: This can be done at the Guest Relations Window (to the right as you face the ticket windows at the Transportation and Ticket Center), or at City Hall, or, from 9 A.M. to 4 P.M. daily, at the Sun Bank in Town Square inside the Magic Kingdom. Currency can be exchanged in the ticket booth in the Train Station on Main Street and at all WDW resort hotels at other times. The Sun Bank in Walt Disney World Shopping Village also exchanges foreign currency.

SHOPPING FOR NECESSITIES: When you finally remember what it was that you left at home, or stay long enough to run out of something, it's useful to know that almost all everyday needs can be satisfied right on the property. Plaza Gifts and Sundries on the Grand Canyon Concourse in the Contemporary Resort, Village Gifts & Sundries on the second floor of the Polynesian Village, Golf Gifts and Sundries in the lobby of the Golf Resort, and the Meadow and Settlement Trading Posts at Fort Wilderness all stock a limited number of brands of a wide variety of toiletries; a broader selection is available at the Walt Disney World Shopping Village area at Gifts and Sundries. In addition, a number of over-the-counter health aids, plus such useful items as adhesive tape, Ace bandages, pocket combs, and nail clippers, can be purchased in the Books and Records section of the Emporium on Main Street; they're kept behind the counter, so it's necessary to ask for the supplies you want. Aspirin and suntan lotion are also available at Mickey's Mart in Tomorrowland.

Reading matter: Newspapers, magazines, best-sellers, and lightweight and inspirational paperbacks are available in a limited selection at Spirit World on the Grand Canyon Concourse of the Contemporary Resort, at News from Civilization on the first floor at the Polynesian Village, and at Golf Gifts and Sundries in the lobby at the Golf Resort. Most carry the daily papers from Orlando and Miami, and the *Wall Street Journal,* and, on Sundays, the *New York Times* and the *Chicago Tribune.*

A larger stock of paperback and hardcover books is available at Read'n & Rite'n in Walt Disney World Shopping Village

The Emporium on Main Street in the Magic Kingdom has a good selection of children's books.

Cigarettes: Smoking items are widely available all over WDW, and Main Street nods to the affection that travelers have for this habit with a special tobacco store, the Tobacconist, which stocks a variety of smokers' aids. It's worth a stop if only to pick up a book of matches; these have particularly handsome covers.

Cigarettes also can be purchased inside the Magic Kingdom at Tropic Toppers in Adventureland, at the Trading Post in Frontierland, at the Royal Candy Shoppe in Fantasyland, at Heritage House in Liberty Square, and at Mickey's Mart in Tomorrowland. In addition, there are cigarette vending machines in the Columbia Harbour House in Liberty Square; at King Stefan's in Cinderella Castle and the Pinocchio Village Haus in Fantasyland; in Tomorrowland Terrace; and in the Mile Long Bar in Frontierland.

In the hotels, you can buy them at Spirit World on the Grand Canyon Concourse in the Contemporary Resorts, at News from Civilization on the first floor of the Great Ceremonial House at the Polynesian Village, and at Golf Gifts and Sundries in the lobby of the Golf Resort.

At Fort Wilderness, they are for sale at the Meadow and Settlement Trading Posts.

PETS: No pets are allowed in the Magic Kingdom or at the WDW resorts. Travelers who bring a pet along can lodge it in one of two attractive air-conditioned kennels—the Walt Disney World Kennel Club, adjoining the Transportation and Ticket Center, and the Fort Wilderness Kennel and Livery, at the campground entrance, next to a huge field where pet owners often take their animals out for a run. In busy seasons, try to arrive before the 9 to 10 A.M. morning rush hour, and note that the Kennel Club closes an hour after the Magic Kingdom.

Bears, cougars, and ocelots have all been accommodated by the WDW kennels, and exotic pets are accepted—if a bit reluctantly. However, owners themselves must put the more unusual animals into the kennel's cages; and snakes, rabbits, birds, turtles, hamsters, and other animals unsuited (because of size) to cat- and dog-sized cages must be accompanied by their own escape-proof accommodations.

Advance reservations are not accepted.

WDW resort guests may board their pet in either kennel; guests at Walt Disney World Village Hotel Plaza establishments (those hotels on the property not owned by Walt Disney World) may board their animals in the Kennel Club. Pets of day guests may not remain overnight. Cost is about $3 for overnight stays, not including food.

Never leave pets in a car.

Also bring along your pet's certificate of vaccination, since Florida law requires proof of immunization for animals involved in biting accidents.

Outside Walt Disney World: A number of hotels in the Orlando and Kissimmee area permit pets. For specific information, phone the Orlando Area Chamber of Commerce, 425-1234.

TIPPING: Walt Disney World is not one of those places where bellmen stick out their hands even before they put down your luggage. Instead, they seem genuinely glad to help out. Oddly enough, however, this pleasant attitude seems to discourage tipping at the same time it arouses the sentiments that make most travelers want to reach for their wallets.

Lack of ostentatious need does not mean that tips are any less valued at WDW than they would be at any other good resort hotel—the standard 50 to 75 cents per bag is appropriate for lugging luggage. Gratuities of about 15 percent are also customary at waitress-service restaurants all over WDW, and at cafeterias such as the Contemporary Resort's Terrace Buffeteria—where waitresses carry trays and keep guests' coffee refilled. At the posh Empress Room, a service charge of 20 percent of the food and drink bill is automatically added to the check.

Gratuities are not required in fast food restaurants or at the attractions, but in the beauty shops, it's usual to leave a tip of about 15 percent of the total bill, and at the spa, to acknowledge the services of the masseur with a tip of $3 to $5.

Cabdrivers in the Orlando area expect a 15 percent tip. Baggage handlers at bus and train stations and at the airport expect at least 50 cents per bag.

TELEPHONE: The folks at home can reach resort guests at the following numbers: 824-1000 for the Contemporary Resort; 824-2200 at the Golf Resort; 824-2000 at the Polynesian Village; and 828-3800 at Lake Buena Vista–area villas.

Public telephones in the Orlando area cost 25 cents. Those in Walt Disney World still cost only a dime.

When calling home, note that it's cheapest to have calls billed to your hotel room. Even though an operator does come on the wire to request your room number, the call is charged at a direct-dial rate rather than at the rates for operator-assisted calls, which prevail when you bill charges to your home telephone or phone-company credit card.

TIME AND WEATHER PHONE: In the Orlando area, the number is 422-1611.

TRANSPORTATION AND ACCOMMODATIONS

Misconceptions about Walt Disney World (like the impression that it's located in the middle of downtown Orlando), and about the surrounding region (like the idea that the park is located on one or another of Florida's coasts), seem to abound. The fact is that Walt Disney World is situated virtually in the center of Florida, and, despite perhaps the most prevalent of nonresident misconceptions, nowhere near Miami or Miami Beach.

But the popularity of Walt Disney World has made the region around Orlando one of the world's major tourist centers, and everything from new airline facilities to a very efficient network of roads and state highways now brings visitors to the area literally by the tens of thousands.

There's no doubt, however, that confusion about getting around the Walt Disney World region is prevalent, and may be exceeded only by the dilemma concerning which sort of specific accommodation is most appropriate for a given family's needs. Just the accommodations facilities that are operated by Walt Disney World itself range from futuristic high-rise towers to treehouses buried deep in piney woods. In between are resorts echoing images of the South Pacific and efficient trailer-type facilities in a nearly perfectly maintained campground. And that doesn't include a sports resort and villas that provide extraordinary luxury. What follows should help any traveler sort out his preferences.

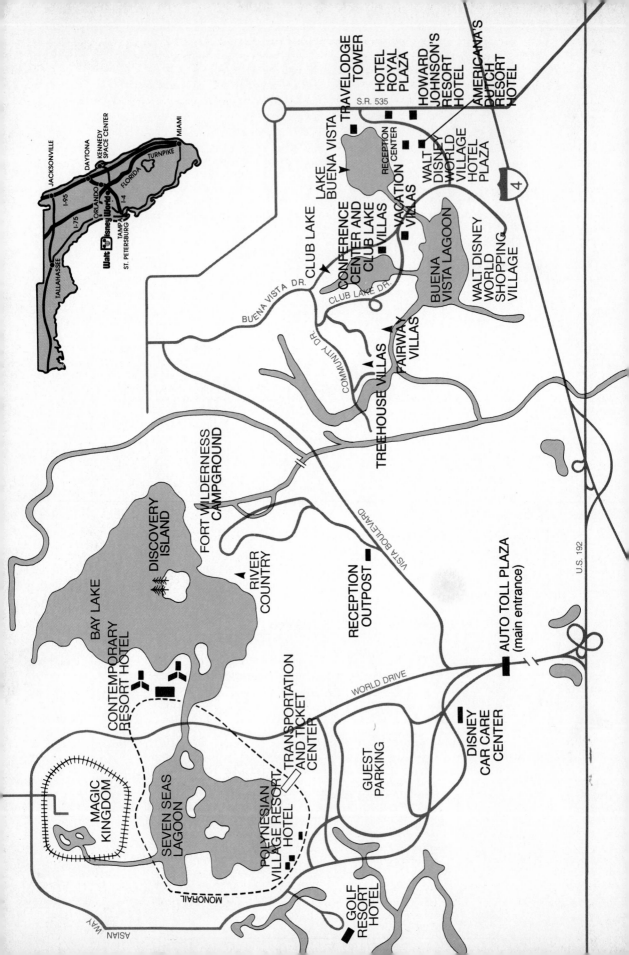

GETTING ORIENTED

Orlando, the Central Florida city of over 120,000 residents, is the municipality with which Walt Disney World is most closely associated. It is not, however, the closest urban community to WDW. That honor belongs to Kissimmee, a far smaller community of 17,000 people located just southeast of the World. Many newish motels are located here, though there are far more in Orlando proper, to the north.

Most of the area's better restaurants are found in Orlando, or in adjacent communities like Winter Park (on its northeastern extremity), Maitland (west of Winter Park), and Altamonte Springs (west of Maitland). Haines City, home of Circus World, is about 8 miles south of WDW's southern border, and Winter Haven, home of Cypress Gardens (described in the *Orlando* chapter), is about 12 miles southwest.

ORLANDO-AREA HIGHWAYS: The most important Orlando traffic artery is I-4, which runs diagonally through the area from southwest to northeast, cutting through the southern half of Walt Disney World, then angles on toward Orlando and Winter Park, ending near Daytona Beach at I-95, which runs north and south along the coast. All the city's other important highways intersect I-4. From south to north, these include U.S.-192, which takes an east-west course that crosses the WDW entrance road and leads into downtown Kissimmee on the east; S.R.-528 (aka the Bee Line Expressway), which shoots eastward from I-4; S.R.-435, also known as Kirkman Rd., which runs north and south and intersects International Drive, where many motels catering to WDW visitors are located; U.S.-17-92-441 (aka Orange Blossom Trail), which runs due north and south, paralleling Kirkman Road on the east; and U.S.-50 (aka Colonial Drive), which runs due east and west.

GETTING AROUND INSIDE WALT DISNEY WORLD: The 43-square-mile tract that is Walt Disney World is roughly rectangular. I-4 runs through its southern half from southwest to northeast; there are two highway exits within WDW. The Magic Kingdom, the Polynesian Village, Contemporary Resort, and Golf Resort hotels, and Fort Wilderness, are all located in the property's northern third. They are located off the Main Entrance Road, a route that is accessible via U.S.-192,which extends due east and west from the more southerly of WDW's pair of I-4 exits. The U.S.-192 exit is four miles from the Toll Plaza, the immediate gateway to the parking lots. The Main Entrance Road is about a mile from the I-4 exit, so that the parking lots are about five miles from the Interstate. Walt Disney World Village has its own exit off I-4 (marked "Lake Buena Vista"), four miles from the one for the Main Entrance. The Walt Disney World Shopping Village parking lots are located about a mile from I-4. Note that many off-property hotels offer free shuttle-bus service to WDW.

There are also a number of roads *inside* the World. In some cases, it is possible to drive from place to place inside the World. Bus transportation is also provided from most points to most other points, and is available to most guests. At the northernmost end of the World, an elevated monorail train operates along a circular route, making stops at the Polynesian Village and Contemporary Resort hotels and at the Magic Kingdom and the TTC. Motor launches and cruisers from those first three points call regularly at Fort Wilderness and Discovery Island.

WDW TRANSPORTATION ROUTES

Route	Destinations	Hours of operation
Red-flagged bus	WDW Shopping Village–Transportation and Ticket Center (TTC)	8 A.M. to 2 A.M.
Red-and-white-flagged bus	WDW Village Hotel Plaza–TTC	8 A.M. to 2 A.M.
Blue-flagged bus	Fort Wilderness–TTC	7 A.M. to 2 A.M.
Green-flagged bus	Polynesian Village–Golf Resort–TTC	7 A.M. to 2 A.M.
Gold-flagged bus	Contemporary Resort Hotel–TTC	7 A.M. to 2 A.M.
Blue-and-white-flagged bus	WDW Shopping Village–WDW Village Hotel Plaza	8 A.M. to 11 P.M.
Green-and-gold-flagged bus	WDW Shopping Village– Conference Center–Town-houses–Lake Buena Vista Club–Treehouses–Club Lake Villas	8 A.M. to 2 A.M.
Blue-flagged watercraft	Contemporary Resort– Discovery Island– Fort Wilderness	9 A.M. to midnight
Green-flagged watercraft	Magic Kingdom– Discovery Island– Fort Wilderness	One half hour prior to Magic Kingdom opening to Magic Kingdom clearing
Gold-flagged watercraft	Polynesian Village–Fort Wilderness–Discovery Island. After 1 P.M., runs in opposite direction: Discovery Island– Fort Wilderness–Polynesian Village	Hours depend on Discovery Island and River Country hours

FROM:	TO: Contemporary Resort Hotel	Polynesian Village Resort Hotel	Golf Resort Hotel	Fort Wilderness Campground
Magic Kingdom	Monorail during operating hours (7) Alternative: Magic Kingdom ferry to TTC (7), then gold-flagged bus (1)	Monorail during operating hours (7) Alternative: Magic Kingdom ferry to TTC (7), then green-flagged bus (1)	Monorail to Polynesian Village (7), then green-flagged bus (1)	Green-flagged watercraft from park opening to park clearing (2, 4) Alternative: Magic Kingdom ferry (7) or monorail (7) to TTC, then blue-flagged bus (
Contemporary Resort Hotel		Monorail (2, 6) Alternative: Gold-flagged bus to TTC (1), then green-flagged bus (1)	Monorail to Polynesian Village (2, 6), then green-flagged bus (1) Alternative: Gold-flagged bus to TTC (1), then green-flagged bus (1)	Blue-flagged watercraft from 9 A.M. to midnigh (2, 4) Alternative: Monorail (2 6) or gold-flagged bus (1) to TTC, then blue-flagged bus (1)
Polynesian Village Resort Hotel	Monorail (2, 6) Alternative: Green-flagged bus to TTC (1), then gold-flagged bus (1)		Green-flagged bus (1)	Gold-flagged watercraft during operating hours (2, 4) Alternative: Monorail (2 6) or green-flagged bu (1) to TTC, then blue-flagged bus (1)
Golf Resort Hotel	Green-flagged bus to Polynesian Village (1), then monorail (2, 6) Alternative: Green-flagged bus to TTC (1), then gold-flagged bus (1)	Green-flagged bus (1)		Green-flagged bus to Polynesian Village (1), then gold-flagged watercraft during operating hours (2, 4) Alternative: Green-flagged bus to TTC (1), then blue-flagged bus (1)
Fort Wilderness Campground	Blue-flagged watercraft (2, 4) from 9 A.M. to midnight Alternative: Blue-flagged bus (1) to TTC, then gold-flagged bus (1)	Gold-flagged watercraft during operating hours (2, 4) Alternative: Blue-flagged bus to TTC (1), then green-flagged bus (1)	Blue-flagged bus to TTC (1), then green-flagged bus (1) Alternative: Gold-flagged watercraft during operating hours to Polynesian Village (2, 4), then green-flagged bus (1)	
Walt Disney World Shopping Village	Red-flagged bus to TTC (2, 3, 5), then gold-flagged bus (1)	Red-flagged bus to TTC (2, 3, 5), then green-flagged bus (1)	Red-flagged bus to TTC (2, 3, 5), then green-flagged bus (1)	Red-flagged bus to TTC (2, 3, 5), then blue-flagged bus (1)
Walt Disney World Village Hotel Plaza	Red-and-white-flagged bus to TTC (2, 3, 5), then gold-flagged bus (1)	Red-and-white-flagged bus to TTC (2, 3, 5), then green-flagged bus (1)	Red-and-white-flagged bus to TTC (2, 3, 5), then green-flagged bus (1)	Red-and-white-flagged bus to TTC (2, 3, 5), then blue-flagged bus (1)
Transportation and Ticket Center (TTC)	Monorail direct to hotel, except before 1 P.M., when it's necessary to change at Magic Kingdom (2, 6) Alternative: Gold-flagged bus (1)	Monorail direct to hotel, except before 1 P.M., when it's necessary to change at Magic Kingdom (2, 6) Alternative: Green-flagged bus (1)	Green-flagged bus (1)	Blue-flagged bus (1)

INSIDE WALT DISNEY WORLD

Walt Disney World Shopping Village	Walt Disney World Village Hotel Plaza	Magic Kingdom	Transportation and Ticket Center
Monorail (7) or ferry (7) to TTC, then red-flagged bus (2, 3, 5)	Monorail (7) or ferry (7) to TTC, then red-and-white-flagged bus (2, 3, 5)		Monorail or ferry (2, 6)
Monorail (2, 6) or gold-flagged bus (1) to TTC, then red-flagged bus (2, 3, 5)	Monorail (2, 6) or gold-flagged bus (1) to TTC, then red-and-white-flagged bus (2, 3, 5)	Monorail during operating hours (7) Alternative: Gold-flagged bus to TTC (1), then Magic Kingdom ferry (7)	Monorail direct to TTC, except before 1 P.M. when it's necessary to change at Magic Kingdom (2, 6) Alternative: Gold-flagged bus (1)
Monorail (2, 6) or green-flagged bus (1) to TTC, then red-flagged bus (2, 3, 5)	Monorail (2, 6) or green-flagged bus (1) to TTC, then red-and-white-flagged bus (2, 3, 5)	Monorail during operating hours (7) Alternative: Green-flagged bus to TTC (1), then Magic Kingdom ferry (7)	Monorail direct to TTC, except before 1 P.M. when it's necessary to change at Magic Kingdom (2, 6) Alternative: Green-flagged bus (1)
Green-flagged bus to TTC (1), then red-flagged bus (2, 3, 5)	Green-flagged bus to TTC (1), then red-and-white-flagged bus (2, 3, 5)	Green-flagged bus to Polynesian Village (1), then monorail (1)	Green-flagged bus (1)
Blue-flagged bus to TTC (1), then red-flagged bus (2, 3, 5)	Blue-flagged bus to TTC (1), then red-and-white-flagged bus (2, 3, 5)	Green-flagged watercraft from park opening to park clearing (2, 4) Alternative: Blue-flagged bus to TTC (1), then Magic Kingdom ferry (7) or monorail (1)	Blue-flagged bus (1)
From the Shopping Village to WDW Conference Center, WDW Village Townhouses, Lake Buena Vista Club, WDW Village Treehouses, and WDW Club Lake Villas, take the green-and-gold-flagged bus.	Blue-and-white-flagged bus (1)	Red-flagged bus to TTC (2, 3, 5), then monorail (1) or ferry (7)	Red-flagged bus (2, 3, 5)
Blue-and-white-flagged bus (1)		Red-and-white-flagged bus to TTC (2, 3, 5), then monorail (1) or ferry (7)	Red-and-white-flagged bus (2, 3, 5)
Red-flagged bus (2, 3, 5)	Red-and-white-flagged bus (2, 3, 5)	Monorail or ferry (2, 6)	

ID REQUIREMENTS: 1) No ID required 2) ID from WDW-owned properties 3) ID from establishments at Walt Disney World Village Hotel Plaza 4) River Country, Discovery Island, or Pioneer Hall ticket 5) Most two- and three-day Passports, including two-day Guest Passport, two-day Magic Kingdom Club Passport, two- and three-day Resort Guest Passports, and three-day Eastern Airlines Guest Passport (One-day Passports, two- and three-day Walt Disney World Village Hotel Plaza Passports, three-day Travel Company Passports, six-day Travel Company Vacation Kingdom Passports, and five-day Magic Kingdom Club Passports are not valid for travel on these buses.) 6) Any Passport 7) Any Magic Kingdom admission media.

HOURS OF OPERATION, FREQUENCY OF SERVICE

Unless otherwise specified, allow 30 to 35 minutes for direct trips, at least 45 minutes for trips involving a change of vehicles.

BUSES: Pickups are made during the following hours:

Red-flagged buses—8 A.M. to 2 A.M.; every 20 minutes

Red-and-white-flagged buses—8 A.M. to 2 A.M.; every 20 minutes

Blue-flagged buses—7 A.M. to 2 A.M.; every 8 minutes

Green-flagged buses—7 A.M. to 2 A.M.; every 15 minutes

Gold-flagged buses—7 A.M. to 2 A.M.; every 15 minutes

Blue-and-white-flagged buses—8 A.M. to 11 P.M.; every 15 minutes

Green-and-gold-flagged buses—8 A.M. to 2 A.M.; every 15 minutes

When the Magic Kingdom is open until midnight, buses operate until 2 A.M.

WATERCRAFT: Service is provided every 20 minutes during operating hours, which are as follows:

Blue-flagged watercraft—9 A.M. to midnight

Green-flagged watercraft—from one half hour prior to Magic Kingdom opening to Magic Kingdom clearing

Gold-flagged launches—Operate according to Discovery Island and River Country hours. For details, phone 824-4457.

No stops are made at Discovery Island after that attraction closes at sundown.

MONORAILS: These operate every five minutes on the average, beginning from the hotels at about 7:30 A.M. and from the Transportation and Ticket Center from about a half hour before Magic Kingdom opening, until about an hour after Magic Kingdom closing. (Service to the hotels, however, is available until at least 11 P.M. year round.) Note: Monorails from the hotels do not stop at the TTC before 1 P.M. daily or at the Magic Kingdom after its official daily closing time.

Rush hours extend from about 30 minutes before the Magic Kingdom opens until 90 minutes afterward for those guests at the Disney-owned resorts. The Magic Kingdom station is busy immediately after closing when the Magic Kingdom closes early; when it's open late, there are occasional crushes between 5 and 7 P.M., and again from the end of the Main Street Electrical Parade at about 9:30 P.M., worsening after the end of the fireworks at around 10:10 P.M.

Special treat: To ride in the cab of the front car, all you've got to do is ask. Your chances are best if you do this when the monorails are not busy.

FERRY: The ferry to the Magic Kingdom from the Transportation and Ticket Center takes a smidgen longer than the monorail, but crowds are often smaller, and in busy periods, it may be your best bet. Ferries operate from about a half hour before the Magic Kingdom opens until roughly an hour after closing.

ACCOMMODATIONS

Orlando and environs have literally thousands of hotel and motel rooms. Few of these, however, whether inside or outside the World, are of a design much beyond the standard Anywhere, USA motel/modern decor, usually with two standard double beds, shag carpeting, simulated wood paneling, color television, and private bathroom.

The biggest differences among groups of accommodations seem to be the power of the shower, the size and thickness of the towels, the dimensions of the room and the adjacent bathroom, the quality of the furnishings, the recreational facilities, the landscaping of the surrounding grounds, and the hotel's location.

Yet in practice, no two are really exactly alike. The differences often are subtle enough, however, that the overall impression is one of unending sameness.

Basically, Walt Disney World–area accommodations fall into two main categories: those owned by WDW and those not owned by the company.

All of the former are located inside the World. Rates are higher than at most other motels in the area, but the convenience is so much greater, the quality of the facilities so far superior, and the additional benefits available to an on-property guest so extensive—closed circuit TV announcing WDW events, a free copy of Walt Disney World News, and the best possible access to Guest Services personnel—that the extra expense is not at all unreasonable. Resort guests, for instance, can reserve tee-off times on the golf courses and places at most of the dinner shows as soon as room reservations are confirmed. They have unlimited access to the World's watercraft transportation system, and can drive on many WDW roads that are off-limits to visitors not staying at the WDW-owned resorts—often a real time-saver. Ticket costs for the Magic Kingdom, as well as River Country and Discovery Island, and green fees and tennis court usage charges, are lower for guests at WDW-owned resorts. Three-day Passports for the Magic Kingdom are available to all guests at WDW-owned resorts—but to few others. (The benefits are so extensive that you should be wary of travel agents who encourage you to stay elsewhere for reasons other than a major difference in price. Since the Disney properties do not pay direct travel agent commissions—as the establishments at the Walt Disney World Village Hotel Plaza and those outside Walt Disney World do—it could be that your agent's advice is influenced by financial considerations.)

Locations of the non-Disney properties are quite scattered. Some are located within the WDW boundaries at Walt Disney World Village Hotel Plaza. The rest are located completely off the property, primarily in Kissimmee, along U.S.-192 (which runs east and west) intersecting the WDW entrance road, and along International Drive (off S.R.-435 at the Orlando city limits). The U.S.-192 establishments are closer to the WDW main entrance—usually only a few miles

away, depending on the individual hostelry. But International Drive, some ten miles from the WDW main gates, is a more pleasant place to stay, thanks to its array of sidewalk-connected lodging places, restaurants, and other minor attractions. Its proximity to still more of the same in Orlando, just a few miles farther north, constitutes an additional benefit.

In choosing a place to stay, you first must decide how much money you want to spend. If your budget permits, try to get reservations at a Disney property. If not, select accommodations outside the World based on what you can afford and on the guidelines given here.

Remember, when examining rate sheets for the best buy for your family, to examine carefully the cutoff age at which children accompanying you (and staying in the same room) will be billed as extra adults. Those with large families should note that villa-type accommodations, which may seem more expensive at first glance, can actually prove less costly in the long run by eliminating the necessity of hiring an additional hotel room—in addition to providing cooking facilities that can provide big savings on meals. If you intend to play golf, find out if the hotel you've chosen offers a Vacationer Golf Membership, which saves money on green fees at the WDW courses.

WDW–OWNED RESORT PROPERTIES

If what you can afford to spend on accommodations approaches the cost of WDW properties, you'll do well to spend the extra money, and to plan far enough ahead to be sure to get one of the rooms here—and to keep trying in hopes of getting a cancellation if you don't secure a reservation the first time around.

In general, rooms at the three hotels—the Contemporary Resort, the Polynesian Village, and the Golf Resort—are quite large and can accommodate up to five without difficulty. Designed expressly with a fair-size family in mind, they're big enough that a cot can be set up or a sofa bed opened up without making the room feel crowded. Most rooms have patios or balconies. And considering the incredibly high occupancy rate here, it's astonishing that things look so fresh. Even the rooms without views have views, if only across the gardens at masses of lovely flowers; none offer you the no-frills panorama of a parking lot that is common at some off-property establishments.

The villa accommodations at Walt Disney World Village, which can accommodate larger groups, are also good for families, especially those who want to cook some of their own meals "at home." Like the hotel accommodations, the villas aren't pretentiously luxurious, but the basics are all there. In fact, some of the utensils and fixtures found in a villa kitchen may be better than those you're using at home. In addition, there are beds that don't sag, big thick towels (and plenty of them), and wisely laid-out bathrooms.

Each resort and villa complex has its own character, and one may hold more appeal for you than another. The Contemporary Resort and the Polynesian Village are right on the monorail and are the most centrally located and most bustling; youngsters love them because there are always other kids around to meet. The Golf Resort, off the monorail and just a bit off the main WDW track, offers a quieter atmosphere and only a slightly less convenient location. The villa accommodations at Walt Disney World Village are remote enough from the heart of things so that you will probably want a car in which to get around. But the Lake Buena Vista Club, with its golf course and tennis courts (described in *Sports*), and the *Empress Lilly* riverboat restaurant are just a short distance away. So for a longer Walt Disney World vacation, one that will not involve spending every day in the Magic Kingdom, the Walt Disney World Village accommodations are probably a good bet.

CONTEMPORARY RESORT HOTEL

Watching the monorail trains disappear into this hotel's enormous, 15-story, A-frame tower never fails to amaze onlookers. The sleek trains look like long spaceships docking as they slide inside; or the sight may bring to mind the story of Jonah being swallowed up by the whale.

Passengers, for their part, are impressed by the cavernous lobby, with its tiers of balconies and, at its center, designer Mary Blair's huge 90-foot-high, floor-to-ceiling, tile mural depicting Indian children, stylized flowers, birds, trees, and other scenes from the Southwest. (Look carefully and you may be able to spot the five-legged goat.)

This imposing establishment is the largest of the WDW properties, boasting over 1,046 rooms in its Tower and the two garden wings that flank it on either side. The hotel has six shops, six complete restaurants, two snack bars, four lounges, large meeting rooms (described in *Meetings and Conventions*), a marina, a beach, a health club, and more. The larger of the hotel's pair of swimming pools, measuring a generous 20 by 25 meters, is a delight for lap swimmers—the best in the World for that purpose. And the Fiesta Fun Center—a vast room full of pinball and other electronic games that's open around the clock—is lively until the wee hours of the morning. For many youngsters, just the presence of this room is reason enough to lodge here. The activity that these installations generate gives the place an urban feeling that is not found elsewhere in WDW; desk clerks who have also done duty at the Polynesian Village and the Golf Resort note that guests arriving at the Contemporary Resort seem more tense and irritable, exhibiting greater anxiety and a defeated-before-they-start mood that Disney personnel surmise is directly related to the environment. Certainly, the place can be a bit intimidating, and the hotel is not to everyone's taste. But you can't deny the Contemporary Resort's vitality, and the sense it gives of being right in the heart of things can prove irresistible.

ROOMS: The hotel's guest rooms are almost evenly apportioned between the Tower and the North and South Garden Wings flanking it on either side. Rooms in the Tower boast exciting views of Bay Lake or the Magic Kingdom, and cost more than the rooms in the garden wings. From rooms on the Bay Lake side, guests can watch the sun rise through the eerie early-morning mists; in the evening, they can watch the Electrical Water Pageant (described in *Good Meals, Great Times*) from their own terrace. Rooms on the Magic Kingdom side, on the other hand, have fine views of the sun setting behind Cinderella Castle (and the Central Florida sunsets are real dazzlers) and of the fireworks exploding around the Castle just after 10 P.M. on nights when the park is open until midnight. Unfortunately, access to Tower rooms is by elevator, and the elevators are slower than molasses in winter. So every trip up and down can become such a chore that impatient folk with some strength may prefer to walk the necessary flights of stairs rather than wait. Except for the views, some guests find it preferable to lodge in the three-storied garden wings.

All rooms can accommodate up to five (plus one additional child under three). Some units have king-size beds; the rest have two queens. Adjoining rooms may be requested, but they cannot be guaranteed.

Bathrooms in the Contemporary Resort are particularly well laid out. Not only are they extremely large, but they also have double sinks, a bathtub with a shower head, plus a separate shower stall, and a toilet slightly separated from the rest of the facilities.

Suites: Several varieties are available. In the Tower, they come with a Bay Lake or Magic Kingdom view, either with one bedroom (and two queen-size beds and two double sleep sofas, to accommodate up to eight), or with two bedrooms (to accommodate up to twelve). Garden Wing suites are available in three types—third-floor Bay Lake–view studio suites that accommodate two, in a parlor and an only slightly separated sleeping area fitted out with a king-size bed; Bay Lake–view one-bedroom suites on the second floor, which sleep up to six in a bedroom, with a king-size bed and a parlor furnished with two double sleep sofas; and garden-view suites, which can accommodate up to seven in the bedroom, which has a pair of queen-size beds, and a parlor furnished with two sleep sofas. (For complete price information, see the chart "Rates at WDW-Owned Properties" in this chapter.)

WHERE TO EAT: Most of the hotel's restaurants are located on the Grand Canyon Concourse on the fourth floor, but there are also restaurants on the fifteenth and second floors, and snack spots beside the marina and in the first-floor Fiesta Fun Center. Special children's menus are generally available at these restaurants. The meal-by-meal specialties of these facilities are described in some detail in the *Good Meals, Great Times* chapter. Here is a brief synopsis:

Terrace Buffeteria: On the Grand Canyon Concourse, this establishment serves breakfast, lunch, and dinner daily.

Terrace Cafe: On the Grand Canyon Concourse. Serves a bountiful, all-you-can-eat Italian buffet every evening; one of the World's best buys. No reservations.

Pueblo Room: On the Grand Canyon Concourse, tucked away behind Coconino Cove. Breakfast, lunch, and dinner are offered. At breakfast, the menu is composed of fairly standard offerings; at lunch, there are salads, hearty sandwiches, and hamburgers; with dinners featuring an assortment of fairly straightforward meat, chicken, and seafood dishes. No reservations.

Outer Rim: On the Grand Canyon Concourse, opposite the Terrace Cafe, with a good view over Bay Lake. Dinner is the only meal usually served here. No reservations.

Gulf Coast Room: One of Walt Disney World's Continental restaurants, this one is on the second floor of the hotel and has a subdued, relaxed atmosphere that seems worlds away from the other bustling areas of this hotel. Dinner is the only meal served. Children might not find the leisurely pace of the service to their taste, but it's possible to send them off to the Fiesta Fun Center

Snack Bar. Reservations are suggested; phone 824-1000, ext. 3684.

Top of the World: This lovely room boasts superb views from the hotel's 15th floor. There's a bountiful, all-you-can-eat buffet for breakfast, lunch, and brunch (on Sunday), and dinner shows either featuring top-name entertainment or a Broadway-style revue nightly. The setting is unique in the World. After dark, the golden spires of Cinderella Castle glitter under the floodlights, and the white lights edging the rooflines of Main Street wink and twinkle like distant fireflies. Reservations are required for the dinner shows and for Sunday brunch; phone the WDW Central Reservations Office at 824-8000.

Fiesta Fun Center Snack Bar: On the first floor; serves light fare until midnight.

Dock Inn: The snack stand at the marina behind the hotel.

WHERE TO DRINK: The no-liquor policy in the Magic Kingdom notwithstanding, tippling is one of the pleasantest pastimes at Walt Disney World, thanks to the settings of many of the bars and lounges and the array of specialty drinks. The Contemporary Resort is no exception.

Monorail Club Car: Near the elevators on the Grand Canyon Concourse, this long, skinny barroom overlooking Bay Lake is a cozy, companionable sort of place for serious drinking. No entertainment but the company you bring.

Coconino Cove: On the Grand Canyon Concourse, just outside the Pueblo Room. Guests waiting to be seated there can have drinks and Mexican-style snacks; there's entertainment nightly.

Top of the World Lounge: Adjoining the Top of the World Restaurant, this spacious, high-ceilinged room offers superb views over the Magic Kingdom. While listening to the dinner show's entertainment just out of sight, it's possible to gaze across the night toward Cinderella Castle. This is a good spot to watch the sunset and, when the park is open until midnight, the fireworks. Dash out onto the more easterly of the two observation decks nearby at 10:05 to see the Electrical Water Pageant blipping and bleeping and glittering on Bay Lake far below.

Sand Bar: Beside the marina, serving a variety of mixed drinks. The specialty is a nifty ice cream piña colada.

ROOM SERVICE: A wide range of offerings suitable for breakfast, lunch, dinner, and snacks can be ordered; consult room service menus for serving times.

Note, however, that room service is generally very slow. To prevent disappointment, pre-order room service breakfasts the night before, using the card hanging from the doorknob; for other meals, count on phoning in an order a couple of hours before you want to be served. When the food finally does arrive, it comes with a smile and, in the morning, with a newspaper.

WHAT TO DO: All by itself, the Contemporary Resort boasts more activities and recreational facilities than many large resorts; it would not be difficult to have a first-class holiday without ever leaving the premises.
Boat rentals: Sailboats, pedal boats, and pontoon

boats, as well as the zippy little motorcraft known as Water Sprites, are all available for rent at the Contemporary Resort marina, near the beach. (See *Sports* for details.)

Water Skiing: Boats with driver and skis can be hired at the hotel marina. (For details, see *Sports*.)

Swimming: There are two main pools here, the big 20-by-25-meter main pool, and the round teen splash pool, deep in the center and shallow on the outside. A toddler's pool is located near the North Wing, and swimming is permitted in the roped-off area of Bay Lake beside the beach. The bottom is delightfully sandy. (For hours, see *Sports*.)

Shuffleboard: Courts are located next to the main pool.

Volleyball: Nets are set up on the beach.

Children's playground: Located near the North Garden Wing.

Jogging: The Fort Wilderness Exercise Trail is only a short run away. Inquire at the desk for directions, and pay careful attention so that you don't miss the turnoff—it's the first road to the left after you pass under the Water Bridge.

Fiesta Fun Center: On the first floor of the hotel, this is one of the World's great indoor recreational facilities, the biggest and most varied of all the Disney hotels' mechanical games rooms, boasting everything from ping pong to skee ball and a couple of different kinds of air hockey, not to mention Asteroids and Space Invaders and all the other current favorites of the pinball-and-electronic-games-playing set. Worth at least a look.

Movies: Three different Disney movies are shown daily (late afternoons and in the early evening) in the theater at the Fiesta Fun Center. A good place to pass a rainy day—or just to get off your feet. (See *Good Meals, Great Times*.)

Shopping: The fourth-floor Grand Canyon Con-

course is full of shops that are not only several cuts above those found in other Orlando-area hotels, but are also interesting enough to make browsing here an amusing way to weather a late-afternoon thundershower. The Fantasia Shop sells kids' stuff and Walt Disney–themed merchandise (china figurines of Mickey Mouse, Minnie, the Cheshire Cat, the Mad Hatter, the White Rabbit, Pluto, and company; T-shirts and sweat shirts; and stuffed animals). Plaza Gifts and Sundries, which adjoins it, is the place for baby food and Pampers, sun hats, and other items, including fresh flowers; and Spirit World, next door, has a selection of newspapers, magazines, books, snack foods, and liquor—just what's needed for a cocktail party on your terrace or aboard a pontoon boat hired at the marina. On the opposite side of the Concourse, the Contemporary Woman offers a range of good-quality women's clothing in all price ranges (and plenty of bathing suits), and the adjoining Contemporary Man stocks casual and beach wear for men. Even tuxedo rentals are available, on 24 hours' notice.

The adjacent Kingdom Jewels, Ltd., displays men's and women's jewelry from around the globe.

TRANSPORTATION: The Contemporary Resort is connected to the Transportation and Ticket Center (TTC) by gold-flagged buses, which operate every 10 to 15 minutes from 7 A.M. until 2 A.M., and less frequently during early morning and late evening hours. The monorail trains, which glide into the hotel with roughly the same frequency, stop just above the Grand Canyon Concourse, inside the atrium area of the Tower; they make stops at the Polynesian Village (from which point you can board a bus to the Golf Resort), the Magic Kingdom, and the TTC.

Blue-flagged watercraft also travel regularly from the marina to Fort Wilderness and Discovery Island.

POLYNESIAN VILLAGE

The Polynesian Village is as close an approximation of the real thing as Walt Disney World Village's *Empress Lilly* riverboat restaurant is an evocation of a genuine stern-wheeler. The vegetation is as lush as anywhere in the World; the architecture speaks of the tropics; and the atmosphere is more subdued than that of even the relatively placid Golf Resort. *Aitea-Peatea*, promises the hotel's motto: "There will be another day tomorrow just like today." Here, that's a pleasant thought.

The mood is set by a three-story-high garden that occupies most of the lobby. To call the construction at the center a fountain is to do it a grave injustice; it's more like a waterfall that a wanderer might suddenly come upon in the jungle. The water cascades over craggy volcanic rocks. Coconut palms tower over 250 square feet of some 75 different species of tropical and subtropical plants—1,500 anthuriums, banana trees, ferns, gardenias, orchids, and other greens. The climatic conditions are nearly perfect, so that everything looks verdant year round.

The structure that contains this mass of greenery, the so-called Great Ceremonial House, is the central building in the Polynesian Village complex. The front desk, the shops, and most of the restaurants are located here. Flanking the Great Ceremonial House on either side are nine 2- and 3-story "longhouses" named for various Pacific islands. These structures house the resort's 637 rooms. On the east side, there is the Tangaroa Terrace restaurant, the resident snack bar, in a building that also houses the game room; on the west, there is Luau Cove, where the Polynesian Revue (described in *Good Meals, Great Times*) is presented nightly. A marina is located just west of the Great Ceremonial House, and a powdery white-sand beach borders the resort property on the north. The fact that the monorail makes stops at this resort makes it a very convenient place to stay; in fact, it's just a couple of minutes' ride to the Magic Kingdom—

the next stop down the line. But because the accommodations are so scattered, and because the hotel is not quite as large as the Contemporary Resort, things seldom feel as hectic, and the Polynesian Village has a loyal following among second- and third-time Disney World visitors. That, coupled with the appeal of the theme as conveyed by the hotel's name, makes the Polynesian Village rooms sell out quickly, and it's the most difficult of the Disney-owned hotels in which to get a reservation.

ROOMS: These are located in the nine longhouses. All rooms have a balcony or a patio, and most have a view of either the Seven Seas Lagoon or of one of the swimming pools; those in the Oahu longhouse, the most easterly of the group, are the largest. Garden-view rooms cost $10 more than pool-view rooms, which in turn are priced at $10 less than lagoon-view units. Most have two queen-size beds, though king-size beds are available on request. As at the Contemporary Resort, all rooms can accommodate five (plus a sixth under age three). Adjoining rooms may be requested, though they cannot be guaranteed.

Suites are available to accommodate from four to eight. Most have a king-size bed in the bedroom and one or two sleep sofas in the parlor. All are located in the Bali Hai longhouse, west of the Great Ceremonial House.

WHERE TO EAT: Some of the more interesting Walt Disney World eating spots are located at the Polynesian Village. (See *Good Meals, Great Times* for more details.)

South Seas Dining Room: Located on the first floor of the Great Ceremonial House. Dinner is served buffet-style at this smallish room.

Papeete Bay Verandah: On the second floor of the Great Ceremonial House, Papeete Bay serves sit-down dinners daily, breakfast and lunch buffets Monday through Saturday, and a massive brunch buffet on Sunday. The room is large and open, and offers fine views across the Seven Seas Lagoon all the way to Cinderella Castle. After dark, Polynesian dancers and a small combo entertain quietly. Reservations are requested for dinner, and are available for all meals; phone 824-5494.

Coral Isle Cafe: On the second floor of the Great Ceremonial House, around the corner from Papeete Bay. This standard coffee shop (with faintly South Seas decor) serves the usual assortment of breakfast items each morning, and does a booming business at lunch and dinner. A good bet when you want a no-fuss meal.

Tangaroa Terrace: This sprawling establishment, on the eastern edge of the property near the Oahu longhouse, has never been as heavily patronized as some of the other Polynesian Village restaurants because of its somewhat remote location. Increasingly, however, good word-of-mouth is spreading, and the restaurant's popularity seems to be rising. Reservations are a good idea at dinner; phone 824-2000.

Barefoot Snack Bar: In the lobby level of the Great Ceremonial House, this is a good spot for Continental breakfasts and for snacks during the rest of the day.

Tangaroa Snack Isle: Most guests discover this snack bar on their way to Tangaroa Terrace, the game room, or the East Pool—to which it is extremely convenient.

WHERE TO DRINK: The resort's Polynesian theme has inspired a whole raft of deceptively potent potables like the Blue Lagoon (creme de banana and blue curaçao), Seven Seas (fruit juice, grenadine, orange curaçao, and rum), Chi Chis (a standard piña colada made with vodka instead of rum), and WDW piña coladas (which include orange juice in addition to rum, pineapple, and coconut cream). There's even a special Polynesian Village non-alcoholic treat—the pink Lei-Lani, a delicious orange juice and strawberry mixture. These drinks are specialties at Polynesian Village lounges, listed below, but can also be ordered elsewhere in WDW. (Details about individual drink menus can be found in the *Good Meals, Great Times* chapter.)

Barefoot Bar: Adjoining the Swimming Pool Lagoon.

Tambu Lounge: Cozy and clublike, this lounge adjoins the Papeete Bay Verandah. A good spot for quiet conversation.

Captain Cook's Hideaway: Off the lobby of the Great Ceremonial House, this small, dark nook also has entertainment nightly.

ROOM SERVICE: It should be noted that while a variety of tempting specialties is available, there is usually a considerable wait between the placing of an order and its arrival. Allow an hour or so at least, so be sure to fill out the card on your doorknob specifying your breakfast desires *the night before*. If this doesn't dampen your enthusiasm for breakfast in your room, the fact that the delicious banana-stuffed French toast is served only in the restaurants might do the trick.

WHAT TO DO: A wide range of activities is available at the Polynesian Village, just as at the Contemporary Resort.

Boat rentals: Sailboats, speedy little Water Sprites, pedal boats, pontoon boats, and outrigger canoes (requiring eight to paddle) are available for rent at the Polynesian Village marina. (See *Sports* for details.) You must go to the Contemporary Resort marina for waterskiing.

Swimming: There are two main pools here, the elliptical East Pool, in the shadow of the Oahu, Tonga, Hawaii, Bora Bora, and Maui longhouses, and the larger, free-form Swimming Pool Lagoon, closer to the marina and the beach. This pool is framed by a large cluster of boulders that forms a water slide much beloved by youngsters; to get to the ladder that takes you to the top, you must duck underneath a waterfall. For swimming laps, the large pool at the Contemporary Resort is best. Toddlers have their own shallow areas in both Polynesian Village pools. Swimming is also permitted in the roped-off areas of the Seven Seas Lagoon. (For hours, see *Sports*.)

Children's playground: Located near the Great Ceremonial House, this assemblage of kid stuff features a small, low, thatch-roofed treehouse affair with the usual assortment of apparatus for climbing and sliding.

Jogging: The Fort Wilderness Exercise Trail and the roads around the Golf Resort are just a short jog away. Ask for directions at the front desk.

Game room: Moana Mickey's Fun Hut, while not as large as the Contemporary Resort's Fiesta Fun Center, usually manages to keep youngsters occupied. Located alongside the Tangaroa Snack Isle.

Shopping: News from Civilization, on the first floor of the Great Ceremonial House, is the only place in Walt Disney World where you can buy a grass skirt, and for that reason alone it's worth a special trip, though most of the other merchandise there—with the exception of a few handsome shells—is of the utilitarian variety—daily newspapers, magazines, tobacco, film, and gifts. Robinson Crusoe Esq., right nearby, sells casual sportswear and swimwear for men, while the Polynesian Princess stocks an appealing assortment of brightly colored resort fashions, bathing suits, and hot-weather accessories. Upstairs, Village Gifts & Sundries sells gift items, souvenirs, and miscellaneous items; Trader Jack's Grog Hut has food, liquor, wine, beer, and other fixings for an impromptu party; and Village Florist can make up a bouquet or a fruit basket to be delivered to your room on request.

TRANSPORTATION: The Polynesian Village is located right on the monorail line, just one stop away from the Magic Kingdom. The entrance is on the second floor of the Great Ceremonial House.

Green-flagged buses, which circulate between the Polynesian Village, the Golf Resort, and the Transportation and Ticket Center, stop at the traffic island in front of the hotel.

Gold-flagged watercraft make regular trips from the Polynesian Village's marina to Fort Wilderness and Discovery Island. Schedule depends on River Country and Discovery Island hours of operation.

GOLF RESORT HOTEL

This 151-room establishment, originally built as a golf clubhouse and later enlarged, is not the hotel that first-time visitors usually choose. "But I don't play golf," they often say. "And besides, it's not on the monorail." Consequently, when there are any empty rooms available in any of the WDW resort hotels, chances are they'll be at the Golf Resort.

Yet guests who stay there for that reason often return enthusiastically on their next visit. For the lack of attachment to the monorail route makes the Golf Resort the most serene of all the Disney-owned hotels. What's more, there aren't so many day guests wandering all over just to see what a Disney hotel is like.

Though the rooms here look about the same as those at the two sister Disney hotels, they're actually a few feet larger. Decorated in subdued earth tones, the Golf Resort also has a pleasantly relaxed atmosphere—more akin to that of the Walt Disney World Village Villas. But the Golf Resort is miles more convenient: buses make the short trip between the Golf Resort, the Polynesian Village, and the Transportation and Ticket Center every ten minutes or so.

ROOMS: These are located in a two-story wing behind the lobby area. All have patios or balconies and views of woods or the golf courses; can accommodate up to five (plus a sixth under age three); and have two queen-size beds and a sleep sofa. (No king-size beds are available here.) Adjoining rooms can be requested, but are not guaranteed.

Two suites, each with two queen-size beds and two sleep sofas, are available as well; they can accommodate up to seven. (For complete price information, see the chart "Rates at WDW-owned Properties" later on in this chapter.)

WHERE TO EAT: The Trophy Room, the hotel's single full-service restaurant, also happens to rank among the most pleasant spots in the World for a meal. Many Disney executives come here for lunch,

because even when there are lines at the Polynesian Village and the Contemporary Resort, the Trophy Room will usually be fairly quiet. Also, the food is quite good. At breakfast and lunch, there are immense all-you-can-eat buffets; at dinner, there is a full, diverse menu. Sunday brunch buffets are also offered. Reservations are suggested; phone 824-2200, ext. 1484.

For snacks, there's the Sand Trap at poolside.

WHERE TO DRINK: The Players' Gallery, adjoining the Trophy Room with a view over the Palm golf course, serves an assortment of specialty drinks and cocktails—Double Eagles (Kahlua on the bottom and a tequila sour floating on the top), Banana Bogeys (light rum, fresh bananas, cream, and vanilla), Unplayable Lies (champagne doused with Southern Comfort and served over a whole frozen apricot), and Lateral Hazards (light rum and Curaçao blended with orange and lime nectar). Beer is available at the Sand Trap at poolside.

ROOM SERVICE: Here, too, it's necessary to plan well in advance when you want to eat in. For breakfast, fill out the pre-order card on your doorknob, and hang it outside your room before retiring.

Pizza is available from room service from 9:30 P.M. until midnight here: deep-dish Sicilian pizza, baked with olive oil, mozzarella, and Parmesan cheeses; or classic 12-inch pizzas topped with mushrooms, onions, green peppers, black olives, pepperoni, and/or sausage. Draft beer is available by the glass or by the pitcher, and wine and sangría by the glass or carafe.

WHAT TO DO: The Golf Resort is landlocked, so when you decide to go boating, you've got to head for the Contemporary Resort or the Polynesian Village. But there are plenty of other activities.

Game rooms: There's a small one located on the lobby level in the guest-room area.

Golf: There are two par-72, Joseph Lee–designed, championship courses—the tree-dotted Magnolia, to the north of the hotel, which plays from 5,903 (ladies) to 7,253 (championship) yards; and, south of the hotel, the Palm, ranked by *Golf Digest* magazine among the United States' top hundred courses—shorter and tighter, with more wooded fairways and nine water hazards, playing from 5,785 to 6,951 yards. Each course has its own driving range. The Wee Links, a 6-hole, 1,525-yard experimental junior layout, occupies a 25-acre corner near the Magnolia. (See *Sports* for details.)

Shopping: The Pro Shop stocks men's and women's golf and tennis togs and gear, some emblazoned with Mickey and Minnie emblems. Golf Gifts and Sundries sells souvenirs, books and magazines, daily newspapers, liquor, tobacco, film, toiletries, and a little bit of a lot of other things.

Swimming: The Golf Resort has its own 60-foot-long swimming pool. For beach action, head for the Polynesian Village.

Tennis: There are two courts tucked away behind the hotel. These are open from 8 A.M. to 10 P.M. daily, and are lighted for night play. (For more information, and for details about fees, instruction, and court reservations, see *Sports*.)

TRANSPORTATION: The green-flagged bus makes regular trips from the Golf Resort to the Polynesian Village and then on to the Transportation and Ticket Center (TTC). To get to the Magic Kingdom or the Contemporary Resort, it's quickest to take the monorail from the second-floor lobby at the Polynesian Village; to get to Walt Disney World Village or Fort Wilderness, stay on the bus until you get to the TTC, and then change for the red-flagged bus for WDW Village or the blue-flagged bus for Fort Wilderness as required.

SPECIAL ROOM REQUESTS

The Central Reservation office (824-8000) can accept *requests* for special rooms or for a particular view, but they cannot guarantee that the resort will be able to honor your request when you arrive.

WALT DISNEY WORLD VILLAGE VILLAS

The area near Walt Disney World Shopping Village is dotted with exceptionally attractive villa-type accommodations, fitted out with fully equipped kitchens and many other amenities. They cost more than individual guest rooms at the three resort hotels, but they accommodate more people as well. For families of more than five (who might otherwise need to rent an extra hotel room), this is the most economical way to stay hereabouts. Smaller families can generally come out even by cooking some of their own meals in their villa.

Aside from the delights of having more space, the villas are exceptionally quiet and secluded; the pace is definitely more relaxed and the atmosphere very low-key. They are not the most conveniently located of WDW accommodations, however, and it's desirable to have a car, since every other type of transportation involves not just one change of bus (as for other WDW hostelries), but two, as described below in the paragraph on transportation.

TYPES OF VILLAS: There are four major types of villas, each one in several sizes. Most have kitchens.

Check in and check out for the Vacation Villas, the Treehouse Villas, and the Fairway Villas, at the Reception Center on Preview Boulevard, between Americana's Dutch Resort Hotel and the TraveLodge at Walt Disney World Village Hotel Plaza. Those staying at the Club Lake Villas should check in and out at the Walt Disney World Conference Center.

Vacation Villas: Located about five minutes' walk from the Lake Buena Vista Club, these apartments, which are fairly formal in feeling, have cathedral-height living-room ceilings; in some, one of the walls is dramatically mirrored. One- and two-bedroom models are available. One-bedroom units can accommodate four, plus an additional child under four; there's a king-size bed in the bedroom and a queen-size sleep sofa in the living room. Two-bedroom units, which can accommodate up to six, plus a seventh guest under age 12, have a king-size bed (or two twins) in each bedroom, and a queen-size sleep sofa in the living room.

The Pool Pavilion in the center of the Vacation Villas is the central recreation area. In addition to the 50-by-30-foot swimming pool, there are bicycle and electric-cart rentals, a laundry, vending machines, and electronic games and pinball machines. Another swimming pool, this one measuring 65 by 30 feet, is located closer to Walt Disney World Shopping Village.

Club Lake Villas: Located slightly northeast of the Vacation Villas area, these units are handsomely done in sophisticated fabrics in reds and blues. The smallest one-bedroom units have a roughly L-shaped configuration, with a special wet-bar-equipped sitting area that is just far enough removed from the sleeping area (with its two double beds) that business travelers who invite their compatriots in for a nightcap don't feel as if they're entertaining in the bedroom. While the layout was drawn up with special care to the needs of those attending conferences at the Walt Disney World Conference Center, it works equally well in providing families with a bit more privacy than they get in the rooms at the three WDW resort hotels. (The single disadvantage for families is the size of the bathrooms—small.) Note that these units, which cost about the same as rooms at the resort hotels, do not have full kitchens—only a small refrigerator and a sink.

For the largest rooms, take a one-bedroom suite, which sleeps five to ten, and includes a Jacuzzi. One-bedroom units have two queen-size beds upstairs and a sleep sofa downstairs, and are priced at a level just slightly higher than the two-bedroom Fairway Villas, Vacation Villas, and Treehouse Villas, all of which sleep at least six.

The Club Lake Villas are all within a ten-minute walk of the Lake Buena Vista Club, across Club Lake, where a 65-by-30-foot swimming pool, golf course, three tennis courts, and restaurants are located.

Fairway Villas: These cedar-sided, slant-roofed, two-bedroom units, located near the tenth, eleventh, seventeenth, and eighteenth fairways of the Lake Buena Vista Club Golf Course, are among the World's most attractive accommodations, bar none, with cathedral ceilings, rough-hewn walls, large windows, contemporary-styled furniture, and an overall feeling of vast spaciousness. They can sleep six, plus a child under 12. Some units for the handicapped are available.

Joggers can loop through the shady Treehouse area or venture forth along Fairway Drive, alongside the golf course, and into the Club Lake Villas area; the nearest swimming pool is the 65-by-30-footer at the Lake Buena Vista Club, within walking distance of some units, a short drive from others.

Treehouse Villas: When you lodge in one of these octagonal, two-bedroom houses-on-stilts scattered along a barbell-shaped roadway at the western edge of the villa area, you go to sleep at night to a cacophony of crickets and wake up to a chorus of bird songs. You're literally in the woods, alongside some of the winding WDW canals, and you feel a million miles from the Magic Kingdom and all its hubbub. Upstairs is the small (but modern) kitchen, with a breakfast bar; the living room (where the television and a sleep sofa are located); two bedrooms (each with a queen-size bed) and two bathrooms; the whole floor is surrounded by a deck where you can eat or just sit and look out into the trees. Downstairs, there's a den and a utility room equipped with a washer and dryer. The canals offer some of the World's best fishing, mainly for bass, and the roadways—shady, flat, and untrafficked as they are—are terrific for jogging. The nearest swimming pool is the 65-by-30-footer at the Lake Buena Vista Club.

Grand Vista Suites: A quartet of ultraluxurious two- and three-bedroom homes—originally designed as model homes for a development project that has been abandoned for the moment—is available for rent in the Vacation Villa area. Bed turndown service and daily newspaper deliveries are provided, refrigerators are stocked with staples when you arrive, and the furniture is first class. (For complete price information, see the chart "Rates at WDW-owned Properties" later on in this chapter.)

WHERE TO EAT: None of the four villa complexes has its own restaurant. But this is not a problem, except for guests lodging in the kitchenless one-bedroom Club Lake Villas, who may want to travel to the Lake Buena Vista Club or to Walt Disney World Shopping Village. (Electric carts that hold four people are available for rent at $15 for each 24 hours.) For breakfast, the options include the Lake Buena Vista Club's main dining room or (for Continental breakfasts only) the snack bar downstairs; or, at Walt Disney World Shopping Village, the Verandah Restaurant or the pastry window at the Gourmet Pantry (open from 9 to 10 A.M.). For lunch and dinner, the selections are broader. (See *Good Meals, Great Times* for more details.)

Groceries: The Gourmet Pantry stocks staples of all sorts, as well as delicacies from around the globe, and good meat, poultry, and fresh green vegetables. Purchases can be delivered to your villa at no charge; if you can't be home to receive them, arrangements can be made for the delivery person to be let in so that perishables can be stashed in the refrigerator. It's also possible to order by phone. Touch "1" on your room telephone (before 2 P.M.), or dial 824-6993 when calling from elsewhere.

WHERE TO DRINK: The Villa area's most convenient drinking spot is the Lake Buena Vista Club's lounge. Otherwise, for liquid refreshment, head for Walt Disney World Shopping Village—Cap'n Jack's Oyster Bar, the Village Lounge, or, aboard the *Empress Lilly* riverboat restaurant, the Promenade Lounge or the Starboard Lounge, or the exceptionally lively Baton Rouge Lounge. (For details about these, see *Good Meals, Great Times* and *Everything Else in the World*.)

ROOM SERVICE: Room service is not available at Walt Disney World Village Villas.

WHAT TO DO: In addition to boating, shopping, and fishing at Walt Disney World Shopping Village (discussed in more detail in *Sports* and *Everything Else in the World*), you can also enjoy a variety of activities in and around the villas themselves.

Biking: The meandering, relatively untrafficked, and quite scenic roads around the Walt Disney World Village Villas, not to mention the eight miles of bike paths there, can make for an enjoyable hour or two of pedaling. Tandems and ordinary two-wheelers are both available for rent at the Pool Pavilion. (See *Sports* for fees.)

Game room: A small arcade with electronic games and pinball machines is located in the Pool Pavilion near the Vacation Villas.

Golf: The par-72 Lake Buena Vista course, which plays from 6,002 to 6,540 yards, is the shortest of the three Disney courses; it's more like the Magnolia than the Palm, but doesn't have the latter's water hazards. There are also practice tees and a driving range, and private lessons (with or without video replay) are available here as well; head pro Rina Ritson, the first woman golf pro ever to hold the top position at a major golf club, is a first-class instructor in her own right, in addition to being married to WDW's Director of Golf, Phil Ritson. First-class clubs, shoes, and balls can be rented at the Pro Shop. (For fees and starting information, see *Sports*.)

Swimming: There are three pools in the Villa area—two near the Vacation Villas (one at the Pool Pavilion, the other close to the shores of the Buena Vista Lagoon) and the third at the Lake Buena Vista Club. Still, they're small; the best for swimming laps is still at the Contemporary Resort Hotel.

Tennis: There are three courts, bordered by the woods and a section of the golf course, at the Lake Buena Vista Club (open 8 A.M. to 10 P.M. daily; lighted for play after dark). Private lessons are available by appointment, and racquets can be rented for a nominal fee; you must buy your own balls. (For fee information, see *Sports*.)

TRANSPORTATION: Green-and-yellow-flagged buses circulate through the Villa areas and to the Lake Buena Vista Club and Walt Disney World Shopping Village, making pickups at bus stops located at regular intervals along the roadways. Sometimes they come every few minutes; sometimes there's a long time lag so you may have to wait as much as twenty minutes—and you never really know when that's going to be. Consequently, although it's indeed possible to get around the World by internal transportation from here, it's not always particularly convenient. You may prefer to rent your own car.

Another option: A $15-a-day electric golf cart can get you from your villa to the WDW Shopping Village or the Lake Buena Vista Club. Or rent a bike. Either can be rented at the Pool Pavilion.

FORT WILDERNESS CAMPGROUND RESORT

The very existence of this 640-acre, canal-crossed expanse of cypress and pines, laced by pleasant blacktop roadways, always surprises visitors who come to WDW expecting the Magic Kingdom and nothing more. If they've heard about Fort Wilderness at all, they often confuse it with the park's Frontierland section.

But the Fort Wilderness atmosphere is relaxed and not at all frenetic. In one corner, a group of kids may be battling it out at tetherball, and on the playing fields there are often a couple of energetic touch football games in progress. In the morning, the campground smells sweetly of dew-wetted pines, then of frying bacon. In the evening, the heat and stillness of the afternoon gives way to dinnertime bustle, and fish and steaks are thrown onto grills as next-door neighbors organize get-togethers. Later on, little clumps of teens and preteens gather alongside the trading posts or at Pioneer Hall, where Fort Wilderness's electronic-games-and-pinball arcade is located. Fort Wilderness also has a marina and a beach, a nature trail, and a number of waterways where fishing, canoeing, and paddleboating are popular; these and other recreational possibilities make Fort Wilderness one of the livelier places to be in WDW.

And you can enjoy the Fort Wilderness experience even if you don't have your own camping gear. Among the 825 campsites, there also are a number of air-conditioned trailers available for rent, complete with kitchen utensils, dishes, microwave oven, linens, color television, daily maid service, and enough other amenities that the woods all around are the only reminders of the fact that you're camping out. The cost is comparable to that of some of the least expensive of the rooms at the resort hotels. (But those don't have kitchens and so don't offer the money-saving option of cooking a few meals "at home.")

CAMPSITES: Fort Wilderness has 825 campsites, ranging in length from 25 to 65 feet, spaced throughout 21 camping loops. Some 200 of them are set up for tent campers, and most of the rest are rented to trailer campers. Each site has a 110/220-volt electric outlet, barbecue grill, picnic table, and a sanitary-disposal hookup; all loops have at least one comfort station equipped with rest rooms, private showers, an ice machine, telephones, and a laundry room. The per-site fee allows for occupancy by up to seven people; beyond that, an additional charge of $2 per extra person is levied.

The various campground areas are designated by numbers. The 100, 200, 300, 400, and 500 loops are the closest to the beach, the Bike Barn, the Settlement Trading Post, and Pioneer Hall; these cost $2 more per day than all the others. The 1500, 1600, 1700, 1800, and 1900 loops are farthest away from the beach and many other Fort Wilderness activities, but they have the heaviest foliage and are quieter and more private.

RENTAL TRAILERS: It used to be that the 176 Fleetwood Travel Trailers scattered through the camping loops at Fort Wilderness were taken only by people who wanted hotel rooms and couldn't get a reservation. Now—mainly as a result of good word-of-mouth—almost every booking is specifically requested. Lodging here provides all the advantages of a villa—and woodsy surroundings to boot.

Trailers are 35 feet long, sleep four or six, and come equipped with pots and pans, dishes, dishwasher, and all the necessary kitchen equipment. There's a bedroom at one end with its own sink, color TV, and a double bed (and, in some trailers, bunk beds); a sofa-bedded living room at the other end (also with its own sink and color TV); and a kitchen and complete bathroom in the center. The bathroom is not the sort of makeshift setup you might expect, but instead compares favorably with, say, a bathroom in the Club Lake Villas or the Treehouses.

Note: No extra camping equipment is allowed on the site; all guests must be accommodated in the rental trailer. (For complete price information, see the chart "Rates at WDW-owned Properties" later on in this chapter.)

WHERE TO EAT: Most people cook their own; supplies are available at the Meadow and Settlement Trading Posts (open from 8 A.M. to 10 P.M. in winter, to 11 P.M. in summer). Deli-style sandwiches can be concocted there for carry-out; you can eat them at your own site, on the beach, or at tables just outside River Country.

When you want to go out, there's the Trail's End Cafe, an informal, log-walled, beam-ceilinged cafeteria inside Pioneer Hall, where home-style fare is served. Beer and sangría are also available, by the glass or the pitcher.

Snacks: The Campfire Snack Bar, in Pioneer Hall, is at the center of the campground and serves hamburgers, cheeseburgers, hot dogs, and the like, from about 11 A.M. until 9 P.M. daily. Down on the shores of Bay Lake, the Beach Shack offers snacks and sodas.

Pizza: Served nightly at Pioneer Hall from 9 P.M. to 12:30 A.M., along with soft drinks, beer, and sangría. Silent movies are shown here then, and a sing-along is staged every night.

WHERE TO DRINK: Beer and sangría are served in Pioneer Hall. Otherwise, take a blue-flagged watercraft to the Contemporary Resort or a gold-flagged watercraft to the Polynesian Village. Be sure to check the operating hours before boarding, however, so you don't miss the last trip back. Or, if you have a car, make the short drive to the *Empress Lilly* riverboat restaurant, Cap'n Jack's, or the Village Lounge at Walt Disney World Shopping Village.

FAMILY ENTERTAINMENT AFTER DARK: In addition to the sing-along and silent movies at Pioneer Hall, there's the Hoop-Dee-Doo Musical Revue, presented three times nightly at 5, 7:30, and 10 P.M.; reservations are required and are so hard to come by that they need to be made well in advance through the WDW Central Reservations Office (824-8000). Cancellations do occur, however. Fort Wilderness guests who can't get a reservation the first time around can have their names added to a waiting list by presenting themselves at the Pioneer Hall Ticket Window before the show. (See *Good Meals, Great Times* for more details.)

There's also a nightly campfire program held at the center of the campground, near the Meadow Trading Post. A sing-along (featuring Chip 'n' Dale) and Disney movies and cartoons are the main goings-on (free). The Marshmallow Marsh Excursion, which begins at the campfire, includes more singing, a marshmallow roast, and a canoe excursion to a secluded lakeside spot from which, at 9:45 P.M., you also can see the Electrical Water Pageant—a procession of waterborne floats, during which an assortment of sea creatures is outlined in a galaxy of tiny colored lights. This can also be viewed from the Fort Wilderness Beach; don't miss it. (For more details, see *Everything Else in the World* and *Good Meals, Great Times*.)

WHAT TO DO: There are more on-site activities at Fort Wilderness than at almost any other area in the World, outside the Magic Kingdom. For golf, of course, it's necessary to travel to the Golf Resort or the Lake Buena Vista Club; for tennis, the Contemporary Resort is most accessible—just a short ride across Bay Lake in the blue-flagged watercraft from the Fort Wilderness marina.

Though it has no swimming pool, Fort Wilderness does have a 315-foot-long, 175-foot-wide beach for swimming in Bay Lake. You can rent tandems, Sting Rays, and other two-wheelers at the Bike Barn for afternoon bicycle excursions or as reliable transportation around the campground. Visits to the Petting Farm, the blacksmith shop, and the horse barn near Fort Wilderness are amusing. Boating is popular; rentals are available at the marina. Canoes can be hired at the Bike Barn. Baseball, basketball, checkers, electric-cart rentals, fishing (on your own in the canals or on organized morning or afternoon angling excursions), horseback riding (on guided trail rides), horseshoes, jogging on the 2.3-mile exercise course, softball, tetherball, volleyball, and water skiing are also available. Or you can just go out for a stroll along the 1½-mile-long Wilderness Swamp Trail, near

Marshmallow Marsh. All of these activities are described in detail in *Everything Else in the World* and *Sports*. There's also a games arcade in Pioneer Hall.

River Country, a major attraction in its own right, with a separate admission charge, is also located at Fort Wilderness; the features of this watery playground—a WDW must right along with the Magic Kingdom—are discussed in detail in *Everything Else in the World*.

TRANSPORTATION: Trams and buses circulating at 7-minute intervals provide transportation within the campground, while buses and watercraft connect Fort Wilderness to the rest of the World. To get to the Polynesian Village, the Contemporary Resort, or the Magic Kingdom, watercraft (which have regular departures from the Fort Wilderness marina) provide the most efficient transportation during their operating hours. At other times, and to get to Walt Disney World Shopping Village, take the blue-flagged bus from the Fort Wilderness bus stop, near the Settlement Trading Post and Pioneer Hall, to the Transportation and Ticket Center. This bus operates at regular intervals. Change to the red-flagged bus for Walt Disney World Shopping Village; the gold-flagged bus for the Contemporary Resort; or the green-flagged bus for the Polynesian Village and the Golf Resort. (For information on watercraft and bus operating hours and frequencies, see the preceding chart under *Transportation* in this chapter.)

Fort Wilderness guests headed for the Polynesian Revue can take special black-flagged buses, which provide service to the Polynesian Village, scheduled for arrival at the Polynesian Village in time for the show. Black-flagged buses also make pickups at the Polynesian Village for guests bound for the Hoop-Dee-Doo Revue at Pioneer Hall. For schedules, inquire at Guest Services.

PRACTICAL MATTERS

The Walt Disney World–owned hotels and villas have some important operating procedures that first-time guests don't always take seriously—much to their later dismay.

Deposit requirements: Deposits equal to one night's lodging (or campsite rental) are required within 21 days of the time that a reservation is made. Personal checks, traveler's checks, cashier's checks, and money orders are acceptable forms of payment. To have deposit charges billed to an American Express or MasterCard account, send your card number, its expiration date, the bank number (for MasterCard), and your signature. Deposits will be fully refunded if you cancel your reservation at least five days before your scheduled arrival. Reservations are automatically cancelled if deposits are not received by the deadline.

Check-in and check-out times: While not unique in the Orlando area, the early check-out time (11 A.M. at Fort Wilderness and the villas, noon for the resort hotels) is almost invariably too early for most WDW guests, while the late check-in times (3 P.M. in the resort hotels, 4 P.M. in the villas) are often painfully late. Even more frustrating is the fact that (except in slow seasons, when the Disney-owned hotels may not be entirely sold out from night to night), these are rules to which all the reservations clerks rigidly adhere. Desk clerks do try to accommodate a guest when possible, but it seldom is.

The management does, however, maintain an efficient luggage-storage operation. So check in and get your ID cards, deposit your suitcases with the bellmen, park your car, and then head off to the Magic Kingdom for the day. (Changing rooms are not abundant; if you don't want to do your sight-seeing in your traveling clothes, you can change in a hotel rest room.)

Payment methods: Hotel bills may be paid with American Express and MasterCard credit cards, with traveler's checks or cash, and with personal checks. Checks must bear the guest's name and address, be drawn on a U.S. bank, and be accompanied by proper identification—that is, a valid driver's license or a government-issued passport, and a major credit card such as American Express, Carte Blanche, Diner's Club, MasterCard, or Visa.

ALL ABOUT WDW RESORT ID CARDS

Issued on arrival at WDW-owned resorts, these unprepossessing little squares of cardboard are among resort guests' most valuable possessions while in WDW. They entitle you to:

- Unlimited transportation by bus, monorail, and watercraft.
- Use of many of the roadways within Walt Disney World.
- Charge privileges: the cards may be used to cover purchases (up to certain credit limits) in shops, lounge and restaurant charges, and recreational fees incurred anywhere in WDW—except the Magic Kingdom.

Note: ID cards are valid for use of the transportation facilities through the end of the last day of your stay, but are not valid for charging past check-out time.

RATES AT WDW-OWNED PROPERTIES

	Charge for single or double occupancy	Charge for additional occupants	Charge for cots	Room capacity	Types of beds	Check out/ check in times
Contemporary Resort Hotel Rooms	$75 to $85 in Garden Wing, $95 in Tower with Bay Lake or Magic Kingdom view	No charge for those under 18; $4 per additional adult	None	Five, plus one additional occupant under age three	Two queen beds. Some king-sized beds available	Noon/3 P.M.
Suites	$170 and $190 in Garden Wings, $240 to $395 in Tower	None	None	Seven to twelve	Most have two queen beds and two sleep sofas	Noon/3 P.M.
Polynesian Village Resort Hotel Rooms	$75 with garden view, $85 with pool view, $95 with lagoon view	No charge for those under 18; $4 per additional adult	None	Five, plus one additional occupant under age three	Two queen beds. Some king-sized beds available	Noon/3 P.M.

Suites	$180 to $275, all in Bali Hai longhouse	None	None	Four to eight	King-sized beds in bedroom and one or two sleep sofas in parlor, usually	Noon/3 P.M.
Golf Resort Hotel Rooms	$75 with woodland view, $85 with pool or golf course view	No charge for those under 18; $4 per additional adult	None	Five, plus one additional occupant under age three	Two queen beds and a sleep sofa in all rooms; no king-sized beds available	Noon/3 P.M.
Suites	$170	None	No cots available; no charge for cribs	Up to seven	Two queen-sized beds and two sleep sofas	Noon/3 P.M.
Club Lake Villas One-bedroom	$85	None	No cots available; no charge for cribs	Five, plus one additional occupant under age three	Two queen-sized beds and one double sleep sofa	11 A.M./4 P.M.
One-bedroom suite	$140	None	No cots available; no charge for cribs	Five	Two queen-sized beds upstairs, one sleep sofa downstairs	11 A.M./4 P.M.
Two-bedroom suite	$280	None	No cots available; no charge for cribs	Ten	Four queen-sized beds and two sleep sofas	11 A.M./4 P.M.
Fairway Villas	$120	None	No cots available; no charge for cribs	Six, plus one additional occupant under age twelve	One queen-sized bed in one bedroom, two double beds (or another queen) in the other, one double sleep sofa in living room	11 A.M./4 P.M.
Vacation Villas One-bedroom	$100	None	None	Four, plus one additional occupant under age three	One king-sized bed in bedroom, queen sleep sofa in living room	11 A.M./4 P.M.
Two-bedroom	$120	None	None	Six, plus one additional occupant under age twelve	King-sized bed (or two twins) in each bedroom, queen sleep sofa in living room	11 A.M./4 P.M.
Treehouse Villas	$120	None	No cots available; no charge for cribs	Six	One queen-sized bed in each bedroom, plus sleep sofa in living room	11 A.M./4 P.M.
Fleetwood trailers at Fort Wilderness Campground	$75	None	No cots or cribs available	Four, for those in 2100 loop	One double bed in bedroom, queen-sized sleep sofa in living room	11 A.M./3 P.M.
	$75	None	No cots or cribs available	Six, for those in 500, 600, 700, and 800 loops	One double bed and bunk beds in bedroom, queen-sized sleep sofa in living room	11 A.M./3 P.M.

Prices subject to change

The four hotels here—Americana's Dutch Resort Hotel, the TraveLodge, the Royal Plaza, and the Howard Johnson's—occupy a unique position among non-Disney-owned Orlando-area accommodations. For they actually are located inside the physical boundaries of Walt Disney World, which makes them especially convenient for anyone intending to spend time in the Magic Kingdom and its environs. And their guests enjoy certain privileges similar (but not equal) to those of guests at WDW-owned properties, such as bus transportation direct to the Transportation and Ticket Center, reduced rates at attractions like River Country and Discovery Island, and the possibility of making reservations for dinner shows before bookings are accepted from the general public.

On the other hand, many of the activities available to guests at WDW-owned properties are not open to guests at Walt Disney World Village Hotel Plaza hotels, and they are not on the whole quite as attractive and appealing as some of the other off-property establishments whose rates are similar. The proximity to WDW attractions, however, not to mention the fact that they are served by an efficient bus system, makes them hard to beat if you can't get a reservation at a WDW-owned hotel.

And while Hotel Plaza establishments don't themselves offer the huge range of facilities found at WDW-owned resorts, the tennis, golf, boating, and fishing available at Walt Disney World Village to all WDW visitors (as described in *Sports* and *Everything Else in the World*) are at your doorstep. WDW Central Reservations (824-8000) can take your bookings for WDW Hotel Plaza hotels (they're also included in several Eastern Airlines packages), but most of these hotels have toll-free numbers that can be called at no charge. Note that all accept a wider variety of credit cards in payment for room charges than do WDW resorts—usually all major credit cards.

AMERICANA'S DUTCH RESORT HOTEL: This gleaming white hotel, its 615 rooms installed in a 19-story tower and two wings, has a tenacious Dutch theme that can be a bit much. The carpets are blue, the bedspreads white, and the rocking chairs and the wallpaper blue-and-white; wooden shoes and windmills are everywhere. The swimming pool is shaped like a windmill; the base of the lamp next to (or on) the bedside table is a wooden shoe. All of this dogged adherence to a single theme is a bit primitive by the standards of the rest of the World; consequently, its appeal is greatest for youngsters. Similarly, the level of maintenance is not up to Disney hotels' standards. The scuff marks, chipped paint, and general aura of wear-and-tear that characterize some of the rooms at Americana's Dutch Resort Hotel simply will not be found at a WDW-owned property.

Restaurants include the Flying Dutchman, which serves breakfast, lunch, and dinner; and the Tulip Cafe, which is open around the clock. (For details on these, see *Good Meals, Great Times*.) There's entertainment and dancing in The Hague Lounge; the Nightwatch Lounge is the hotel's cozy just-for-drinking spot. Two lighted tennis courts, the racquetball and shuffleboard courts, miniature golf, a playground for children, and a game room are also available. Rates are about $96 for two in high season, $84 in low season ($5 in cots). There are no rooms specially equipped for handicapped travelers. More information: Americana's Dutch Resort Hotel; 1850 Preview Blvd.; Lake Buena Vista, FL 32830; 828-4444 (toll-free 800-327-2994; from Florida, 800-432-2926).

HOTEL PLAZA

TRAVELODGE TOWER: This oddly curvilinear, 325-room hotel-tower has exceptionally large and pleasant rooms done in shades of sea green or coral, each one with two queen-size beds, an AM/FM radio, and a private balcony that offers glorious views of the flat central Florida countryside—a sea of pines. A game room and a swimming pool are about the extent of the on-premises recreation here, but the tennis, golf, fishing, and boating in Walt Disney World Village are all available.

There's one restaurant, the Coral Grotto, and for snacks there's the Sleepy Bear Ice Cream Parlor (in season only). The Top of the Arc Lounge, on the hotel's 18th floor, offers a superb panorama of the World—including Cinderella Castle in the Magic Kingdom and the fireworks displays that take place in the park at about 10 P.M. every night that the park stays open until midnight. Rates are about $76 in low season, $88 in high season (no additional charge for children under 19 sharing their parents' room; $6 for cots). There are six rooms for handicapped travelers. More information: TraveLodge Tower; Walt Disney World Village Hotel Plaza; Box 22205; Lake Buena Vista, FL 32830; 828-2424 (toll-free 800-255-3050).

HOTEL ROYAL PLAZA: The liveliest of the four Walt Disney World Village Hotel Plaza properties, and the hotel with the biggest swimming pool, it also boasts 400 exceptionally commodious rooms located in a 17-story high rise and in two-story, garden-style wings. (Choose rooms in the tower or away from the pool if you like to sleep with the windows open, since things stay active down there until very late on occasion.) Each room has its own balcony and safety deposit box; youngsters will be intrigued by the innovative punch-card door "keys." In addition, there are saunas, a Jacuzzi, a game room, shuffleboard courts near the pool, four tennis courts, and special children's programs.

El Cid specializes in Continental-style cuisine, the Knight's Table offers standard coffee-shop fare, and there are two bars—La Cantina, which serves shrimp, crab, and fresh oysters along with its cocktails, and Giraffe, a locally popular disco—the only one in the World—which attracts an energetic young crowd (many of them Disney employees). A barber shop, beauty salon, and a one-day film-developing service are also available on the premises. "Premium" rooms on the hotel's lower floors run $80 per night; "deluxe" rooms on the middle floors go for $86; and "preferred deluxe" poolside and tower rooms cost $92; room rates apply for up to four guests in a room, no matter what their ages ($5 for cots). Handicapped visitors should be advised that while all first-floor rooms have wider doors, there are no grab rails in bathrooms. More information: Hotel Royal Plaza; 1905 Preview Blvd.; Lake Buena Vista, FL 32830; 828-2828 (toll-free 800-327-2990; from Florida, 800-432-2920).

HOWARD JOHNSON'S RESORT HOTEL: An exceptionally handsome establishment, this HoJo has 323 rooms spread through a six-story annex building, and a fourteen-story tower whose rooms are arrayed around a balcony overlooking a plant-filled atrium served by a glass-walled elevator. There are two swimming pools—plus a kiddie pool—and the hotel has its own game room; guests can use the Royal Plaza Jacuzzi and the TraveLodge playground. A standard Howard Johnson's Restaurant (a coffee shop with a dining room attached) is on the premises; it's open around the clock. Five special rooms are equipped with wider doors and grab rails for handicapped guests. Rates range from $75 to $85 in low season and $85 to $95 in high season (no additional charge for children under 18; $8 for cots). More information: Howard Johnson's Resort Hotel; Box 22204; Lake Buena Vista, FL 32830; 828-8888 (toll-free 800-654-2000).

FLORIDA CENTER ACCOMMODATIONS

This area, ten miles north of the WDW main gates–a 15-minute drive—is the best-developed of the several areas where guests not staying in WDW-owned properties usually lodge. It comprises Sand Lake Road (S.R.-528A), which intersects I-4 (and runs eastward all the way to the airport); International Drive, the sidewalk-bordered boulevard that runs roughly northward off Sand Lake Road; and Kirkman Road (S.R.-435), which heads north off Sand Lake Road.

The densest concentration of lodging and eating places is on International Drive. Most of the best-known motel chains are represented here, and many restaurant chains also have branches: Arby's, Baskin Robbins, Burger King, Cork and Cleaver, Denny's, Dino's Pizza, The Golden Corral, International House of Pancakes, Long John Silver's, McDonald's, Perkins Cake and Steak, Pizza Inn, Pizza Hut, Steak and Ale, Wendy's, and Western Sizzlin' among them. Bennigan's, a somewhat tonier chain with a restaurant here, is known among some Disney employees for its particularly good "happy hours."

Most of these facilities on Sand Lake and Kirkman Roads are clustered close to their intersections with International Drive. The city's more interesting restaurants are too far away to reach on foot, however, and the cost of shuttle transportation for a family of four is so close to that of renting a car that it seems pointless not to do so.

It's also worth noting that the distance to the WDW main gates from here (you have to figure an hour from Main Street to your hotel swimming pool) is such that leaving the Magic Kingdom for a rest at your hotel—a good idea, especially in the heat of summer—is not always practical unless the park is open late and you can muster the energy to go early, stay for a few hours, and then return after dinner to savor the nighttime delights of the park for a few hours more. This takes stamina; young children may not always have it.

The area is, however, one of the livelier places to lodge outside WDW. Florida Center is also relatively accessible to downtown Orlando (ten to fifteen minutes' drive away), and Winter Park (about 20 minutes from parking space to parking space), where there are more than a dozen interesting little shops and nearly as many intriguing restaurants, including one of the most pleasant ice-cream parlors around.

A selection of some of the more attractive properties (in a variety of price ranges) follows:

COURT OF FLAGS: This lively, 820-room establishment in the Kirkman Road area of Florida Center has facilities for meetings of up to a thousand people, but the family trade wasn't forgotten either, and the place is as bright and cheery and appealing as any in the area, especially considering the price. Rooms are arranged in four 3-story buildings. There are three swimming pools—two small round ones and another that is shamrock-shaped (but large enough for swimming laps); and they all have plenty of palm trees and chairs. Saunas for men and women are located near the larger pool, and there are two tennis courts nearby that are lighted for night play. The somewhat secluded location, inside a complex of hotels where the roads are little used, off busy Kirkman Road, makes for good (if unshaded) jogging. The children's playground is nothing out of the ordinary. Doubles cost $49 to $53, depending on the location (no additional charge for children under 18; $7 per cot). This is a little more than the neighboring Caravan Resort Inn and considerably less than the Sheraton–Twin Towers Complex nearby (which does a big convention business)—but a better choice than either. (The Howard Johnson's, the fourth in the Kirkman Road quartet, has some rooms that are less expensive than any offered at the Court of Flags, and if price is a prime consideration, it is your best bet.) Pet owners are permitted to bring animals inside, but only after paying a $50 deposit. Details: Court of Flags Hotel; 5715 Major Blvd.; Orlando, FL 32805; 351-3340 (toll-free 800-327-0721; from Florida, 800-432-1171).

DAYS INN-SAND LAKE ROAD: Orlando's several Days Inns rank among its most economical accommodations. The complexes tend to be large, and the architectural finesse and the landscaping are minimal; but there are pools and game rooms enough to go around. This 718-room facility on Sand Lake Road, one of the largest, is attractively located on the shores of Spring Lake, and the view from some of the rooms is particularly nice. There are three swimming pools, laundry facilities, a playground, and a restaurant-and-cafeteria (though its food is of a caliber that makes one seek out even the nearest McDonald's). Rates are $27.88 from June through May ($1 extra per additional occupant under 18). Single rates, which cost $2 less, are even more advantageously priced. There are no facilities for handicapped travelers. Details: Days Inn; 7200 Sand Lake Rd; Orlando, FL 32811; 351-1900. (A variety of toll-free reservation numbers are available; for the one to call from your location, phone directory assistance at area code 800.)

HILTON INN-FLORIDA CENTER: Comparable to the Marriott (described below), this 420-room establishment has two restaurants, private safes and refrigerators in each room, free in-room movies, two large swimming pools (one of them Olympic-size and under an open-air pavilion), a well-kept (but hardly huge) game room with about a dozen machines, and a large convention center. This means a certain amount of hubbub that may not appeal to all family vacationers, but the hotel itself is quite pleasant.

Rates are $55 to $75 in summer, around Christmas, and from February through April; off-season rates, which prevail in January, in May, during the first two weeks of June, and from September through mid-December, are $44 to $63. Efficiencies go for $85 in season, $70 the rest of the year. No charge for up to three children, regardless of age, sharing accommodations with parents. Cribs and rollaway beds are free, and an entire section of the hotel was designed with handicapped travelers in mind. Details: Hilton Inn Florida Center; 7400 International Dr; Orlando, FL 32809; 351-4600 (toll-free 800-327-1363; from Florida, 800-432-5141).

HOLIDAY INN-INTERNATIONAL DRIVE: This 642-room property's 13 tropically landscaped acres are occupied by six buildings—a 14-story tower, a 5-story annex, and four other buildings two stories high. There is a free-form pool (with a water slide and a landscaped island in the center), a playground, an excellent game room that looks appropriately Space Age, and shuffleboard and volleyball courts. There are two restaurants—Gomba Joe's, which serves Italian and American specialties every evening, and the Pipers Restaurant, one of the handsomest of area coffee shops, with its blond-wood Windsor chairs and glassed-in alcove overlooking the swimming pool. Twelve special rooms for the handicapped are available. Every room has a digital clock-radio and a color television set wired to receive Home Box Office. Rates for doubles in the hotel are about $52 to $63 (no charge for children 19 and under; rollaways $6). Details: Holiday Inn-International Drive; 6515 International Dr.; Orlando, FL 32809; 351-3500 (toll-free 800-238-5000).

LA QUINTA MOTOR INN: It's not exactly a Spanish hacienda, but the rates are low enough—about $32 to $40 for doubles, depending on the season (with no charge for children under 17 sharing their parents' quarters)—that you wouldn't expect fancy accommodations, and the establishment is quite pleasant and well-kept. The 160 rooms are arranged in four 2-story wings that wrap around a small (but tidy) pool. Entrances to the rooms are in hallways inside; there's no at-door parking. Ground-floor rooms are suitable for handicapped travelers. Denny's Restaurant, open around the clock, is next door. Details: La Quinta Motor Inn; 5825 International Dr.; Orlando, FL 32809; 351-4100 (toll-free 800-327-1366; from Florida, call collect).

ORLANDO MARRIOTT: Located at the corner of Sand Lake Road and International Drive, near the exit to I-4, this is one of the choicest of the lodging spots outside the World. It's not cheap—the appeal is primarily to businessmen and vacationers willing to pay for WDW-level accommodations but unable to get a reservation—though there is value here. The Marriott has two outdoor pools—one quite large and dogleg-shaped, the other barbell-shaped and relatively small—near the six lighted tennis courts and the playground, an innovative complex of wooden structures for climbing and swinging. There's also miniature golf and a game room. The 640 smartly decorated guest rooms are arranged in ten 2-story, cream-colored, stucco-walled "villas" scattered around grounds that are handsomely landscaped with ferns, palms, and all manner of other tropical vegetation. These can be opened up to adjoining rooms or suites to form spacious quarters with one or two bedrooms, living room (or third bedroom), two or three baths, and a full apartment-size kitchen. Rates are $60 to $75 in high season, about $10 less the rest of the year. Two rooms for the handicapped are available. The attractive Samantha's, one of two restaurants on the property, is a favorite local restaurant and has live entertainment Monday through Saturday nights. More information: Orlando Marriott; 6700 Sand Lake Rd.; Orlando, FL 32809; 375-2420 (toll-free 800-228-9290).

QUALITY INN INTERNATIONAL: Adjoining Morrison's Cafeteria, this 320-room property is extremely pleasant, if not fancy, and quite well-kept. Most rooms are in two-story structures flanking the reception building. The pool is Y-shaped (*not* Olympic-size as the Quality Inn directory states), but adequate for all but the most ambitious lap swimmers. The game room is small, with only about half a dozen machines. The Family Restaurant, one of two eateries on the premises, is ornamented with pretty antiques. There's good value here: rates are about $36 to $40 for two during the summer and over the Christmas holidays, $24 to $30 from September until mid-December, with no extra charge for children under 17 occupying the same room as their parents. Some facilities for the handicapped are available. Details: Quality Inn at International Drive; 7600 International Dr.; Orlando, FL 32809; 351-1600 (toll-free 800-228-5151; 800-642-8700 from Nebraska).

SHERATON WORLD: Particularly attractive and situated off to itself, well south of Sand Lake Road, just a stroll from Sea World, this 319-room establishment has a good-size swimming pool, a game room, two lighted tennis courts, and a miniature golf course. The surrounding area is undeveloped and is ideal for early-morning jogging. Several rooms are suitable for the handicapped. Rates are particularly reasonable: $42 to $52 (no charge for youngsters under 18). For details, contact the Sheraton World, 10100 International Dr.; Orlando, FL 32809; 352-1100 (toll-free 800-325-3535).

U.S.-192 ACCOMMODATIONS

The motels along this four-lane divided highway, which intersects I-4 in the community of Kissimmee, are closer to the WDW main gates than those along Orlando's International Drive, but the area itself is far less attractive and lacks International Drive's abundance of eating places. Still, the accommodations here can't be faulted for convenience, and on stays of short duration, that may be a consideration. Also, this area lies closer to Circus World (about 8 miles distant) and Cypress Gardens (some 12 miles beyond Circus World).

DAYS LODGE-192 EAST: As a rule, establishments in this budget chain offer the best value for your money in the area, and this 609-room property is a case in point. There's plenty of concrete and no landscaping of which to speak. But there are three swimming pools, and each unit is an apartment, complete with a bedroom, kitchen, and sofa bed—equipped living room—ideal for a family that has had it with the togetherness of two double-bed rooms. And for all this you pay only about $40 to $50, depending on the season—a very good buy indeed, especially after you consider the additional savings available in fixing your own meals. (Even a lousy cook should be able to do better than the chef at the adjacent restaurant-and-cafeteria.) There are no special facilities for handicapped travelers. Details: Days Lodge; 5820 E. Spacecoast Pkwy.; Kissimmee, FL 32741; 846-7900. (A variety of toll-free reservation numbers are available; for the one to call from your location, phone directory assistance at area code 800.)

HOLIDAY INN-MAIN GATE EAST: Situated 2½ miles from the WDW main gate, this 512-room property is not the most attractive of the local inns, yet it can easily be counted among the best-looking in its price range—about $35 to $46, depending on the season, and the facilities are somewhat broader than those you usually get for that kind of money. For instance, there are two lighted tennis courts, and in a somewhat perfunctorily landscaped courtyard at the center of each of the squares where the 512 rooms are located, there's a medium-size swimming pool. A children's dinner theater (open to youngsters 4'10" and under) operates every evening; grown-ups can park kids there and eat elsewhere in peace if they desire. Drinks in the Mason Jar Lounge and at the pool bar are served in Mason jars that you can keep. A few rooms are equipped for handicapped travelers. Details: Holiday Inn-Main Gate East; 5678 E. Spacecoast Pkwy.; Kissimmee, FL 32741; 846-4488 (toll-free 800-238-5000).

HYATT ORLANDO: This hotel, the closest non-Disney owned resort to the WDW main gates, is large, with some 960 rooms grouped in four clusters of buildings so complexly arranged that it takes many people a couple of days to find their way around. But it's one of the few hotels outside WDW that can even begin to compete with the Disney properties in terms of service, facilities, and amenities. The tastefully decorated rooms, with their sophisticated, subdued coloring and sleek modern furniture, are a cut above even Disney's. Each guest room has color TV, AM/FM radio, and in-room movie capacity, and there are three tennis courts and a 1.3 mile jogging-and-exercise trail right on the property. The game room here stands out, even in a town full of terrific competitors. Each of the four clusters has its own medium-size swimming pool and an innovative playground. There are also several restaurants—Limey Jim's, whose Continental-style menu makes it some Orlando residents' favorite destination for a night on the town; the Big Bicycle Buffet, pleasant and informal, serving meals buffet-style; and Gatsby's, the multileveled, intriguingly designed coffee shop. The Bus Stop Deli serves snacks and light sandwiches from morning until late evening, and Limey Jim's Pub and Show Lounge has entertainment every night except Sunday. The gift shops may not excite you the way those in the Disney hotels can, but there are plenty of them. The hotel provides complimentary shuttle service to WDW. Room rates are high—$60 to $80 per room, $160 to $320 for suites. Facilities for handicapped travelers are available. Details: Hyatt Orlando; 6375 Spacecoast Pkwy.; Kissimmee, FL 32741; 846-1234 (toll-free 800-228-9000).

KING'S MOTEL: There is a handful of nonchain establishments on U.S.-192 as you head toward downtown Kissimmee and away from Walt Disney World. This 96-room establishment is among the better ones. Its small rectangular pool sits on the shore of a lake, and boats can be rented at the motel office (or you can fish from the dock). In addition to standard motel rooms, efficiencies accommodating four or six also are available. Many units have lake views. Rates are a reasonable $25 to $35. Handicapped travelers should note that while doors are wide enough for wheelchairs, bathrooms lack grab rails. More information: King's Motel; 4836 W. Spacecoast Pkwy.; Kissimmee, FL 32741; 847-4762 (toll-free 800-327-9071).

KNIGHTS INN: The royal purple, crushed-velvet bedspreads of this establishment (down the road from the Holiday Inn-Main Gate East) may take some getting used to, but this small hostelry offers an excellent choice of rooms—standard two-double-bed ones; efficiency apartments (fitted out with a bed, a sofa bed, and a completely furnished kitchen); and deluxe rooms (equipped with just one bed and a sofa). Both smoking and nonsmoking units are available in every style. The pool is small, but everything is on one story, and you can park right outside your door; it seldom happens that someone else parks in your space. Rates are about $35 to $38 for two (no charge for children under 18). All rooms are accessible to wheelchair travelers. Details: Knights Inn; 2800 Fountain Park; Kissimmee, FL 32741; 846-8186.

RAMADA INN: Attractive landscaping makes this 386-room establishment, just west of I-4, another very pleasant spot. There are two medium-size, heated swimming pools—roughly L-shaped to make for good lap swimming; plus a pair of lighted tennis courts; an excellent game room (with 30 electronic machines, two pachinko games, two football games, an air hockey game, and two pool tables); and two restaurants—the elegant Mayan Restaurant and the Aztec Terrace, where buffet breakfasts and dinners are served daily. The Mayan Lounge has entertainment nightly except Sunday. The hotel has two rooms for the handicapped. Details: Ramada Inn Southwest; 2950 Reedy Creek Blvd.; Kissimmee, FL 32741; 846-4466 (toll-free 800-327-9127; 800-432-9195 from Florida).

SHERATON–LAKESIDE INN: One of a pair of fancy resorts on U.S.-192, the Sheraton-Lakeside, located west of I-4 (not far from the Ramada Inn), has 476 rooms arranged in several buildings around two good-sized trapezoidal swimming pools and along the shores of Black Lake, where guests go paddle boating (though swimming is not permitted). Playgrounds are located poolside, and there are four tennis courts and a good miniature golf course as well. Restaurants include Max's Deli, which serves high-piled sandwiches to eat at lakeview tables; Sadie's Seafood Saloon, which offers fresh Florida fish and crustaceans; and the Cafe Lakeside, a coffee-shop-with-class. The cost, about $42 to $65 per couple (no charge for children under 18), is lower than at the Orlando Hyatt and the WDW hotels, and there are enough amenities to make this a fairly good deal. Wide doors and ramps make most of the hotel accessible to wheelchair-bound travelers. Details: Sheraton-Lakeside Inn; 7711 Vine St.; Kissimmee, FL 32741; 846-3221 (toll-free 800-325-3535).

MISCELLANEOUS

The following six establishments are located outside the U.S.-192 and Florida Center/International Drive areas. Each of the six has appealing features that make it stand out among Orlando-area hostelries.

HARLEY HOTEL OF ORLANDO: Lodging in downtown Orlando puts vacationers close to some of the more interesting local restaurants, and the Harley—one of the best among the Greater Orlando–area hotels—is the establishment of choice. You're only a few minutes' drive from Winter Park—a fact best appreciated when, at the end of a long day of sight-seeing, you can have a late meal there. And you're only a couple of minutes from Rosie O'Grady's, an Orlando night spot so lively that it's easy to party there until the very wee hours of the A.M. (For a further description, see *Orlando*.) On the other hand, you are not quite as close to the Magic Kingdom. But driving the 17 miles or so to the WDW main gates early in the day is not difficult. Adults traveling without children will especially enjoy the atmosphere at this hotel, which is one of the few in the Orlando area that doesn't cater primarily to a family crowd. Reflections, the mirrored eatery on the Harley's top floor, is a dazzler, and the Cafe on the Park, the hotel's restaurant, is almost equally lovely, with its rosy salmon-pink color scheme and its fine view out over Lake Eola and the municipal fountain at its center. The hotel's swimming pool, which shares the view, is also an especially relaxing place to be. And the guest rooms' handsome decor warrants special mention. Rates—$46 to $58 for two, depending on the room—stay the same all year round, which makes the hotel an especially good deal in high season, when other establishments raise their prices. Some rooms are equipped for handicapped travelers. Details: Harley Hotel of Orlando; 151 E. Washington St.; Orlando, FL 32801; 841-3220 (toll-free 800-321-2323).

BEST WESTERN WORLD INN: Located on the edge of WDW's 27,400 acres, next to the Orange Vista Hospital, this pleasant 248-room stopping place is a good bet among off-property establishments. Though slightly farther from the WDW main gate than some of the U.S.-192 lodging places, the World Inn is still quite close, and it's only a couple of minutes' drive from Walt Disney World Shopping Village and all of its excellent restaurants (described at length in *Good Meals, Great Times*). There's a fine rectangular swimming pool (good for laps); and the peaceful country roads nearby, not to mention the WDW roads around the Shopping Village and the WDW Village Villas, are fine for jogging. Free shuttle buses make round trips to WDW's Transportation and Ticket Center five times daily, and there are vans to take guests

ACCOMMODATIONS

into the Shopping Village. The hotel's lounge has nightly entertainment and a "happy hour" that attracts many Disney employees. Doubles cost from $48 to $58, depending on the season (with no additional charge for children under 17). The hotel has no special facilities for the handicapped. More information: Best Western World Inn; I-4 and Rte. 535; Lake Buena Vista, FL 32830; 876-3636 (toll-free 800-327-6954).

GRENELEFE GOLF AND TENNIS RESORT: Located some 22 miles from the WDW main gates, this 950-acre resort—a fine destination in its own right with its pair of 18-hole golf courses, its dozen tennis courts, golf and tennis instruction programs, its lakefront marina, beach, pools, saunas, Jacuzzis, and 1.6-mile-long fitness course—is primarily of interest to those who want to add a visit to the Magic Kingdom to the beginning or end of a vacation in a country club–like atmosphere that is less oriented to the family trade than WDW's own resorts—not to mention lots less frenetic. The 800-odd rooms here are located in clusters of buildings scattered along winding drives next to the fairways of the golf courses; some are like standard hotel rooms, with one or two double beds, while one- and two-bedroom parlor suites with fully equipped kitchens are also available. The program of golf instruction, the Andy Bean Golf Studio, is particularly interesting: private, semi-private, group, and playing lessons that use videotape recordings, as well as private lessons without video and free clinics for juniors (under 18), are offered. There are three restaurants and three lounges. Cost is $55 for hotel rooms, $85 for suites with one bedroom, $115 for those with two bedrooms; about twice that during the high season, which lasts from January to mid-April. Grenelefe is a real bargain for WDW visitors in summer. For details: Grenelefe Golf and Tennis Resort; Grenelefe, FL 33844; 813-422-7511 (toll-free 800-237-9549; from Florida, 800-282-7875).

JOHN NEWCOMBE'S VACATION RESORT: Occupying 85 acres on U.S.-27 just over a mile from its intersection with U.S.-192 and close to eight miles from the WDW main gates, this 230-room establishment designed for active families stands out for its variety of recreational offerings, the most striking of which is tennis on the 17 courts (a half dozen of them lighted for night play) and the sophisticated tennis instruction programs. But the low rates ($40 in low season, $46 in high season; no additional charge for children under 17) also merit mention, especially since they include shuttle service (operated two or three times a day) to WDW's Transportation and Ticket Center. The resort's Misty Harbor Restaurant, designed around a New England theme, serves fine dinners; another eatery, the Greenhouse, is available for breakfast and lunch. There are minimal facilities for handicapped travelers. More information: John

Newcombe's Vacation Resort; Box 2527; Orlando, FL 32802; 656-8181 (toll-free 800-874-9064 from outside Florida).

PARK PLAZA: Orlando's closest approximation of a cozy country inn occupies a prominent location on genteel Park Avenue in the toney community of Winter Park. The guest rooms don't quite measure up to the lobby, which is done up in mirrors, old tiles, brass, antiques, and potted palms. But with their thick new carpet, subdued color scheme, and polished wooden moldings, they're attractive enough—particularly the two-room suite ($75 nightly), with its sitting area and a balcony overlooking Park Avenue, where you can rock away for an hour or two in a gleaming white wicker rocking chair. Smaller rooms, more suitable for one, could be cramped for two; they're available with courtyard or parkside views at $45 to $55 nightly. Continental breakfast is included in the rates. No children under five are permitted—but this is basically not set up for families because of the size of the rooms and bathrooms. (Nor is the hotel set up for handicapped travelers.) The distance from Walt Disney World, a half-hour's drive or so, makes it a good choice only for those who don't plan to spend a great deal of time in the World. Details: Park Plaza; 307 Park Ave. S.; Winter Park, FL 32789; 647-1072.

LANGFORD RESORT HOTEL: This esteemed 220-room hotel is set on its own tree-shaded grounds, just off the beaten path in the ritzy community of Winter Park. The Park Avenue shopping district is a block away, but the hubbub of commerce (what little hubbub is allowed in the exclusive shops there) never reaches the guests at Langford—even those lounging by the side of the Olympic-size pool. It has two dining rooms, the Anchor Room and the Empire Room Supper Club; the latter has a show every night that includes plenty of opportunities for ballroom dancing. Rates are $35 to $46 a night for a single; $42 to $46 for a double. Information: Langford Resort Hotel; 300 E. New England Ave.; Winter Park, FL 32789 (644-3400).

CAMPING OUTSIDE WALT DISNEY WORLD

The lush, cypress-hung woods of WDW's Fort Wilderness are not duplicated at any other Orlando-area campground. But not everyone can get a reservation at Fort Wilderness, and in any case, not everyone wants to spend the money. If you fall into one of these groups, consider some of the other local campgrounds. Most offer planned activities, swimming pools, conventional electricity and water hookups, hot showers, and other amenities.

CAMPING WORLD CAMPGROUND: This campground is big, with some 488 sites, and it has an expansive list of activities and facilities: fishing, shuffleboard, a playground, a game room, movies, bike

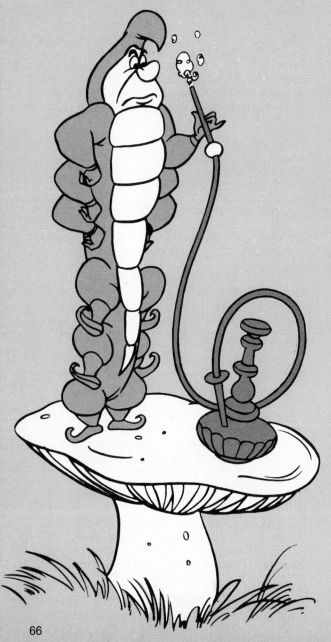

and paddle boat rentals, nightly movies and weekend entertainment (a circus, for example), and a large swimming pool with a water slide built into the rocks, very much like the one at WDW's own Polynesian Village. And you can't beat the location, just five miles east of the main gates. But there's not much shade. Rates are $9.95 for two adults and any number of children under 18 the year round, $1.50 per additional adult per night, including all hookups. Tenters are welcome. Details: Camping World Campground; 5175 U.S.-192; Kissimmee, FL 32741; 846-3424 (toll-free 800-327-9153, or 800-432-9196 from Florida).

ORANGE GROVE CAMPGROUND: Though not the biggest or fanciest of Orlando-area campgrounds, this one does boast plenty of shade—as much as the 700 citrus trees on the site can provide. There's also an oversized rectangular swimming pool, a game room, playground, horseshoe and shuffleboard court, and, in winter, an activities program that includes bingo, movies, and square dancing. There are 192 sites. Two people pay $8 (for sites with water and electric hookups) or $9 (for those with sewage hookups as well) in high season; $7.25 and $8 respectively the rest of the year. There's an additional charge of $1 for each of the next three guests. Tenters are welcome. Located five miles east of the WDW main gates. Details: Orange Grove Campground; 2425 Old Vineland Rd.; Kissimmee, FL 32741; 847-6655.

YOGI BEAR'S JELLYSTONE PARK CAMP-GROUND: Located 4½ miles west of the WDW main gates on U.S.-192, this partially wooded 700-site campground has a lake, mini-golf course, boating and fishing facilities; a fully stocked store, restaurant, and gift shop; and a range of planned activities. Rates ($11 to $15.50 year round, for families with up to seven children) include water, electric, and sewage hookups; tent sites are also available. Tenters are welcome. Details: Yogi Bear's Jellystone Park Campground; 8555 W. Spacecoast Pkwy.; Kissimmee, FL 32741; 351-4394 (toll-free 800-558-2954).

YOGI BEAR'S JELLYSTONE PARK CAMP-GROUND: This 500-site campground, located 10 miles east of the WDW main gates just off I-4, has less shade than its U.S.-192 relative, but the facilities, rates, and range of activities are about the same. Details: Yogi Bear's Jellystone Park; 9200 Turkey Lake Rd.; Orlando, FL 32809; 351-4394 (toll-free 800-558-2954).

YOGI BEAR'S JELLYSTONE PARK CAMP-GROUND: Activities and many of the facilities are identical to those at the other Orlando Jellystone Park locations, except that the swimming pool here is Y-shaped rather than rectangular, and the site is completely wooded rather than open. It's also farther away—30 miles to the northeast of the WDW main gates, in Apopka. Rates are $10 for up to six on each of the 455 campsites, year round. Details: Yogi Bear's Jellystone Park Campground; Rte. 1, Box 2000; Apopka, FL 32703; 889-3048 (toll-free 800-558-2954).

THE MAGIC KINGDOM

Though occupying just 98 acres of Walt Disney World's 27,400 total acres, the Magic Kingdom is the main drawing card for most visitors. Few who have traveled the four miles from the main highway to see it are disappointed, and even the most blasé travelers manage a smile. Every day is like a great fair. The sight of the soaring spires of Cinderella Castle, the gleaming woodwork of the Main Street shops, the tiny white lights that edge their rooflines after dark, and the crescendo of music that follows the parades never fail to have their effect. Even when the crowds are thick and the weather is at its warmest, a visitor who has toured this wonderland dozens of times still can look around and think once again how satisfying this place is for the spirit.

The delight that most guests experience on first sight of the Magic Kingdom can quickly disappear when disorientation sets in, however. There are so many nooks and crannies, so many bends to every pathway, and so many sights and sounds clamoring for attention—not to mention the 45 attractions and adventures and the dozens of shops and restaurants—that it's too easy to wander aimlessly and miss the best that the Magic Kingdom has to offer. So we earnestly suggest that you peruse this chapter carefully before you make your own visit.

At the same time, it's also interesting to learn a little about how the Magic Kingdom works. This wonderland started out as little more than swampland. When the Seven Seas Lagoon was dredged, the leftover soil was used to build up the level of the Magic Kingdom site, to provide proper drainage, to supply dry land on which to plant trees and flowers, and to accommodate a vast subterranean system of rooms and hallways where the magic of the Magic Kingdom is manufactured. One vast room of the underground warren is given over solely to computers, used in everything from food planning to the timing of the presidents' nods in Liberty Square's Hall of Presidents. Another area houses a photo library and darkrooms. Yet another whole network of rooms houses the world's largest working wardrobe, where the thousands of costumes worn by the young Magic Kingdom hosts and hostesses hang on dozens and dozens of racks. The place looks like the world's gaudiest department store. Another room is given over solely to the wig department. And that's only the beginning.

Every land has a theme, which is carried through from the hosts' and hostesses' costumes to the food served in the restaurants, the merchandise in the shops, and even the design of the trash bins. Thousands of details contribute to the effects; paying attention to these small touches makes any visit more enjoyable.

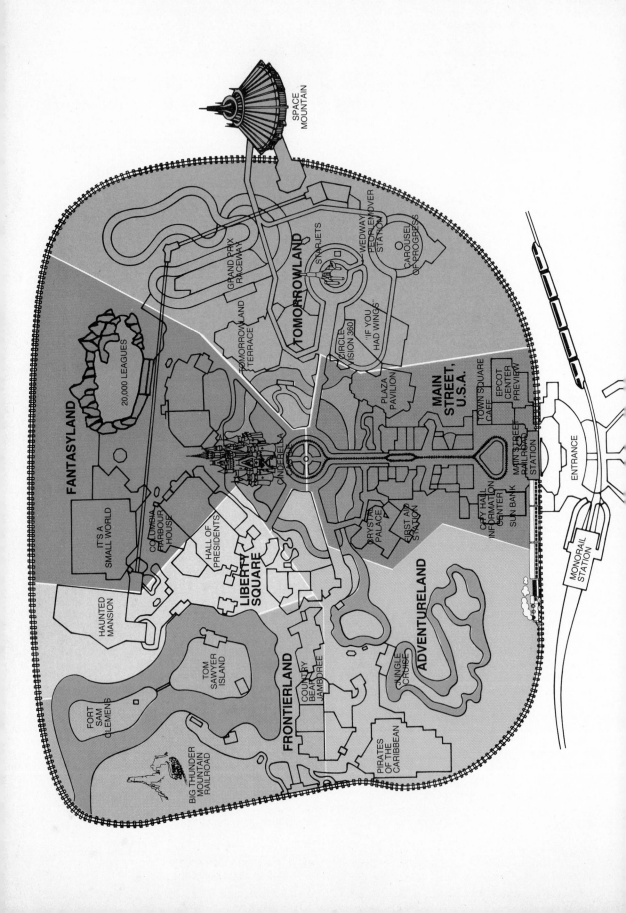

GETTING IN: One of Walt Disney's greatest disappointments was the fact that the citrus groves that originally rimmed the Disneyland site in Anaheim, California, soon gave way to unsightly commercial development. Finally, only the berm rimming the park protected it from surrounding eyesores. When planning Walt Disney World, he pledged to prevent a repeat of that situation, and set the Magic Kingdom some four miles from the nearest interstate highway—so far that it's not even possible to see the towers of Cinderella Castle from the road.

From the Disney World exit off Highway I-4, it's a mile and a half to the Toll Plaza; from there, it's another 2½ miles to the main entrance complex known as the Transportation and Ticket Center (TTC). Even then, the Magic Kingdom visitors have not completed their journey: there remains a five-minute ride by ferry across man-made Seven Seas Lagoon, or a slightly shorter trip by monorail around its shore. Each section of the trip—the drive from the I-4 exit to the Toll Plaza and then to the parking lot, then the lake crossing—serves to heighten the suspense, and by removing guests from the workaday world, to prepare them for the visual delights that follow.

HOW TO GET TO THE MAGIC KINGDOM FROM WHEREVER YOU ARE

From the Contemporary Resort Hotel or the Polynesian Village: The monorail is the easiest way to go.

From the Golf Resort: Take the green-flagged bus in front of the hotel to the Polynesian Village, walk through the lobby to the second floor, and then out to the monorail boarding area.

From Walt Disney World Village: Red-flagged buses make the trip from here to the TTC on a regular basis.

Guests at the Treehouses, the Vacation Villas, the Club Lake Villas, and the Fairway Villas can take green-and-yellow-flagged buses from bus stops located at frequent intervals throughout the villas area to the Walt Disney World Shopping Village area. From there, a red-flagged bus goes to the TTC. Since the whole trip involves two transfers and three separate vehicles, guests at all of these establishments may prefer to drive. Resort IDs can be used to get you through the checkpoints along the back roads (thereby avoiding the occasional traffic jams on I-4 and U.S.-192); maps are available at villa check-in desks.

From Fort Wilderness: Blue-flagged buses make the trip from the campground to the TTC; depending on the location of your campsite, it may be easier to take one of the boats that call at the dock.

From the hotels at Walt Disney World Village Hotel Plaza: Take the red-and-white-flagged buses that stop at the front door of your hotel. Because WDW's private roads are off limits to all but guests at WDW-owned establishments, guests who are staying at one of the four Hotel Plaza properties and who

want to drive must go out onto I-4, drive 4½ miles west, then enter the park via the Toll Plaza along with other day visitors; this can mean grappling with traffic (see *When to Arrive*, below), so in most cases it's more efficient to take the bus—even though it may mean a wait at both ends.

From Orlando or Kissimmee: Follow the signs for Walt Disney World on I-4, take the U.S.-192 west turnoff, and proceed to the Toll Plaza. Go straight ahead and then turn left into the parking lots. Gray Line and Rabbit shuttle buses serve most hotels, but the per-person charges are so high relative to the low local car-rental rates that it makes sense to drive. Some hotels have free shuttle service to WDW.

A Note on Transportation Costs: Parking in the Magic Kingdom lots costs 50¢ (free to guests at WDW-owned resorts, upon presentation of their IDs). Most WDW buses provide transportation to most visitors at no extra charge. Gold-, green-, and blue-flagged buses are courtesy vehicles. To ride the red-and-white-flagged bus between Walt Disney World Village Hotel Plaza and the Transportation and Ticket Center, and to board the red-flagged bus between Walt Disney World Shopping Village and the Transportation and Ticket Center, it is necessary to show an ID card from a Hotel Plaza establishment or a WDW-owned property; all kinds of two- and three-day passports will also get you onto the buses. (For details on the bus and monorail system, see *Transportation and Accommodations*.)

WHEN TO ARRIVE

WHEN TO ARRIVE: Especially during the busy summer and holiday seasons—when the highways leading to the Toll Plaza can look like a Los Angeles freeway during rush hour, and when there are long queues at WDW monorails and ferries—it's advisable to plan on reaching the park by 7:30 or 8 A.M. Eat breakfast at your hotel, if you will—or wait and eat inside the park. Or if this just seems too early, wait until later—about 1 P.M.—or even later than that during the seasons when the park is open late. During less congested periods, when the park closes at 7 P.M., plan to arrive around 10 A.M.

PARKING: After passing through the Toll Plaza, drive straight ahead and bear left for the parking lots. Parking attendants will direct you to a spot in one of a dozen areas. Each lot is named for a Disney character—Daisy, Donald, Sneezy, Bashful, Grumpy, Happy, Goofy, Pluto, Chip & Dale, Minnie, Sleepy, and Dopey. Bashful, Sneezy, Donald, and Daisy are within walking distance of the Transportation and Ticket Center (TTC); other lots are served continuously by tractor-drawn trams that make periodic stops to pick up and discharge passengers.

When leaving your car, note the name of your section and your aisle number; there is a spot for noting this information on the back of your parking ticket. Roll up all windows and lock all doors. Also, do not leave your pet in the car! The Walt Disney World Kennel Club—which is air-conditioned, far more comfortable for the animal, and far safer for him—is conveniently located right at the TTC, just a few steps from the ticket sale windows. The charge is $2 per day for any pet.

Guests who leave the park at midday for their hotels should keep their parking tickets; the tickets are good for reentry to the park throughout the day.

FERRY VS. MONORAIL: Once you've bought your admission ticket or passport and made your way through the TTC turnstiles, it's necessary to decide whether to travel to the Magic Kingdom by ferry or by monorail.

The monorails make the trip in a bit less than the five minutes required by the ferries—but the latter often will get you there more quickly in the busier season, because long lines can form at the monorails; most people just simply don't make the short extra walk to the ferry landing. When there's no line for the monorail, it's your best choice.

Wheelchair vacationers should note that while the monorails are accessible, the ramp leading to the boarding area is a bit steep.

Guests staying at the Golf Resort may take a bus to the Polynesian Village, where they can join guests from that resort and from the Contemporary Resort Hotel on the monorail, which links the two hotels directly to the Magic Kingdom.

MONEY MATTERS

TICKETS: A complicated ticket system has recently been replaced by one that is far easier to understand: instead of paying a general admission charge and then buying additional individual tickets for individual attractions, one now need purchase only a single Passport to gain admission and enjoy unlimited access to all Magic Kingdom rides, shows, and attractions (with the exception of the Shootin' Gallery) for the duration of the ticket. Passports are good for one, two, or three days. The three-day incarnations are sold only to guests at Walt Disney World–owned hotels and to vacationers who have bought certain Eastern Airlines or other packages; they often include admission not only to the Magic Kingdom, but to River Country (at the Fort Wilderness Campground) and to the Discovery Island bird sanctuary as well.

A general admission ticket, which includes all transportation, is also still sold for those return visitors who may have retained some of the old ride and attraction coupons.

All tickets may be purchased at the Transportation and Ticket Center (TTC) and at many local resorts and hotels, including WDW-owned establishments.

WDW resort guests who buy their tickets at WDW resorts may charge Passports to their rooms by using their resort IDs. At the TTC, however, only cash, traveler's checks, or personal checks are accepted as payment for Magic Kingdom admission media; personal checks must be imprinted with your name and address and must be accompanied by a driver's license and a major credit card (that is, American Express, Visa, MasterCard, Diner's Club, and Carte Blanche). Note, however, that only American Express and MasterCard charge cards are ac-

cepted in payment for food (in table service restaurants only) and merchandise in the Magic Kingdom and the rest of the World.

Tickets may also be purchased by mail by sending a check or money order in the exact amount to:

Admissions
Walt Disney World
Box 40
Lake Buena Vista, FL 32830

Remember to include your return address. Allow at least 15 *working* days for ticket requests to be processed.

Airport ticket purchase: Admission passports may also be purchased at the guest services counter of "Walt Disney World On Parade" at the new Orlando Airport.

Walking tours: Three-and-a-half-hour guided walking tours of the park are also available. These include the services of a guide, admission to four attractions, and a Passport to use for the balance of the day. These tours are terrific for first-time visitors, especially those without a great sense of direction, and the cost is quite reasonable. For details, call Guest Services or Guest Relations (at 824-4321), or inquire at the Transportation and Ticket Center.

For tickets: Only cash, traveler's checks, or personal checks are accepted in payment for Passports; personal checks must be imprinted with the bearer's name and address and must be accompanied by a driver's license and a major credit card (American Express, Visa, MasterCard, Diner's Club, and Carte Blanche only). Department store charge cards or oil company credit cards are not accepted for check-writing purposes.

At sit-down restaurants and for merchandise: American Express and MasterCard are accepted, as are cash and traveler's checks. WDW resort identification cards are not accepted as payment for food and merchandise purchases inside the Magic Kingdom.

At fast food restaurants: no credit cards are accepted at fast food eating spots. You must pay cash. Traveler's checks are accepted.

TICKET PRICES

A Guests at WDW-Owned Resorts/Villas
B Guests at Establishments in WDW Village Hotel Plaza
C Guests at Hotels/Motels Outside WDW

	A	B	C
ONE-DAY PASSPORT			
Adult	11.50	11.50***	13.00
Junior*	10.50	10.50***	12.00
Child**	9.50	9.50***	11.00
TWO-DAY PASSPORT			
Adult	20.50	21.75	22.50
Junior*	18.50	19.75	20.50
Child**	16.25	17.75	18.50
THREE-DAY PASSPORT			
Adult	31.50	34.50	Not Available
Junior*	29.00	32.00	to Off-Property
Child**	23.75	26.75	Guests
GUIDED TOURS (Includes One-Day Passport)			
Adult	14.50	14.50	15.00
Junior*	14.50	14.50	15.00
Child**	11.00	11.00	11.50

*12 to 17 years of age.   **3 to 11 years of age.
***Transportation not included.
NOTE: These prices were in effect at press time, but are subject to change.

THE LAY OF THE LANDS

Not long ago, one Magic Kingdom visitor spent an entire day in Tomorrowland—thinking it was the full extent of the place. To avoid having a similar experience, it's essential to understand the lay of all the lands *before* you arrive on Main Street.

There are six sections, or "lands," in the Magic Kingdom—Main Street, U.S.A.; Adventureland; Frontierland; Liberty Square; Fantasyland; and Tomorrowland. The monorail stations and ferry docks at which all guests arrive are just outside the Magic Kingdom gates; just inside them is Town Square, at the head of Main Street, which runs straight to Cinderella Castle. The area in front of the Castle is known as the Central Plaza, or, more aptly, the Hub. It is surrounded by small canals, the Hub Waterways, which are crossed by bridges to enter each of the lands. The first bridge to your left goes to Adventureland; the next, to Liberty Square and Frontierland. On your right, the first bridge heads to Tomorrowland, the second to Fantasyland. The end points of the avenues leading to the lands are linked by a roadway that is roughly circular, so that the layout of the Magic Kingdom resembles a wheel. All of the attractions, restaurants, and shops are arranged in various buildings along the rim of the wheel and along its spokes.

In theory, it couldn't be simpler; in practice, it's all too easy to get confused because of the many bends and curves in the pathways, the many entrances to each shop and restaurant, and the somewhat angular placement and architecture of many of the buildings. But if you keep mental notes of your own route, losing your bearings becomes fairly difficult. If you still manage to get confused, however, any park employee can help set you straight—and there are information booths prominently located in each land.

A note on north, south, east, and west: when you stand at the Magic Kingdom entrance and face Cinderella Castle, you're looking north. Main Street is straight ahead, with Fantasyland beyond the Castle. Adventureland, Liberty Square, and Frontierland are to the west (your left). Tomorrowland flanks the Hub on the east.

MAIN STREET, U.S.A.

This is the Disney version of turn-of-the-century small-town Main Streets all over the country—freshly painted, full of curlicued gingerbread moldings and pretty details, and, with its baskets of hanging plants and genuine gaslights, a showplace both in the bright light of high noon and after nightfall, when the tiny white lights edging all the rooflines are flicked on.

What's particularly amazing is that all the variety of furbelows and frills that a real Main Street would have enjoyed as a result of normal growth have been assimilated into the Disney version. Most of the structures along the thoroughfare are given over to shops, and each one is different, from the wallpaper and layout of displays to the flooring material, the style of chandeliers, and even the lighting level. Some emporiums are big and bustling, others are relatively quiet and orderly; some are spacious and airy, others are cozy and dark. Floors are made of black-and-white tile, or of wide-oak planks set in with wooden pegs; some are covered with Victorian-patterned carpet. Where wallpapers are used, they are striped, or gaudily flowered; in contrast, some walls are paneled in subdued mahogany or oak. In one shop, you find a potbellied stove; others boast slowly turning ceiling fans. The effect is far more sophisticated than first-time visitors probably would have imagined, and it doesn't really matter that some of the "wood" is fiberglass.

Inside and outside, maintenance and housekeeping are superb. White-suited sanitation men patrol the street to pick up litter and quickly shovel up any droppings from the horses who pull the trolley cars from Town Square to the Hub. The pavement, like all in the Magic Kingdom, is washed down every night with fire hoses. There's one crew of maintenance men whose sole job is to change the little white lights around the roofs; another crew devotes itself to keeping the woodwork painted. As soon as these men have worked their way as far as the Hub, they start all over again at Town Square. Epoxy, acrylic, and more ordinary varieties of paints are used, depending on the area to be painted. The greenish, horse-shaped, cast-iron hitching posts are repainted 20 times a year on the average—and totally scraped down each time. It's no wonder the painters who visit here marvel at the quality of work they see.

Visitors from outside the United States find all these details so fascinating that it takes them a good deal longer than the 40 minutes spent by the average guest to get from one end of Main Street to the other. There are only four real "attractions" along Main Street, and they are relatively minor compared to the really big deals such as Tomorrowland's Space Mountain and Frontierland's Big Thunder Mountain Railroad. But each and every shop has its own quota of merchandise that is meant as much for fun and show as for sale—the monster masks at the House of Magic, for instance, or the large Hummel figurine at Cup'n Saucer. It's also entertaining to stand and just watch the candlemakers at the Wonderland of Wax; the magicians at the House of Magic; the cake-decorators turning frosting into roses at the Sara Lee Bakery; and the cooks stirring up batches of peanut brittle at the Confectionary. The windows at the Emporium and the Mickey tableaux in the Christmas Shop and the House of Magic are also musts.

While walking along the street, note the names on the second-story windows. Above Crystal Arts, you can see the names of Roy Disney, Walt's brother, and Patty Disney; above the Shadow Box, those of Ron Miller, who married Walt's daughter Diane and is now president of Walt Disney Productions, and Dick Nunis, who heads Outdoor Recreation (the company's theme parks division). Above the House of Magic are the names of Ted Crowell, WDW's vice-president of facilities, who, among other things, is responsible for maintenance and for the World's own electric generating plants, and John de Cuir, the Disney artist in charge of the production of the paintings filmed for the Hall of Presidents show. Card Walker, the "practitioner of Psychiatry and Justice of the Peace" mentioned nearby, is the company's Chairman of the Board. Other names, as well as those on signs elsewhere in the Magic Kingdom, are also those of real people connected with the company.

Finally, some advice. Before heading toward the Castle, stop at City Hall and inquire about the times and places that live entertainments are scheduled to take place all around the park that day and night. Also, do your shopping in the early afternoon, rather than at day's end when the shops are jammed; purchases can be stored in lockers under the Walt Disney World Railroad's depot, or, in the case of very large items, behind the desk at City Hall.

PENNY ARCADE: Scarcely a motel in Orlando lacks its blipping, bleeping, squeaking room full of electronics games; the one at the Contemporary Resort ranks among the largest in the country. The Magic Kingdom also has its games room—but here on Victorian Main Street, in addition to the modern machines, there are authentic old-time games—a Kiss-O-Meter, tests of strength, and an antique football game.

In addition, in the center of the front section of the arcade, there are a number of machines that show very early "moving pictures"—that is, stacks of cards on a roller that can be turned to flip the cards and thereby "animate" the images they contain. There are two types of viewing devices—Mute-o-scopes, first introduced around 1900, whose rollers must be turned by hand, and Cail-o-scopes, developed about a decade later. These are turned automatically. Both of these are worth your while. Most stories here are comedies; the humor is broad and slapstick—good for at least a smile (if not a roar) and as amusing comments on the changing ideas about what tickles a funny bone. On the Cail-o-scopes, you can see such stories as *Yes, We Have No Bananas*, in which a suitor slips on a banana peel and is ridiculed; *Tough Competition*, in which sailors come to blows over a pretty girl; *Texas Rangers*, where the good guy lassoes the robber; and *Run Out of Town*, in which one unfortunate man has paint dumped on him, falls into a manhole, is knocked over by a car, sits on a freshly painted bench, and knocks over a paint bucket—all in a single day. During *A Raid On A Watermelon Patch*, two fellows do and are discovered. *Oh Teacher* concerns the antics of a teacher's pest. *Brigitte On A Bike* shows a real sourpuss taking a tumble; it might be subtitled, "Or The Trials of Riding In A Long Skirt." Particularly interesting is

Captain Kidd's Treasure, in which a pirate lass shows knees, bare arms, and ankles. The display of skin—which would rate a solid *G* today—must have looked positively risqué three quarters of a century ago.

Among the Cail-o-scopes, the best are probably *Expecting*, which is a funny cartoon about people waiting, and *Knock Out*, which documents a World's Heavyweight Boxing Championship between Joe Louis and German fighter Max Schmeling; but some of the others are also worth a peek—and the cost is only a penny.

While you're looking, you can be pumping the big coin-operated antique band organ against the Arcade's south wall; its ringing tones almost block out the clatter and clacks of the pinball and electronic games machines (at least when it's not out of order; it's as temperamental as a prima donna, and even the ministrations of the resident musical-instrument caretaker can't always keep it singing). Before leaving, also note the paintings that hang on the walls. They depict a roadster race, the Wright Brothers and an early flying machine, a Victorian-era amusement arcade, and a rural Illinois river valley scene. All of these were created for the film that precedes the chief executives' roll call in Liberty Square's Hall of Presidents.

MAIN STREET CINEMA: The beauty of this prominent attraction on Main Street is that most vacationers bypass it in their rush to get to 20,000 Leagues Under The Sea in Fantasyland or Pirates of The Caribbean in Adventureland, or other thrill-a-minute attractions. Yet on a steamy summer afternoon—when everyone else is standing in line for these blockbusters—this air-conditioned theater is a fine place to relax. Five short silent films are shown here simultaneously: an early film version of Robert Louis Stevenson's *Dr. Jekyll and Mr. Hyde*; Thomas A. Edison's *The Great Train Robbery*; *The Rounders*, starring Fatty Arbuckle and a balletic Charlie Chaplin in a vignette about two wayward husbands and their wailing wives; *Crashing Through*, a steamy melodrama about baby-napping in Poker Flat, starring one Ford Sterling; and *Steamboat Willie*, the first sound cartoon, in which a little mouse named Mickey, making his film debut, meets Minnie and then makes beautiful music on (among other instruments) a cow's udder, a feat which drew one of the film's biggest laughs at the time of its September 1928 release.

WALT DISNEY WORLD RAILROAD: The best introduction to the layout of the Magic Kingdom, the 1½-mile, 15-minute journey on this rail line is as much a must for the first-time visitor as it is for railroad buffs. For the former, it offers an excellent orientation, as it passes through Adventureland and Frontierland and skirts Fantasyland and Tomorrowland. En route, viewers see hippos, and other Audio-Animatronics animals, and pass an Indian settlement, as well as the flooded mining town glimpsed on the fly from the cars at the runaway Big Thunder Mountain Railroad. Aficionados of railroadiana may remember that Disney himself was among their number, and perhaps, during the early years of television, saw films of him circling his own backyard in a one-and-one-half-scale train named for his wife, Lilly Belle. The Walt Disney World Railroad also has a *Lilly Belle* among its quartet of locomotives. All of these were built in the United States around the turn of the last century and later were taken down to Mexico to haul freight and passengers in the Yucatan, where Disney scouts found them in 1969; the United Railways of Yucatan was using them to carry sugar cane.

Brought north once again, they were completely overhauled, and even the smallest parts were reworked or replaced. New boilers and fiberglass cabs were built, along with new tenders and tanks. (The cast-iron wheels, side rods, frames, and parts of the hardware, however, are original.) Originally designed to burn coal or wood, then converted by the Mexicans to use oil, they now consume diesel fuel—considerably less dirty than either of the former fuels.

The *Lilly Belle* is a Mogul-type engine, with two small front wheels and six drive wheels, while the *Roy O. Disney* is an American Standard eight-wheeler (with four small wheels forward and four drive wheels), and the *Walter E. Disney* and the *Roger Broggie* (named for a Disney imagineer who shared Walt Disney's enthusiasm for antique trains) are both two-wheelers, with four small forward wheels and six large drive wheels.

EPCOT PREVIEW: Housed in the yellow building on the east side of Town Square, in the film theater that once hosted *The Walt Disney Story*, this presentation gives visitors to the 98-acre Magic Kingdom a taste of what they'll see on October 1, 1982, on the 600 acres of the new EPCOT Center, which is presently being built on a site just a few miles south of the Magic Kingdom. The EPCOT Center—the acronym stands for Experimental Prototype Community of Tomorrow—will have two major sections: World Showcase, which will show off the best of the culture of nations from all over the globe; and Future World, which will highlight technology of the future. At the Preview, a film shows models and describes the features of each area.

In the waiting area outside the screening room, there are a number of exhibits dealing with Walt Disney, his honors, and his life: letters from Harry Truman, Dwight Eisenhower, Richard Nixon, U Thant, Winston Churchill, Dag Hammarskjold, and Leopold Stokowski; posters from old Disney movies, photos of the Mouseketeers (and a real Mouseketeer hat), Zorro's cape, and—among the other medals and honors—the Oscar presented for *Snow White and the Seven Dwarfs*, the familiar tall golden figure with seven miniature versions arranged alongside. Note the photo of Walt Disney with Stan Laurel and Oliver Hardy against the wall to your right as you pass through the turnstiles.

Special three-day souvenir tickets are currently being sold to commemorate the opening of EPCOT Center on October 1, 1982. These tickets will be good for three days admission to EPCOT and the Magic Kingdom, and cost $30 (adult), $24 (juniors), and $18 (children). They will be on sale to August 1, 1982.

Swan Boats: At the busiest times during the summer, these swan-shaped boats—which are named for Disney characters from Snow White to Pollyanna and kept in the Hub near the Tomorrowland Bridge—take guests on trips through the Hub Waterways. A good alternative to relaxing on a park bench.

Old-Fashioned Vehicles: A number of these can be seen traveling up and down Main Street—horseless carriages and jitneys patterned after turn-of-the-century vehicles (but fitted out with Jeep transmissions and special mufflers that make the putt-putt-putting sound); double-decker buses; a spiffy scarlet fire engine, which can be seen in the Firehouse adjoining City Hall when not in operation; and a troop of trolleys drawn by Belgians and Percherons, two strong breeds of horses that once pulled plows in Europe. These animals—aged between six and ten, weighing in at about a ton each, and shoed with plastic (easier on their feet)—pull the trolley the length of Main Street about two dozen times during each of their three to four working days; afterward, they're sent back to their homes at the barn at the Fort Wilderness Campground.

CINDERELLA CASTLE

Just as the courtly little mouse named Mickey stands for all the joy and merriment in the whole of Walt Disney World, the many-spired Cinderella Castle, childhood's storybook castle made real, represents the hopes and dreams of those youthful years when anything seems possible.

This Castle is different from Disneyland's Sleeping Beauty Castle: Measuring some 180 feet in height, the Florida castle is more than a hundred feet taller; and with its slender towers and lacy filigree work, it's also more graceful, taking its inspiration not only from the architecture of twelfth- and thirteenth-century France, the country where Charles Perrault's classic fairytale originated, but also from the mad Bavarian King Ludwig's castle at Neuschwanstein, and from the designs prepared some three decades ago for the motion-picture version of Perrault's story—and the imaginations of a whole troupe of creative Disney imagineers who have collectively spent several lifetimes turning fantasies into reality.

Unlike real European castles, this one is not made of granite, but of steel beams, fiberglass, and some 500 gallons of paint. There are no dungeons underneath it, but rather service tunnels for the Magic Kingdom's day-to-day operations. In the Castle's upper reaches there are broadcast facilities, security rooms, and the like; toward the top, there's the apartment originally meant for members of the Disney family (but never occupied).

When mounting the curving staircase to the parapet-level restaurant King Stefan's Banquet Hall, or when passing through the Castle's main gateway—or as seen by night from the Contemporary Resort's observation deck, with fireworks exploding all around those slender towers—the Castle looks as if it had come straight out of some never-never land of make-believe.

The mosaic murals: The elaborate murals in the five panels beneath the Castle's archway-entrance rank as one of the true wonders of the World. Measuring some 15 feet high and 10 feet wide, these creations of the Disney artist Dorothea Redmond, crafted by the mosaicist Hanns-Joachim Scharff, tell the familiar story of a little cinder girl, a hardhearted stepmother, two ugly stepsisters, a fairy godmother, a pumpkin transformed, a handsome prince, a certain glass slipper, and one of childhood's happiest happily-ever-afters, using a million bits of Italian glass in some 500 different colors, plus real silver and 14-carat gold. The renderings of the stepsisters and of the many small woodland animals are particularly faithful to images from the Disney film; but every passerby has favorite sections. Don't fail to stop and look.

Coats of arms: The one above the Castle on the north wall belongs to the Disneys. Others belonging to assorted Disney executives hang in the waiting hall just inside the door to King Stefan's; the hostess keeps a book behind the desk that details which belong to whom for any interested party to see. Some of the same names show up as on the second-story windows of the Main Street shops.

ADVENTURELAND

Adventureland seems to have even more atmosphere than the other lands. That may be a result of its neat separation from the rest of the Magic Kingdom, by the bridge over Main Street on the one end and by a gallery-like structure where it merges with Frontierland on the other; or possibly it's because of the abundance of landscaping. There are Canary Island date palms, the small Cape Sable palms, as well as Pigmy date species, and more. On the Adventureland Bridge alone, visitors will see Cape honeysuckle from South Africa, flame vines from Mexico, bougainvillea from Brazil, Chinese hibiscus, hanging sword ferns, spider plants, and Australian tree ferns, to name just a few. It's hard to imagine that just ten years ago, the landscape of this little piece of real estate was as bare and flat as that flanking the WDW entrance road.

As for the architecture, even though it derives from such diverse areas as the Caribbean, Polynesia, and Southeast Asia, there's a strong sense of being in a single place, a nowhere-in-particular that is both exotic and distinctly foreign, smacking of island idylls and tropical splendor. Shops offer imports from India, Thailand, Hong Kong, Africa, and the Caribbean islands. The Adventureland Veranda serves food cooked in the Magic Kingdom's most exotic style (never mind that it happens to be simple Chinese fare).

Strolling away from Main Street, you hear the beating of drums, the squawk of a couple of parrots, the regular boom of cannon. Paces quicken. And the wonders you soon encounter do not disappoint.

TROPICAL SERENADE (ENCHANTED TIKI BIRDS): The first of the AudioAnimatronic attractions, the one that laid the foundation for attractions such as *Great Moments With Mr. Lincoln* at the 1964-65 New York World's Fair, this one, introduced at Disneyland in 1963, features four emcees—José, Michael, Pierre, and Fritz—plus some 225 birds, flowers, and Tiki-god statues singing and whistling up a tropical storm with such animation that even the most blasé folks can't help but smile. Presented by the Florida Citrus Commission.

PIRATES OF THE CARIBBEAN: One of the very best of the Magic Kingdom's adventures, this cruise through a series of sets depicting a pirate raid on a Caribbean town—a Disneyland original added to WDW's Magic Kingdom, in revised form, because of popular demand—remains strangely uncrowded in the afternoons, even when guests are lining up at Frontierland's Big Thunder and Liberty Square's Haunted Mansion, which resemble Pirates in attention to detail. Here there are flowerpots that explode and mend themselves, drunken pigs whose legs actually twitch in the porkers' soporific contentment, chickens that look for all the world like the real thing (even when seen at close range); the observant will note that the leg of one swashbuckler, dangled over the edge of a bridge, is actually hairy. Each pirate's face has remarkable personality, and the rendition of

"A Pirate's Life"—the attraction's theme, originally composed for the 1953 Disney film *Peter Pan*—makes what is actually a rather brutal scenario into something that comes across as good fun.

Before entering the plaza-queue area, be sure to stop and give a nod to the parrot in the pirate costume sitting near the Pirates of the Caribbean sign.

JUNGLE CRUISE: Inspired in part by the 1955 documentary *The African Lion*, this ten-minute cruise adventure is one of the crowning achievements of Magic Kingdom landscape artists for the way it takes guests through landscapes as diverse as a Southeast Asian jungle, the Nile valley, the African veldt, and Amazon rain forest. Along the way, passengers encounter zebras and giraffes, impalas, lions, vultures, and headhunters; they see elephants bathing and tour a Cambodian temple—and listen to the funny spiel delivered by the boatman. For most passengers, this is all just in fun. Gardeners, however, are especially impressed by the variety of species coexisting in such a small area. To keep some of the more sensitive of subtropical specimens alive, 100 gas-fired heaters and electric fans concealed in the rocks pump hot air into the jungle at the rate of 25 million BTUs per hour when temperatures fall to 36° F. This adventure, which is best enjoyed by daylight, is one of the Magic Kingdom's most popular attractions, and it does tend to be crowded from late morning until late afternoon, so plan accordingly.

SWISS FAMILY ISLAND TREEHOUSE: "Everything we need right at our fingertips" was how John Mills, playing the father in Disney's 1960 remake of the classic novel *Swiss Family Robinson*, described the treehouse that he and two of his three sons constructed to house the family after the ship transporting them to America was wrecked in a storm. When given a chance—several adventures later—to leave the island, all but one son decided to stay on. That decision is not hard to understand after a tour of the Magic Kingdom's version of the Robinsons' banyan-tree home. This is everybody's idea of the perfect treehouse, with its many levels and many comforts—patchwork quilts, lovely mahogany furniture, candles stuck in an abalone shell, even running water in every room. (The system is ingenious.)

The Spanish moss draping the branches is real; the tree itself—unofficially christened *Disneyodendron eximus*, which translates roughly as "out-of-the-ordinary Disney tree"—was constructed by the props department. Some statistics: the roots, which are concrete, poke 42 feet into the ground; and some 800,000 leaves and flowers (vinyl) grow on 600-odd branches, which stretch some 90 feet in diameter. "Boy, Dad sure went out on a limb for that one," quipped a Disney props worker's son on hearing of his father's task.

FRONTIERLAND

With the Rivers of America lapping up at its borders, and Big Thunder Mountain rising toward the rear, even higher than Cinderella Castle at the center of the park, this re-creation of the American Frontier encompasses the area from New England to the Southwest, from the 1770s to the 1880s. Hosts and hostesses wear denim, calf-length cut-offs, long skirts, or similar garb. The shops, restaurants, and attractions have unpainted barnboard siding, or stone or clapboard walls, and outside there are a few of the kind of wooden sidewalks down which Marshall Matt Dillon used to stride.

Near Pecos Bill's the landscape seems desertlike (even on humid summer days), with mesquite providing shade, and Peruvian pepper trees nearby; the latter's twisted branches boast clusters of bright red berries in fall and winter. Jerusalem thorns blossom with sweet-smelling yellow flowers in the spring. Century plants and Spanish bayonets also can be seen. Farther down the Frontierland avenue, slash pines provide some shade, along with other evergreens of a variety known as cajeput, which can be recognized by its spongy, light-colored bark and white flowers.

DIAMOND HORSESHOE REVUE: The half-hour-long show presented in this re-creation of a Western dance hall saloon is the kind of thing that makes sophisticated folk laugh despite themselves. As at the Hoop-Dee-Doo Revue, which takes place nightly at Fort Wilderness's Pioneer Hall, the jokes range from corny to absolutely preposterous, yet seldom fall flat, thanks to the enthusiastic, energetic efforts of the talented crew of singers, dancers, ventriloquists, and comedians who perform here several times each day. As at Hoop-Dee-Doo Revue, reservations are necessary; here they must be made in person at the saloon's porch on the morning of the day of the performance. Since they are dispensed on a first-come-first-served basis, it's essential to show up within an hour of park opening. Those who arrive too late may be able to snag a cancellation by showing up at the door a half hour or so before seating time, which is 40 minutes before the entertainment begins; but you can't count on it. Presented by Del Monte.

FRONTIERLAND SHOOTIN' GALLERY: Sharpshooters never fail to delight in testing their skills against the sitting ducks and fleeing rabbits, buffalo, deer, moose, and cougars here. Unlike most shooting galleries, this one never shows its age, since the whole thing is repainted *every day*. This is one of the only attractions in the park whose cost—a quarter for 12 bullets—is not covered by the all-inclusive Magic Kingdom admission-and-attractions ticket known as the Passport.

COUNTRY BEAR JAMBOREE: An occasional determined sophisticate will remain impervious to the charms of this country-and-western hoedown (aka, informally, the Teddy Bear Jamboree) in Frontierland's big stone-walled Grizzly Hall. But most guests call it one of the Magic Kingdom's best attractions. Ostensibly concocted by one Ursus D. Bear after an especially inspiring season of hibernation, it is performed mainly by a cast of close to 20 life-size Audio-Animatronics bruins, with results more believable than almost anywhere else in the park outside the Hall of Presidents. Henry, the debonair, seven-foot-tall master of ceremonies, introduces the Five Bear Rugs (a C&W plinking group made up of Zeke, Zeb, Ted, Fred, and Tennessee); a big-bodied, tiny-headed pianist named Gomer; the girthy Trixie, the Tampa Temptation, who laments her transformation from cubby to chubby in particularly plaintive C&W tones; the feather boa-wrapped, long-lashed Teddi Barra; the three little bears in blue—Bubbles, Bunny, and Beulah (singing a little like the Andrews Sisters); and assorted other bruins, including Terrence, the shank shaker; Wendell, the overbearing baritone; Liver Lips McGrowl; and Big Al, who demonstrates such force of personality as he deadpans his way through "Blood on the Saddle" that he nearly stops the show. The fact that Big Al postcards are hot sellers at souvenir stands throughout the park ought to convey some idea of his popularity.

Since the Country Bear Jamboree is a top attraction, lines can get quite long during busy periods. They usually seem longer than they are, however, and it's worth noting that huge bunches of people are admitted all at once so that once a line starts moving, it dwindles fast. Seats in the rear of the house are just as good as seats toward the front, if not a little better. In fact, the only marginal seats in the house are those on the far right-hand side, where Teddi Barra's one-in-a-million face can't be seen. When entering the auditorium, hostesses always request that you slide all the way to your right. Consequently, it's best not to try to be the first one in, but instead to tarry a bit so as to have the pick of center seats. Presented by Frito-Lay and Pepsi-Cola.

TOM SAWYER ISLAND: Opened in April of 1973, this small landfall in the middle of the Rivers of America has hills to scramble up, a working windmill Harper's Mill with an owl in the rafters and a perpetually creaky water wheel, and a pitch-black (and scary) cave in which kids can get lost.

There are oaks, pines, and sycamores here, red maples and elms, and a number of small plants—dwarf azaleas; firethorn, an evergreen shrub that sprouts bright red berries in December; Brazilian pepper trees, which also grow berries at the end of the year; and American holly plants, which acquire their masses of berries in fall. Dirt paths wind this way and that, and it's easy to get disoriented, especially the first time around. There also are two bridges—an old-fashioned swing bridge and a so-called barrel bridge, which floats atop some lashed-together steel drums. When one person bounces, everybody lurches—and all but the most chicken-hearted laugh. Both bridges can easily be missed, so keep your eyes peeled and ask for directions if the path eludes you.

Across the bridge is Fort Sam Clemens, where there is a guardhouse in which the figure of a ratty-looking drunk is AudioAnimatronically snoring off his last bender, accompanied by a mangy-looking dog, chickens, and a pair of horses. On the second floor of the fort, there are close to a dozen air guns for youngsters to trigger into ceaseless cacophony. This area gives a fine view across the Rivers of America to Big Thunder Mountain. Keep poking around, and near the refreshment stand you'll find the twisting, dark, and occasionally scary escape tunnel out of the fort. Walk along the pathway on the banks of the Rivers of America, and you're back at the bridges.

The whole island seems as rugged as backwoods Missouri, and probably as a result, it actually feels a lot more remote than it is, enough to be able to provide some welcome respite from the bustle of the Magic Kingdom. One particularly pleasant way to pass an hour here is over lemonade and a sandwich on the porch at Aunt Polly's. While adults in the party are giving their feet some rest, watching the stern-wheelers plying the Rivers of America, kids can go out and burn up some more energy. Rest rooms are located at the refreshment stand in the fort and at the main raft landing. Note that this attraction closes at dusk.

WALT DISNEY WORLD RAILROAD: The old-fashioned steam trains also pick up and discharge passengers at the depot in Frontierland. There's seldom a waiting line, and the breezy, open-sided passenger cars are good places to cool off from the heat of summer afternoons, for putting up your feet, and for getting from Frontierland to Main Street without expending too much energy. The vegetable-like plants in front of the depot, flowering cabbage, are edible but not tasty—and are mainly ornamental; the trees flanking this Victorian station are laurel oaks, and, behind it, towering slash pines, long-leaf pines, and evergreen elms.

BIG THUNDER MOUNTAIN RAILROAD: This attraction, located partly inside the 197-foot-high redstone mountain that pokes into the sky behind the Tom Sawyer Island rafts landing, is something of a cross between Tomorrowland's Space Mountain (an honest-to-goodness roller coaster) and Adventureland's Pirates of the Caribbean (a tame but very exciting and scenic boat tour). As any true coaster buff could tell you, this three-minute ride is a relatively mild one, despite the posted warnings; the thrills are there, but the experience is not so extreme that you'll be left with a determination never to subject yourself to it again. The pleasant rush of adrenaline that comes with some of the swoops and curves, as well as the attractive scenery along the 2,780 feet of track, gives most visitors the opposite reaction. There are the bats; the phosphorescent pools and waterfalls; and best of all, Tumbleweed, the flooded mining town (best seen to your right during one of the uphill climbs). There are some 20 AudioAnimatronics figures here—including real-looking chickens, donkeys, possums, a goat, and a rainmaker, clad in long underwear, whose name is Professor Cumulus Isobar. Careful observers will note a party still going on in a not-yet-sunken second-story room of a saloon, whose weathered look (like that of some other sections of the Magic Kingdom) derives from a judicious mixture of plant food and paint. The $300,000 worth of real antique mining equipment sprinkled around the attraction's 2.5 acres—an ore-hauling wagon, a double-stamp ore crusher, a wooden mining flume, and an old ball mill used to extract gold from ore—were picked up at auctions all over the Southwest, at something less than bargain prices, since the high price of gold and the resulting profitability of small-scale mining operations had boosted demand by genuine miners themselves. As with Pirates of the Caribbean, every trip yields new sights, and even a second or third trip in a matter of days is as amusing as the first time around.

The summit of the mountain, whose name refers to an old Indian legend about a certain sacred mountain in Wyoming that would thunder whenever white men took out its gold, is entirely Disney-made. It was in the planning for some 15 years and under construction for two, and required some 650 tons of steel, 4,675 tons of cement, and 16,000 gallons of paint; hundreds of rock-makers contributed, applying multiple coats of cement and paint, throwing stones at the mountain, kicking dirt on it, and banging on it with sticks and picks to make the whole thing resemble the rocks of Monument Valley, Utah—that is, as if Mother Nature herself had created it. Design was largely by Tony Baxter, a Disney imagineer who started his career with the company with a job at a Disney ice-cream parlor while in high school. (His name now can be seen on one of the doors in the unloading and boarding area.) The area inside the mountain that does not house the tunnels of the ride itself is occupied by the machinery that makes the ride go—pumps, electronic equipment, and part of the computer that runs the show. The total cost was about $17 million, which, give or take a few million, was as much as it cost to build all of California's Disneyland in 1955. Incidentally, that park's version of the attraction, which opened in 1979, is similar, but lacks the flash-flood scene and a few other details.

Note on timing: Certain aspects of the ride are more convincing after dark. Optimally, you should experience it first at night, then have a second go-round by the light of day. Since the trip is extremely popular, plan to take it in during the 9 P.M. running of the Main Street Electrical Parade (in season), or just before park closing, when the lines are generally shorter. By day, go early in the morning or around dinnertime.

LIBERTY SQUARE

The transition between Frontierland on one side and Fantasyland on the other is so smooth that it's hard to say just when you arrive, yet ultimately there's no mistaking the location. The small buildings are clapboard or brick and topped with weather vanes; the decorative moldings are Federal or Georgian in style; the glass is sometimes wavy, and there are flower boxes on shop windows, bright-colored gardens, neatly trimmed borders of Japanese yew, and masses of azaleas in a number of varieties— George Tabor azaleas, which blossom white and pink in March and May; redwing-hybrid Kurume azaleas, which boast red blossoms in winter; southern charms, which from February to April turn rosy pink; and more. There are a number of good shops, most notably the Yankee Trader, Mlle. Lafayette's Parfumerie, and Olde World Antiques; plus two of the park's most popular attractions—Haunted Mansion and the Hall of Presidents—and the Liberty Tree Tavern, one of the few Magic Kingdom restaurants to offer waitress service, and one of just two to take reservations (though only at dinner). Liberty Square also is home of one of the most delightful nooks in all the Magic Kingdom—the small, secluded area just behind the Silversmith Shop near the Fife and Drum. There are tables with umbrellas, plenty of benches, and big trees to provide shade—and the sound of the crowds seems a million miles away.

THE LIBERTY TREE: Not an attraction per se, this 130-year-old live oak (*Quercus virginiana*)—which recalls trees all over the colonies, on which the Sons of Liberty used to hang lanterns after the Boston Tea Party of 1773—was found on the southern edge of WDW's 27,400 acres, and then moved to its present site in one of the more complex of the Magic Kingdom's landscaping operations. Since the tree was so large (weighing an estimated 35 tons, with a root ball that measured some 18 by 16 by 4 feet around), lifting it by cable was out of the question—the cable would have sliced through the bark and into the trunk's tender cambium layer, injuring the tree. Instead, two holes were drilled horizontally through the sturdiest section of the trunk; the holes were fitted with dowels, and a 100-ton crane lifted the tree by these rods, which were subsequently removed and replaced by the original wood plugs. Unfortunately, these had become contaminated, and an infection set in and rotted out a portion of the inside of the trunk. To save the tree, the plugs again were removed, the holes were filled with cement, diseased areas cleaned out, and a young *Quercus virginiana* was grafted onto the tree at its base, where it grows even today. Careful observers will be able to spot the plugs and the portions of the trunk that were damaged. The thirteen lanterns hanging on the branches represent the thirteen original states.

HALL OF PRESIDENTS: This is not one of those thrill-a-minute attractions, like the Pirates of the Caribbean or the Country Bear Jamboree; it's long on patriotism and short on humor. But the detail certainly is fascinating. After a film (presented on a sweeping 70 mm screen) discusses the importance of the Constitution from the time of its framing through the dawn of the Space Age, the curtain goes up on what some guests have mistakenly called the "Hall of Haunted Presidents." A portion of today's Hall of Presidents presentation derives from the Disney-designed Illinois Pavilion's presentation *Great Moments with Mr. Lincoln* from New York's 1964-65 World's Fair.

At the Magic Kingdom show, Lincoln's remarks are prefaced by a roll call of all 39 American presidents, including Ronald Reagan, who debuted in 1981. Each chief executive responds with a nod; careful observers will note the others swaying and nodding, fidgeting, and even whispering to each other during the proceedings.

Costumes were created by two famous film tailors who were coaxed out of retirement. Not only are the styles those of the period in which each president lived, but so are the tailoring techniques and the fabrics. Some had to be specially woven for the purpose. Each figure has at least one change of clothes, and jewelry, shoes, hair texture, and even George Washington's chair are all re-created exactly as indicated by the results of careful research using paintings, diaries, newspapers, and government archives. The observant should be able to see the brace on Franklin Delano Roosevelt's leg. The effect is so lifelike that the figures look almost real, even at close range.

The paintings in the waiting area outside the hall are just a few of the 85 created for the pre roll–call film—in the style of the period during which the event depicted took place—by a dozen artists working under the direction of the Academy Award–winning artist John De Cuir. Other paintings can be seen in Main Street's Penny Arcade and Liberty Square's Liberty Tree Tavern and Columbia Harbour House.

LIBERTY SQUARE RIVERBOATS: The *Admiral Joe Fowler* and the *Richard F. Irvine*, built in drydock at WDW and named for two key Disney designers, are real steamboats. Their boilers turn water into steam, which is then piped to the engine, which drives the paddle wheel that propels the boats. They are not the real article in one respect, however: they move through the half-mile-long, seven-foot-deep Rivers of America on an underwater rail. The ride is more pleasant than thrilling, but it's good for beating the heat on steamy afternoons. En route, a variety of props create a sort of Wild West effect: moose, deer, cabins on fire, and the like. (Many of these are also visible from the Walt Disney World Railroad.) Best

ing parts were expunged and a pleasant voice-over keeps things from getting too serious. Even then, the experience that's left is among the Magic Kingdom's best. Special effect is piled upon special effect, and just when you think you've seen it all, there's something new: the raven who appears over and over again; the bats' eyes on the wallpaper; the plaque that reads "Tomb, Sweet Tomb"; the suit of armor that comes alive; the horrible transparent specter in the attic; the terrified cemetery watchman and his mangy mutt; the ghostly teapot pouring ghostly tea; the difficult-to-identify flying objects above the image in the crystal ball (which is actually of a woman who works in the wardrobe department).

seats are in front or rear and center, so that you can see both river banks equally well.

The trees framing the entrance to Riverboat Landing, which bear crinkly blossoms of bright red throughout much of the year, are crepe myrtles; these can also be seen in other areas of the park.

MIKE FINK KEEL BOATS: Named for a riverboat captain who lived from 1770 to 1823 and once met up with Davy Crockett, the pair of squat, oddly shaped Mike Fink Keel Boats—*Bertha Mae* and the *Gullywhumper*—also traverse the Rivers of America. Since they take in the same scenery as the Liberty Square Riverboats (though from a slightly different angle), you wouldn't want to do both in the same day.

HAUNTED MANSION: Those who expect to get the daylights scared out of them inside this big old house, modeled on those built by the Dutch in the Hudson River Valley in the seventeenth century, will be a tad disappointed. In deference to the number of small children and other easily frightened souls who tour the Magic Kingdom every day, the most terrify-

In the portrait hall (which you enter after passing through the mansion's front doors), it's amusing to speculate: is the ceiling moving up—or is the floor descending? It's one way here, and another way at the New Orleans–style Haunted Mansion in Disneyland.

At both places, one of the biggest jobs of the maintenance crews is not cleaning up, but keeping things nice and dirty. Since each mansion's attic is littered with some 200 trunks, chairs, dress forms, shovels, harps, rugs, and assorted other knickknacks, it requires a good deal of dust. This is purchased from a West Coast firm by the five-pound bagful and distributed by a device that looks as if it were meant to spread grass seed. Local legend has it that enough has been used since the park's 1971 opening to bury the mansion. Cobwebs are bought in liquid form and strung up by a secret process.

When waiting to enter, be sure to note the amusing inscriptions on the tombstones in the overgrown cemetery.

FANTASYLAND

Walt Disney called this a "timeless land of enchantment," and his successors term it "the happiest land of all"—and it is, for some. Although it's not precisely a kiddieland, it is the home of a number of rides that are particularly well-liked by younger children. The nursery-song cadences of "It's A Small World" appeal to them, as do the bright colors of the trash baskets, the flowers, and the tentlike rooftops; and they delight in the fairy-tale architecture and ambience, reminiscent of a king's castle's courtyard during a particularly lively fair. Fantasyland is also one of the most heavily trafficked areas of the park.

CINDERELLA'S GOLDEN CARROUSEL: Not everything in the Magic Kingdom is a Disney version of the real article: this carrousel, discovered at the now-defunct Maplewood, New Jersey, Olympic Park, was built for the Detroit Palace Garden Park (also long gone) by Italian-born wood-carvers of the Philadelphia Toboggan Company back in 1917, toward the end of the golden century of carrousel-building that began around 1825 (when the Common Council of Manhattan Island, New York, granted one John Sears a permit to "establish a covered circus for a Flying Horse Establishment"). "Liberty"—as the Philadelphia Toboggan Company's red, white, and blue creation was called during that patriotic era—originally featured 72 horses on an oversized moving platform measuring 60 feet in diameter, plus several stationary chariots. During the Disney refurbishing, these were removed, and many were replaced with additional horses made of fiberglass. Also, the original horses' legs, which were arranged in a rather decorous pose, were ingeniously rearranged to make the steeds look like real chargers. (Careful examination seems to reveal some of the cracks by which this change was effected.) Also, for the wooden canopy above the horses, Disney artists handpainted 18 separate scenes (each measuring about two by three feet) with images of the little cinder girl from Charles Perrault's fairy tale and Disney's 1950 film. Additionally, the original mechanical wooden parts were replaced by metal ones; the thick layer of paint that had obscured some of the finer points of

the original carving was stripped away, and the horses were repainted. The painting alone required about 48 hours per horse. All the horses are white, Disney spokespeople will tell you, because all the riders are good guys!

While waiting to mount the carrousel's steeds, it's worthwhile to take the time to study the animals carefully. One is festooned with yellow roses, another carries a quiver of Indian arrows, and yet another sports a portrait of Eric the Red on its back. No two are exactly alike. The band organ, which plays favorite music from Disney studios (such as the Oscar-winning "When You Wish Upon A Star," "Zip-a-dee-doo-dah," and "Chim-Chim-Cheree"), was made in one of Italy's most famous factories.

SNOW WHITE'S SCARY ADVENTURES: This attraction near the carrousel retells the scary part of the Grimm Brothers' fairy tale, which Walt Disney made into the world's first full-length animated feature in 1937 and 1938. Though basically a ride for kids, Snow White's Scary Adventures features two skeletons and plenty of spooky darkness; also, the wicked witch—evil, long-nosed, and practically toothless—appears more than once with such suddenness and menace that some youngsters end up really frightened. At the end, the hag dumps a rock on the passengers; the stars you see are among the attraction's best special effects.

MAD TEA PARTY: The theme of this ride—in a group of oversized pastel-colored teacups that whirl and spin as wildly as many carnivals' Tubs of Fun—derives from a scene in the Disney studio's 1951 production of Lewis Carroll's novel *Alice in Wonderland*. During the sequence in question, the Mad Hatter hosts a tea party for his un-birthday. Unlike many of the other rides in Fantasyland, this attraction is not strictly for the younger children; the 9-to-20-crowd seems to like it best. Be sure to note the soused mouse that pops out of the teapot at the center of the platform full of teacups.

DUMBO, THE FLYING ELEPHANT: This is purely and simply a kiddie ride—though personages as varied as Romanian gymnast Nadia Comaneci and Muhammad Ali have loved it. The character of the flying elephant was developed for the 1941 film release of *Dumbo*, one of the shortest of Disney's animated features and one of the best, starring a baby elephant born with inordinately large ears and an ability to fly that is discovered after he accidentally drinks a bucket of champagne. The mouse that sits atop the mirrored ball in the middle of the circle of the ride's flying elephants is the faithful Timothy Mouse, who in the film becomes Dumbo's manager after the circus folk who had once laughed at the flying elephant hire him to be a star.

SKYWAY TO TOMORROWLAND: Entered from near Peter Pan's Flight, this aerial tram transports guests one-way to Tomorrowland. En route it's possible to see the clear aquamarine pool traversed by Captain Nemo's ship, the striped tent tops of Cinderella's Golden Carrousel, Tomorrowland's Grand Prix, and the not-so-wonderful rooftops of the buildings where many Magic Kingdom adventures actually take place. This attraction is best boarded at its Tomorrowland terminus, where the lines are usually shorter.

PETER PAN'S FLIGHT: The inspiration for this attraction was the Scottish writer Sir James M. Barrie's play about the boy who wouldn't grow up, which appeared as a Disney movie in 1953. Riding in flying versions of Captain Hook's ornate ship—which are suspended from an overhead rail once they leave the boarding area—visitors swoop and soar through a series of scenes that tell the story of how Wendy, Michael, and John get sprinkled with pixie dust and, heading for "the second star to the right and straight on till morning," fly off to Never-Never-Land with Tinkerbell; and meet Princess Tiger Lilly, the evil Captain Hook, his jolly-looking sidekick Mr. Smee, and the crocodile—who has already made off with one of Hook's hands and is on the verge of getting the rest of him as you sail out into daylight. As in the movie, one of the most beautiful scenes—one that makes this attraction a treat for adults as well as for littler folk—is the sight of nighttime London, dark blue and speckled with twinkling yellow lights, complete with the Thames, Big Ben, London Bridge, and vehicles that really move on the streets. The song that accompanies the trip is "You Can Fly, You Can Fly, You Can Fly" by Sammy Cahn and Sammy Fain.

IT'S A SMALL WORLD: Originally created for New York's 1964–1965 World's Fair, with a tunefully singsong melody written by Richard M. and Robert B. Sherman (the Academy Award–winning composers of the music for *Mary Poppins*, among other Disney scores), this favorite of young children and senior citizens involves a boat trip through several large rooms where stylized AudioAnimatronics dolls—wooden soldiers, cancan dancers, balloonists, chess pieces, Tower of London guards in scarlet beefeater uniforms, bagpipers and leprechauns, gooseherds, little Dutch kids in wooden shoes, Don Quixote and a goatherd, yodelers and gondoliers, houri dancers, dancers from Greece and Thailand, snake charmers, Japanese kite flyers, hippos and giraffes and frogs, hyenas, monkeys, and elephants, hip-twitching Polynesians, surfers, and even dolphins—sing and dance to a melody that will run through your head for hours after you float out of their wonderland. Of the two queues that are usually found here, the one to the left is almost always shorter.

20,000 LEAGUES UNDER THE SEA: Jules Verne, on whose novel Disney based the 1954 release that provides the theme for this attraction, described the Machiavellian Captain Nemo's ship as an undersea monster, with headlights that appeared as eyes in the dark water. The 61-foot-long, 58-ton, 38-passenger craft that ply the beautiful, blue Fantasyland lagoon are far too handsome to fit the description, but—at least on the outside—they bear a remarkable resemblance to the craft piloted by the nefarious Nemo toward Vulcania. In the course of the trip, visitors tour an 11½-million-gallon pool filled with sea grass, kelp, giant fishes, clams, seahorses, coral, icebergs, and rock formations fashioned of fiberglass, plastic, steel, stucco, and epoxy paint. The ship's course passes by the lost city of Atlantis and under a rather attractive "polar ice cap"; as in the film, passengers listen to Nemo playing the organ, and endure an attack by a giant squid. The special effects aren't the Magic Kingdom's best, and the queues outside move rather slowly—so don't line up unless it's not too busy.

Incidentally, the nautical flags above the entrance—which now spell out the word "Leagues" in the attraction's name—read S-E-U-G-A-E-L 0-0-0, 0-2 when the park first opened. A Navy visitor pointed out the mistake. The queue area, which is done up with Disney-made rocks, is meant to resemble the volcanic boulders that would have been found on Nemo's Vulcania. The area is also graced by a large Senegal date palm and a Southern magnolia, which were so heavy that the ceiling of the Magic Kingdom basement down below had to be specially reinforced to support them. The cliffs into which the submarines disappear, on the far side of the lagoon, conceal the backstage area where much of the scenery is set up; a better view of the layout is available from the Skyway above.

MR. TOAD'S WILD RIDE: Wild in name only, this attraction is based on the October 1949 Disney release *The Adventures of Ichabod and Mr. Toad*, which itself derives from Kenneth Grahame's classic novel *The Wind in the Willows*. It seems that a gang of weasels has tricked that memorable man-about-town Mr. J. Thaddeus Toad into trading the deed to his ancestral mansion for a stolen motorcar. In the attraction, flivvers modeled on this very car take guests zigging and zagging along the road to Nowhere in Particular, through dark rooms painted in neon colors and illuminated by black lights where the redoubtable Mr. Toad is trying to get out of the scrape. In the process, you crash through a fireplace, narrowly miss being struck by a falling suit of armor, go hurtling through haystacks and barn doors and into a coop full of squawking chickens, then ride down a railroad track on a collision course with a huge locomotive. Some of this is scary enough that some small children end up momentarily frightened. By and large, though, this is a ride for kids.

TOMORROWLAND

With its vast expanse of concrete, Tomorrowland offers a picture of the future that is a little less than wonderful, since the architecture looks a bit too much like yesterday's version of Tomorrow: As Disney planners have discovered, it isn't easy to portray a future that persists in becoming the present. Mission to the Moon, for instance, became Mission to Mars in 1975, when the earth's lunar neighbor began to seem almost as close-to-home as the neighborhood McDonald's. But the extreme forms into which many of the trees and bushes have been pruned do look vaguely futuristic. Note the ligustrums between the Grand Prix Raceway and the Tomorrowland Terrace—shrubs that have been shaped into single-trunked trees topped with spheres; the oleanders, another type of shrub pruned like a tree, located in raised planters near the Carousel of Progress; and many others. One of the most interesting of the plantings, the ligustrum near Tomorrowland Terrace—which looks a bit like an octopus balancing many green trays—was found by a Disney landscape artist in the 1960s on the front lawn of a Sarasota home whose owner was persuaded to give up her pet for a check and a promise to repair any damages incurred in the transplanting operation. (Eventually, that meant not only fixing the lawn, but also repaving the lady's driveway.)

Also, Space Mountain—which anchors this land at its eastern edge (with the bulky contours of the Contemporary Resort Hotel rising just beyond)—has a shape that seems almost timeless. Though this attraction is usually very crowded in the afternoon, most others—high-capacity adventures that they are—may require no waits then, so Tomorrowland is a good area to visit during a busy time on one of the Magic Kingdom's busier days.

SPACE MOUNTAIN: Rising to a height of over 150 feet, just a few inches shy of the peak of Big Thunder Mountain, and extending some 300 feet in diameter, this gleaming white steel and concrete cone (shaped vaguely like Japan's Mount Fuji) houses an attraction that most people call a roller coaster. Actually, it bears the same sort of resemblance to the traditional thrill ride that the Magic Kingdom does to the garden variety of theme park. It's the Disney version—a roller coaster and then some. While the 2-minute, 38-second ride does not exactly duplicate a trip into outer space, there are

some truly phenomenal and quite lovely special effects—shooting stars and strobe-like flashing lights among them; and the whole ride takes place in an outer space–like darkness that gets progressively inkier—and scarier—as the journey progresses. The eight-passenger rockets that roar through this blackness attain a maximum speed of just over 28 miles per hour. Just how terrifying this actually is to any given passenger depends on his or her level of tolerance. In general, the Space Mountain trip seems to inspire in lovers of thrill rides an immediate desire to go again; it's just wild enough to send eyeglasses, purses, wallets, and even an occasional set of false teeth plummeting to the bottom of the track (and turbulent enough to upset the stomachs of those so unwise as to ride it immediately after eating)—but not so harrowing that passengers' shake and the weakened knees persist for more than a minute or two after "touch-down." Those in a quandary about whether or not to line up can get a preview from the WEDway PeopleMover described below; and those who decide to pass after hearing the shrieks and the clatter of the cars from the queue area have their own special exit.

After experiencing the space journey, it's interesting to note some statistics. The mountain itself—which occupies a 10-acre site and contains 4,508,500 cubic feet, enough to accommodate a small skyscraper—is composed of 72 pre-stressed concrete beams cast nearby, then hoisted into place by mammoth cranes. Each rib weighs 74 tons, and measures 117 feet in length and, in width, 4 feet at the top and 13 feet at the bottom. With the work lights on, the interior of Space Mountain looks humdrum and almost commercially common, with its tangled array of track and supporting scaffolding. Some of the shooting stars are produced quite simply, by aiming a beam of light at a mirrored globe; and

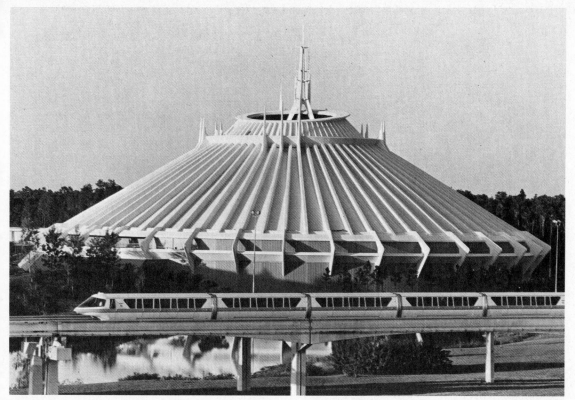

legend has it that the meteors visible to guests in the queue area are actually projections of chocolate chip cookies! The whole ride is controlled by a Nova-2 computer (with another Nova-2 in backup) and is monitored on a board full of dials and a battery of closed-circuit television screens by Disney hosts and hostesses sitting in a control room (whose eerie blue glow is another striking feature of the queue area). As a result, any guest caught disobeying posted rules will be seen—and his or her rocket stopped so that the offender can be escorted out of the park. Children under seven must be accompanied by an adult; no children under three are permitted; and as the many signs at the attraction warn, "You must be in Good Health, and Free from Heart Conditions, Motion Sickness, Weak Back, or Other Physical Limitations" to ride. It is also suggested that expectant mothers pass up the trip. Presented by RCA.

HOME OF FUTURE LIVING: The moving sidewalk that takes guests out of Space Mountain also carries them past scenes in which some of the Magic Kingdom's less-sophisticated AudioAnimatronics figures demonstrate the uses of the electronic media in the future, in business and in the home. Far more interesting are the RCA Broadcast Systems ($70,000 to $80,000 each) that allow guests to see themselves on television—in living color.

SKYWAY TO FANTASYLAND: This aerial cable car takes guests from Tomorrowland to a point near Peter Pan's Flight in Fantasyland. The trip takes five minutes, and the cable car—built by Von Roll, Ltd., of Bern, Switzerland, then shipped to Miami and on to Orlando—is notable for being the nation's first conveyance of a type able to make a 90-degree turn. If you're going to ride the Skyway, this is the place to get on: The lines at the Fantasyland end are usually much longer.

STARJETS: Towering high over Tomorrowland, this is purely and simply a thrill ride and ought to delight anyone who loves Space Mountain, but doesn't necessarily want to get in line all over again.

WEDWAY PEOPLEMOVER: Boarded near the StarJets, these small, five-car trains move at a speed of about ten miles per hour along close to a mile of track, alongside or through most of the major attractions in Tomorrowland. If you have any doubts about riding Space Mountain, a trip on the PeopleMover — which travels through the queue area inside and offers a view of the rockets as they hurtle through the darkness—will probably help you make your decision. Just as important, from an intellectual standpoint, is the fact that the WEDway PeopleMover shows off an innovative means of transportation operated by a linear induction motor that has no moving parts, uses little power, and emits no pollution. Presented by the Edison Electric Institute.

IF YOU HAD WINGS: Located behind Circle-Vision 360 (described below), this five-minute-long adventure takes guests along a track where, to the accompaniment of the very catchy song that gives the attraction its name, some 83 projectors show scenes of the tropics (a waterfall in a Trinidadian tropical forest, a bluer-than-blue Caribbean sea, a Mexican marketplace, and the like). Most of these effects are a bit tame, but the next-to-last shot, which features some you-are-there film taken from speeding planes and cars, is the sort of footage that makes you want to go all over again—something that is blessedly easy to do, since the lines here are usually minimal. No admission charge; no ticket needed. The attraction's sponsor, Eastern Airlines (the Official Airline of Walt Disney World), maintains an airline ticket office near the exit.

CIRCLE-VISION 360 "MAGIC CARPET 'ROUND THE WORLD": This 21-minute film, the first attraction on the far right just over the Tomorrowland Bridge, is a travel film like few others. Instead of showing only what's in front, it also lets viewers see what's behind and to either side, thanks to an unusual filming technique that involves nine 35mm cameras mounted in a circle on a pole-like affair. Part of the footage was filmed by a ground crew of seven, who did their shooting from a station wagon; the rest was taken from a modified B-25 bomber plane emblazoned with the face of Mickey Mouse himself. Both crews spent two months on the road and brought back 200,000 feet of film, which was edited down to the 17,000 feet. This footage is shown in the big theater by an equally innovative arrangement of nine projectors, nine 20-by-30-foot screens, and 12 channels of sound reproduced through nine different speakers (one mounted behind each screen), plus six others, affixed to the ceiling, which carry the narration. Consequently, the experience is really impressive (and a few of the flight scenes are realistic enough to make some guests airsick). The journey includes stops at London's Tower Bridge and the Thames River, Copenhagen's Tivoli Gardens, Paris's Notre Dame Cathedral, the Swiss Alps, Germany's castles on the Rhine, Vienna (to hear the celebrated Vienna Boys' Choir), Rome's ancient Colosseum, a bull ring in Madrid, Jerusalem's Wailing Wall, the Sahara Desert, the Valley of the Nile (to see the Pyramids and the Sphinx), the big-game country of Africa, India's Taj Mahal, Hong Kong Harbor (aboard a Chinese junk), and more. The grand finale involves a tour of the United States, from San Francisco Bay to the Statue of Liberty. The attraction can accommodate up to 3,700 people an hour, so don't be discouraged if you see a crowd outside: it disappears every 20 minutes or so. This is generally one of a handful of spots where the queues on a busy afternoon are the least discouraging.

MISSION TO MARS: After a pre-flight briefing in a room styled to look like Mission Control, and a narration by an AudioAnimatronics flight engineer who looks just like the father in the Carousel of Progress family, guests enter a round cabin for a simulated trip to Mars that was developed in cooperation with NASA. Seats tilt and shake, sub-audible sound waves are sent out, and oversized speakers let out great roars and hisses that sound like a washing machine during the spin cycle; corny though the idea is, the realization is okay. The attraction is located opposite Circle-Vision 360 (below). Films screened during the flight, some developed from photos taken during the Mariner Nine space program, show a section of Mars's surface called Mariner Valley and its 40-mile-wide Olympus Mons, the universe's largest known volcano. The best viewing is from the third and fourth rows. Presented by McDonnell Douglas Corp.

CAROUSEL OF PROGRESS: First seen at New York's World's Fair of 1964–1965 and moved here in 1975, this 22-minute show features a number of tableaux starring an AudioAnimatronics family, and demonstrates the great improvements in American life that have come about as the result of increased use of electricity. The sheet music for the song "Now

GRAND PRIX RACEWAY: The little cars that *vroom* down the four 2,760-foot-long tracks at this attraction opposite the Tomorrowland Terrace provide most of the background noise in Tomorrowland—and that's another grim thought about the future. Older kids and teenagers love the ride and will spend as many hours driving the Mark VII-model gasoline-powered cars as they can; one 87-year-old grandmother comes here just to watch. Like true sports cars, the vehicles—which cost about $6,000 each—have rack-and-pinion steering and disc brakes; unlike most sports cars, these run on a track. Nonetheless, even expert drivers have a hard time keeping them going in a straight line until the technique is mastered: just steer all the way to the right, or all the way to the left, and you've got it made. One lap around the track takes about five minutes, and the cars (which are manufactured by a Disney company called MAPO, short for Mary Poppins) can travel at a maximum speed of about 7 miles per hour. You must be at least 4'4" to ride. Presented by Goodyear.

SHOPS IN THE MAGIC KINGDOM

No one travels all the way to the Magic Kingdom just to go shopping. But as many a first-time visitor has learned with some surprise, shopping is one of the most enjoyable pastimes there. Donald Duck key chains and Mickey Mouse lapel pins, Alice-in-Wonderland dresses for little girls and Walt Disney World sweat shirts, and other Disney souvenir items make up a large portion of the merchandise you see on display. Most of this Disney merchandise has been custom-made for the park and is not available elsewhere.

But the Magic Kingdom's boutiques and stores stock much more than just Disneyana, and it's possible to buy antiques and silver-plated tea services, escargot holders and cookbooks, mock pirate hats and toy frontier rifles, 14-carat gold charms and filigreed costume jewelry in Main Street shops that also sell magic tricks and film, peanut brittle and Droste chocolate apples. In Adventureland, you can buy imported items from around the world—hand-carved elephant statues from Africa, inlaid marble boxes from India, batik dresses from Indonesia, and much more. Shops stock items that complement the themes of the various lands (and so, in Tomorrowland, one finds contemporary wall hangings and futuristic-looking table lamps). Every store offers a selection of items from the inexpensive to the costly: in Tinkerbell's Toy Shop in Fantasyland, for instance, kids can beg for a $5 windup toy after requests for the larger-than-life-sized $1,500 stuffed animals are denied. In the Cup'n Saucer, a china shop on Main Street, a four-foot-high Hummel figurine costs thousands of dollars; a music box in the shape of the Taj Mahal can be seen in Adventureland's Magic Carpet. And in many shops, you can watch craftsmen at work—peanut brittle being poured in the Main Street Confectionary, perfume being mixed at Mlle. Lafayette's Parfumerie in Liberty Square, a glass blower in Main Street's Crystal Arts and Adventureland's La Princesa de Cristal, and the like.

Consequently, there's no need to spend a fortune to have a good time. Budget-watchers should note, though, that most buying in the Magic Kingdom is impulse buying, and that the retail operation here is one of the most successful of any in the United States. The temptation to nickel-and-dime yourself into penury is very strong, and you need to be careful. It's a good idea to set a spending limit for each member of your party in advance—and try to stick to it.

MAIN STREET

East Side

STROLLER SHOP: Just after the turnstiles into the Magic Kingdom, to the right as you face Cinderella Castle. Strollers and wheelchairs can be rented here, and assorted souvenirs purchased.

THE CHAPEAU: This Town Square shop is the place to buy Mouseketeer ears and have them monogrammed, and to shop for visors, cowboy hats, straw hats, Confederate soldier hats, and other headgear. The shop sells literally truckloads of ridiculous bubble-head hats made out of colored, stiffened netting material—fun to try on, if not necessarily worth the investment.

POLAROID CAMERA CENTER: Gleaming glass-fronted mahogany cases show off the Canon, Minolta, Pentax, Nikon, and the other 35mm, instant-load, quick-developing cameras for sale at this high-ceilinged shop near Town Square. Flash cubes, film, and other photo supplies are also available, and very minor repairs can be made. A wide variety of cameras is available for rent (a deposit is required).

You can also have an 8-by-10 Polaroid portrait taken in old-fashioned costumes that look for all the world like something a favorite grandmother would have worn–except that the backs of the costumes are treated like hospital gowns; sitters pose on the rear end of a caboose. Even if you decide not to spend the money (under $10), it's amusing just to stand and watch other guests lining up to say "cheese."

MAIN STREET CONFECTIONARY: The store is an old-fashioned pink-and-white paradise, a delight at any time of day, but especially when the cooks in the shop's glass-walled kitchen are pouring peanut brittle onto a huge tabletop to cool, and the candy is sending up clouds of scent that you could swear was being fanned right out into the street. Some 18 to 20 batches are made each day. The sweet product is for sale in small bags, along with chocolate apples and oranges and pastilles by the Dutch candy maker Droste, Irish toffee, jellies by the Scottish company

Davidson of Dundee, thick glacéed apricots from Australia, Toblerone, dried fruits, macadamia nuts and pistachios, plain old marshmallows and jelly beans, marshmallow peanuts and nougats, mints and kisses, rock candy, M&Ms, and dozens of other nemeses for a sweet tooth. When your stomach is growling and there are long queues in the ice-cream parlor, this is a good place to grab a snack.

THE CUP'N SAUCER: Fine china and other gift items—china birds and figurines, swans, china flowers, Lalique figurines, and all manner of pretty teacups, Disney character figurines, and Wedgwood boxes and plates—priced at $5 to $13,000—are the stock-in-trade of this airy establishment. The most expensive item, at last look, was a giant Hummel statue, depicting two ruddy-cheeked peasant children in an apple tree; at least peek at it, even if it is a bit rich for most pocketbooks.

WONDERLAND OF WAX: The warm wax that the candlemakers use to produce Easter bunnies, and other creations-with-wicks, perfumes this area of the Christmas Shop, behind the Cup'n Saucer (the china shop). Fun to watch, even if you're not out to buy.

CHRISTMAS SHOP: The honor of being possibly the best Christmas store on earth is most likely to belong to the Christmas Chalet in Walt Disney World Shopping Village. But this red-and-green shop boasts an intriguing tableau—not for sale—with Mickey Mouse napping next to the fire, in front of a Christmas tree, set up in a miniature library complete right down to the cuckoo clock. Surrounding Mickey is a variety of Christmas souvenirs, mouse-themed and otherwise, that has proved well-nigh irresistible to more than one budget-conscious guest—Santa Clauses and wooden soldiers, bells and drums and Christmas sleighs, plus trinkets in velvet, clothespins, dough, and china to decorate next year's tree.

DISNEY & COMPANY: The wallpaper at this shop on Center Street (the cul-de-sac just off Main) is bright and Victorian, the floors are parquet, and the woodwork elaborate; and old-fashioned ceiling fans twirl slowly overhead. But this is a souvenir stand, purveying sweat shirts and T-shirts, hats and bags, pens and pencils, stuffed animals, and other items by the dozen. The selection is not as vast as at the Emporium, but neither is Disney & Company quite so overwhelming.

UPTOWN JEWELERS: Not far from Disney & Company. The selection of good-quality costume jewelry here is excellent, particularly for pins, necklaces, pendants, bracelets, and earrings with an old-fashioned look. One counter in the corner of the shop stocks wonderful souvenir charms in 14-carat gold and sterling silver: Tinkerbell, Cinderella Castle, and the Walt Disney logo (a globe with mouse ears).

MARKET HOUSE: An old-fashioned spot, with displays of Smucker's jams and jellies in more varieties than supermarket shoppers would have imagined even existed, plus Mrs. Butterworth's syrup, Cracker Jacks, pretzels, pickles, honeys, and all kinds of tea

and snack items arranged in old-fashioned oak cases flanking a sturdy, black potbellied stove. The floors are oak and pegged, the lighting comes in part from brass lanterns dangling above the stove, and in one corner there's a real old-fashioned hand-crank telephone.

THE SHADOW BOX: Watching silhouette cutters snip black paper into the likenesses of children is one of Main Street's more fascinating diversions, and there's always a crowd on hand—some folks waiting their turn, some just inspecting the progress and the results. Framed silhouettes cost about $3.

CRYSTAL ARTS: Cut-glass bowls and vases, urns and glasses, plates and shelves glitter in the mirror-backed glass cases of this high-ceilinged, brass-chandeliered emporium. Genuine Waterford crystal is also offered for sale. Occasionally, an engraver and a glassblower are at work by the bright light flooding through the big windows. The wares available at Adventureland's La Princesa de Cristal are similar.

WEST SIDE

NEWSSTAND: No newspapers are sold in the Magic Kingdom—even at its Newsstand, which is opposite the Stroller Shop, to your left as you face Cinderella Castle, just after you've passed through the turnstiles at the entrance to the Magic Kingdom. Character merchandise and souvenirs are for sale; the selection is fairly limited, but you can usually pick up items you've forgotten during your travels through the rest of the park.

THE EMPORIUM: Framed by a two-story-high portico, this Town Square landmark, the Magic Kingdom's largest gift shop, stocks a little bit of everything—flower pots and silk flowers, all kinds of candles, including some in animal shapes, some done up like hot dogs or ice cream sundaes; stuffed animals and toys; a doll-lover's array of Madame Alexander dolls, as well as five or six other kinds; and more. Everyone seems to have an armload of Walt Disney World T-shirts and sweat shirts, towels and handbags, Mouseketeer ears and other hats, and various items emblazoned with Mickey, Minnie, or Walt Disney World logos. The cash registers almost always seem to be busy, especially toward the end of the afternoon and before park closing. It's a good place to souvenir-shop, though, since it's only a few steps from lockers (under the train station) where purchases can be stowed. Don't forget to note the window displays, which usually feature AudioAnimatronic displays ranging from themes of the season to the most recent Disney movie.

THE GREENHOUSE: While inside the Emporium, it's sometimes hard to tell where this sprawling store ends and the next shop begins. The Greenhouse is the corner of the Emporium devoted to growing things. There are intriguing little clay pots for sale, some with fruits and vegetables molded onto the sides in relief, alongside some animal-shaped ceramic potters in bright colors; plus hundreds upon hundreds of lovely silk and plastic flowers that spill out into Center Street (and make the view from the Harmony Barber Shop next door particularly colorful). Guests who have come by car may be interested in buying one of the mock topiaries—animal-shaped

forms made with moss and wire and planted with a kind of small-leafed vine that will cover completely in about six months. A must.

NEW CENTURY CLOCK SHOP: Clocks and watches in all shapes and sizes, not to mention Mickey Mouse watches in a variety of configurations, are displayed in the polished wood cases at this establishment adjoining the Emporium. There are clocks for the kitchen and clocks for the living room, clocks with chimes and clocks without them, alarm clocks for bedside tables and others for travel, digital watches and watches with hands, and even some pocket watches and a Mickey Mouse telephone—with rotary dial or Touch Tone. Purchases can be shipped on request. Presented by Elgin-Helbros.

HARMONY BARBER SHOP: The setting is quaint and old-fashioned, worth a peek even if you've no need for a trim. Nostalgic shaving items and mustache cups are for sale.

HALLMARK CARD SHOP: Hallmark stocks this boutique near the Emporium on Main Street with cards, wrapping paper, and pretty party items, such as paper plates, napkins, and tablecloths.

HOUSE OF MAGIC: Magicians can make ordinary playing cards simply disappear, balls pass through cups, water pours out of a jug that looks empty, coins pass through solid sheets of rubber, and a wand turns into two silken handkerchiefs. Some believers can produce coins from thin air, or pour the milk from a whole pitcher into a thimble. This Main Street emporium sells the kind of magician's tools that can turn everyday travelers into magicians, along with party-joke items such as phony arm casts, slimy reptiles, and similar stuff.

TOBACCONIST: The sign outside ranks among the Magic Kingdom's handsomest; the matchbooks given out with purchases are especially attractive; and the smell of all the pipe tobaccos is heavenly. Even nonsmokers will at least want to breeze through.

ADVENTURELAND

HOUSE OF TREASURE: The only spot in the Magic Kingdom that sells pirates' hats, this swashbucklers' delight adjoins Pirates of the Caribbean on the west and stocks piratic merchandise—toy rifles and brass dolphins, a Pirate's Creed of Ethics printed on parchment, Jolly Roger flags, shell rings, old-looking maps, pirate dolls, and an assortment of books (one on how to build ships in bottles, others on whalers and frigates and men-of-war). There's as much for adults as for youngsters.

GOLDEN GALLEON: A real antique diver's helmet is the centerpiece of this neighbor of La Princesa de Cristal, a low-ceilinged, tile-floored shop full of golden treasures—handsome nautical items worthy of a luxurious living room, globes and brass door knockers, brass cannons, ships' wheels, and a spyglass—not to mention some of the most dazzling rhinestone necklaces this side of Bloomingdale's.

LA PRINCESA DE CRISTAL: The cut-glass items, custom-engraved goblets and bowls, and blown-glass baubles sold at this emporium tucked away behind the snack stand called El Pirata Y El Perico, opposite Pirates of the Caribbean, are about the same as those in Crystal Arts on Main Street—but the ceilings here are lower and beamed, and the floors are red tile instead of linoleum—so the feeling is totally different.

Warning to the squeamish: the sound made by the engravers is for all the world like fingers scraping on a chalkboard. Eek!

TRADERS OF TIMBUKTU: This shop is in a marketlike complex in the plaza opposite the Enchanted Tiki Birds, and displays a fine selection of the sort of handsome (but inexpensive) trinkets that travelers find while visiting the erstwhile Dark Continent—carved wooden giraffes and antelopes, ethnic jewelry (including carved bangles, wooden combs, and shark's-tooth necklaces), dashikis, and khaki shirts. The great child-pleasers here are the plastic pith helmets.

TIKI TROPIC SHOP: Hawaiian and Caribbean clothing—polyester caftans, terry rompers, and other such items, plus a fine assortment of bathing suits—is the specialty at this establishment located near Traders of Timbuktu, opposite the exit to the Swiss Family Treehouse.

THE MAGIC CARPET: Not all guests manage to wander into this tiny, low-ceilinged shop tucked away in Adventureland, near Traders of Timbuktu and the Sunshine Tree Terrace. But the showpiece here, a two-foot-high music box replica of India's onion-domed Taj Mahal, makes the fragrant shop well worth a detour, even if you don't flip over the other Middle Eastern and Asian imports (carved tea trays, cotton and silk dresses made in India, brass bells and baubles, leather items, jingle bells in three sizes, incense, and more) displayed on glass shelves against elaborate damask backdrops.

ORIENTAL IMPORTS: This shop, hung with silk-tasseled Oriental lanterns, stocks the sort of goods that merchants in Hong Kong sell in quantity: lovely satin change purses and eyeglass cases, slinky women's dresses, straw boxes made in China, Chinese-style hand-embroidered pajamas for kids, figurines, and hand-gilded and engraved copper plates, done by the so-called Chokin method, which was originally used to decorate Samurai warriors' helmets.

TROPIC TOPPERS: This simple shop near Traders of Timbuktu is the spot to find the kind of safari hats worn by the pilots at the Jungle Cruise. Assorted other straw hats and handbags and other knick-knacks are also for sale.

COLONEL HATHI'S SAFARI CLUB: This emporium near the entrance to the Swiss Family Treehouse, named after the elephant in the 1967 film *The Jungle Book*, smells sweetly of the rattan and straw goods that give it its tropical character. Merchandise here is all summer stuff: sunglasses and wind chimes, thongs and terry-cloth rompers, straw handbags and shells, coral bangles, palmetto fans, and the like.

PLAZA DEL SOL CARIBE: This market next to the Pirates of the Caribbean sells candy and snacks, a variety of straw hats (including colorful oversized sombreros), and artificial flowers.

LAFFITE'S PORTRAIT DECK: Hidden away near the Plaza del sol Caribe, this is the Adventureland counterpart of the photography studio in Main Street's Camera Center. Here, though, instead of posing in the genteelest of Gay Nineties garb, you dress up as swashbucklers and pirate maids amid what look to be pieces of eight and chests brimful of pearls and precious jewels.

FRONTIERLAND

FRONTIER TRADING POST: This is the place to outfit a youngster like a true son of the Great Frontier: cowboy hats and boots or feathered headdresses and moccasins, hefty brass belt buckles, sleeve garters, calico sunbonnets, sombreros, sheriff's badges, old-fashioned spatterware enamel coffeepots, gold nugget jewelry, and reproduction pistols and rifles should do the trick. Also available are Western items like tom-toms, peace pipes, plastic toy horses, forts, Big Al stuffed bears, books on American folklore, and C. M. Russell paintings. Don't miss the doll-sized model store against the rear wall at the eastern end of the emporium.

LIBERTY SQUARE

OLDE WORLD ANTIQUES: One of the first of the Liberty Square shops that visitors pass after crossing the bridge from the Hub area in front of Cinderella Castle, this little, lace-curtained emporium stocks real antiques—grandfather clocks and rocking chairs, hutches, drop-leaf tables, and assorted decorative items in brass, pewter, copper, mahogany, oak, and pine—as well as some reproductions. Prices run into thousands of dollars, and bargains are nowhere to be found, but every item is in tip-top condition, and is tagged with a description of its origin, so the browsing is good.

MLLE. LAFAYETTE'S PARFUMERIE: Few spots in the Magic Kingdom smell quite as fragrant as this tiny neighbor of Olde World Antiques, where perfume

blenders turn six basic fragrances into hundreds of different combinations, using an assortment of giant eyedroppers, tiny paper blotters, glass funnels, and graduated cylinders; the process is fun just to watch. Each formula is recorded so that guests can reorder at will. Those who decide to stick with traditional fragrances can shop for dozens of perfumes by makers as varied as Nina Ricci, Hermès, Worth, Patou, Chanel, Madame Rochas, Charles of the Ritz, and Myrurgia. Pretty glass atomizers are also available.

HERITAGE HOUSE: Among the Early American reproductions that predominate in the stock of this store next to the Hall of Presidents, youngsters may go for the parchment copies of famous American documents, while homeowners might snap up pewter plates and candlesticks, creweled items, wooden candlesticks and pepper mills, busts of the presidents, souvenir spoons, mugs in Early American motifs, wrought-iron knickknacks, or lovely enameled paintings of clipper ships. Most wonderful of all— more for grown-ups than for kids—are the dolls, the quaint and intensely personable creations of a Poughkeepsie, New York, doll maker: elegant ladies in Victorian garb, as well as characters from Early American life such as the chimney sweep, the peddler, the pottery vendor, the soap fat man carrying a tub of tallow.

YANKEE TRADER: No first-time visitor to the Magic Kingdom would expect to be able to buy stoneware soufflé dishes and espresso makers, cast-iron muffin tins and escargot holders. But this wonderfully fragrant shop, immediately to the right after you turn into the lane leading to the Haunted

Mansion, is crammed like a too-small kitchen cabinet with just these kitchen knickknacks, and more: cookie cutters and choppers, graters and spatulas, French-fry slicers, wooden-handled whisks, egg timers, and wall plaques made of dough, to name just a few of the sorts of items available here. Cookbooks are also for sale—not only the old favorites like *Joy of Cooking*, but also unusual volumes of historic recipes. The store is located near the archway-entrance to Fantasyland.

TRICORNERED HAT SHOPPE: One of the Magic Kingdom's most profitable shops per square foot, this one offers hats of all descriptions (especially Western ones), plus feathered hatbands and leather goods. It's tucked away near the arcade leading to Adventureland, between the ornamental Frontierland stockade, alongside the Shootin' Gallery and the Diamond Horseshoe saloon.

KEEL BOAT SHOPPE: This small shop, situated next to Mike Fink's Keel Boats, gives guests on their way to the Haunted Mansion a taste of things to come with a stock of horrific monster masks and assorted ghoulish goodies. Some magic tricks and party jokes (in a more limited selection than at Fantasyland's Merlin's Magic Shop and Main Street's House of Magic) are also available.

SILVERSMITH: The sign above the entrance to this tiny shop adjoining Olde World Antiques (just next to the Liberty Square bridge to the Hub) reads "J. Tremain, Prop." That refers to the main character in the 1957 Disney film of the Esther Forbes novel about a silversmith's apprentice who joins the Boston

Tea Party and helps hang the lights on the Liberty Tree during America's colonial days. At this low-ceilinged, plank-floored establishment, antiquey-looking cabinets display tongs and teaspoons, Revere-style bowls, tea sets, silver-coated roses, candelabra, and more—all in silver plate.

FANTASYLAND

THE KING'S GALLERY: Situated inside Cinderella Castle, near the entrance to King Stefan's Banquet Hall, this shop is one of the Magic Kingdom's best. The walls are dark and the ceilings beamed, and the stock includes a huge and imaginative selection of wonderful handmade dolls, music boxes, cuckoo clocks, Russian lacquer boxes, Spanish-made swords and leather handbags, German beer mugs with lids, chess sets, and more—very little of it at rock-bottom prices. Also here, practiced artisans demonstrate the art of Damascene, a form of metalworking originated by the inhabitants of Damascus in the sixth century A.D.; it is mastered today by only a handful of specialized craftsmen around the world. Painstakingly, these skilled workers dip steel pendants into acid to create tiny pores, then use a combination of sterling silver and 24-carat gold wire to outline butterflies and other intricate designs onto the acid-blackened steel.

MERLIN'S MAGIC SHOP: Another really wonderful place near the Cinderella Castle archway. In addition to ogre fangs, monster makeup, and all manner of bizarre masks costing up to $40 (some of them really horrific), the store stocks Chinese rings, cups and balls, and other staples of the magician's trade, plus magic books by Houdini and other masters of prestidigitation. There are party jokes as well: rubber fried eggs, bald-skull caps, bloodshot eyeballs-on-springs that pop out of the wearer's head, Slinkies, ventriloquists' dummies, fake scorpions and lizards, and other knickknacks much loved by youthful Magic Kingdom visitors.

95

CASTLE CAMERA: This shop, near Cinderella Castle opposite Cinderella's Golden Carrousel, is one of two in the Magic Kingdom that specialize in photographic materials. In addition to film and flash materials, you can buy simple Polaroid and Kodak cameras, video cassettes, slides of Magic Kingdom scenes, camera straps with Mickey Mouse's face woven into the cloth, home movies of such attractions as the Haunted Mansion and Pirates of the Caribbean. No cameras are available for rent; for that, visit the Camera Center on Main Street.

MAD HATTER: Another place to buy Mouseketeer ears and other souvenir hats and have your name embroidered on them on the spot. This shop was named for the Mad Hatter, who held the tea party for his un-birthday in Disney's 1951 film version of Lewis Carroll's classic *Alice in Wonderland*.

TINKERBELL TOY SHOP: One of the more wonderful boutiques in the Magic Kingdom, and a fine toy store by any standards. One of the sales counters is shaped like a section of a pirate ship, and behind the counter there's a velvet-cloaked Captain Hook and his cohort, Mr. Smee. For sale are stuffed animals, miniature model cars and trucks, character patches, windup toys and wooden toys, bar soap emblazoned with Disney scenes, Mickey and Minnie toys and clothing, Alice-in-Wonderland dresses, Snow White dresses (with Dopey on the skirt), and a positively marvelous array of Madame Alexander dolls. A must.

THE ARISTOCATS: Most of the lands have one store that specializes in Disney souvenirs; this stone-walled, vaguely Gothic shop alongside Merlin's Magic Shop, slightly to the northeast of Cinderella Castle, is Fantasyland's spot for Donald and Mickey key chains, sweat shirts and T-shirts, china Disney figurines, salt and pepper shakers, Donald Duck needlepoint kits, Minnie tote bags, tennis balls with a Mickey logo, and more.

THE ROYAL CANDY SHOPPE: This souvenir stand next to the Lancer's Inn sells assorted Disneyana, including Mickey Mouse back scratchers, key chains, and stuffed animals, plus a selection of jelly beans and peppermint sticks, Tootsie Rolls, lollipops, and other hard candy.

TOMORROWLAND

MICKEY'S MART: One of the best places in the Magic Kingdom for Disney-themed items, along with Main Street's Emporium.

SKYWAY STATION SHOP: A small spot tucked away near the Tomorrowland terminus of the Skyway to Fantasyland. Disney souvenirs are the stock-in-trade.

SPACE PORT: Sells the kind of contemporary decorative gifts that teens and pre-teens seem to love: lamps whose plastic filaments, when lighted, look like falling water; modern wire statues of golfers and other sportsmen; and other such items. This is one of the Magic Kingdom's most popular shops.

WHERE TO BUY A RAINCOAT: The show doesn't stop just because of a storm. Instead, shops all over the Magic Kingdom stock raincoats to outfit guests who have left their own back home, at their hotel, or in the car. Among them are:

> Main Street: The Emporium
> Adventureland: Tropic Toppers
> Frontierland: Frontier Trading Post
> Fantasyland: Tinkerbell's Toy Shop,
>   Mad Hatter, AristoCats
>   (also umbrellas)
> Tomorrowland: Mickey's Mart

MAIL-ORDER MICKEY: T-shirts, Mouseketeer ears, stuffed animals, and any other souvenir items for sale in Walt Disney World shops can be ordered by mail. For details, write:

> Mail Order Department
> Walt Disney World
> Box 40
> Lake Buena Vista, FL 32830

Or call: 305-824-4718

WHERE TO EAT IN THE MAGIC KINGDOM

A complete listing of all Magic Kingdom eateries—full restaurants with waitress service, fast food emporiums, snack shops, and food vendors—will be found together with all other WDW eating spots in the *Good Meals, Great Times* chapter.

HAPPENINGS AND LIVE ENTERTAINMENT

Before heading down Main Street, check at City Hall to get times for live shows and other special Magic Kingdom happenings. Others may be encountered serendipitously in the course of the day, and occasionally shows scheduled for a given place or time may be changed or canceled at the last minute—but more often than not, the shows proceed as planned.

DAPPER DANS: Are likely to be encountered while you're strolling down Main Street. This barbershop quartet, its members clad in straw hats and striped vests, tap-dance and let one-liners fly during their short four-part harmonic performances. Occasionally, they bring out their set of bamboo organ chimes.

WALT DISNEY WORLD MARCHING BAND: This concert band performs daily at the 5:15 P.M. flag retreat ceremony, and on occasion in the Fantasyland Theater as well.

REFRESHMENT CORNER PIANIST: Tickles the ivories of a snow-white upright at busy periods at this centrally located hamburgers-and-hot-dogs restaurant.

ALL-AMERICAN COLLEGE MARCHING BAND: Featuring college students. Performs on Fantasyland's Fantasy Faire stage only during the summer. Part of a 12-week summer program.

KIDS OF THE KINGDOM: Perform daily in the Castle Forecourt, in a show featuring lively singing and dancing to popular melodies—plus appearances by Disney characters such as the portly Winnie the Pooh and Mickey Mouse himself. The hand motions during the "Lady America" medley repeat the words of the songs in sign language for the deaf. The pressing of hands over the heart signifies "love."

FLAG RETREAT: Daily at 5:15 P.M., a small band and color guard march into Town Square, take down the American flag that flies from the flagpole there, then release a flock of snowy homing pigeons symbolic of the dove of peace. Watch carefully lest you miss them: as one wag quipped, these are union pigeons; they flap away toward their loft-home (behind the Castle) practically before you can say "Cinderella." The whole flight takes just 20 seconds. Some trivia: the carts in which the birds are transported are fashioned from authentic peddlers' carts bought in England for the 1971 film *Bedknobs and Broomsticks*.

J. P. AND THE SILVER STARS: Play familiar tunes on the instruments so well-known in the Caribbean Islands, steel drums—oil barrels whose sides have been cut to a foot or less from the bottom (which itself has been pounded hollow). On a stage near Adventureland's Pirates of the Caribbean.

HANDPICKED: Can occasionally be found fiddling and banjo-picking in busy season in Frontierland and Liberty Square, near the Rivers of America.

DIAMOND HORSESHOE SALOON: A dance hall such as might have been found in nineteenth-century Missouri. Several times a day, there's a lively vaudeville show. Reservations are required; to get them, appear in person at the Diamond Horseshoe in the morning shortly after park opening.

FANTASY IN THE SKY: Even those rare recalcitrant souls who resist fireworks displays as though they were other people's home movies have little quarrel with this spectacular show, which is presented nightly when the park is open until midnight. The 150-odd shells that were mortarized over a 15-minute period when the program was first introduced are now ignited in a period of just four minutes—a rate of one shell every two seconds. They're detonated electrically, so that firings coincide perfectly with the announcer's voice on the P.A. system. The big symmetrical starburst shells are generally Japanese-made, while the ones whose explosions look as if they had been poured from a pitcher (with a concentrated area of particularly vivid color at the center) are of English manufacture.

CHARACTER SHOW: A variety of different shows featuring singing and dancing and appearances by favorite Disney characters such as Alice in Wonderland, Goofy, and Mickey himself. Presented several times a day at the Fantasy Faire stage, opposite Cinderella's Golden Carrousel.

PEARLY BAND: Plays Dixieland on the Fantasy Faire stage and occasionally along Main Street. Named after a group from the movie *Mary Poppins*.

MARDI GRAS SOUND COMPANY: Plays popular music and rock at the Tomorrowland Terrace and at the Plaza Pavilion.

BANJO KINGS: Play specialty songs and comic ditties from the Roaring Twenties on washboards and banjos, mostly on Main Street.

MICHAEL ICEBERG: Master of a battery of electronic instruments, this zany Disney star—a real person—entertains regularly at the Tomorrowland Terrace restaurant, opposite the Grand Prix Raceway in Tomorrowland. He's by turn melodic and schmaltzy, corny, truly funny, whimsical, and serious; like Steve Martin, he's the sort of comedian who will do anything to get a laugh—and he does. A must.

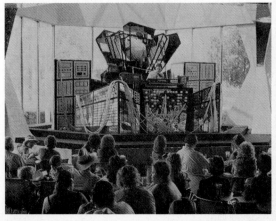

HOLIDAYS AND PARADES

Every day in the Magic Kingdom feels like a celebration, from the moment the park opens until the last
guest has gone home. But that's never more true
than over holiday periods, and during one of the
many parades that wend their way along the Magic
Kingdom parade route daily—usually down Main
Street, around the east half of the Hub, across
Liberty Square Bridge, through Frontierland.

THE GREAT MAIN STREET ELECTRICAL PARADE

Since it premiered on June 9, 1977, this dazzler
has been WDW's biggest hit. Featuring a million
twinkling lights, some 100 performers, and nearly
30 floats, it is presented in busy seasons—usually
during Easter, summer vacations, and when the
park is open until midnight, usually at
9 and 11:30 P.M. each evening—and it's a little like
all the world's best Christmas trees rolled into
one, so undeniably, incredibly, supercalifragilistic-
expialidociously spectacular that it's well worth
enduring the Magic Kingdom's busiest periods to
see. In 1982, there will also be a parade staged
every Saturday night (at 9 P.M.) during the month
of January. Part of the fascination is the presentation: one minute the lights are twinkling along the
edges of the Main Street roofs; the next, as soon
as the announcer heralds its arrival, everything
is black. The crowds, already impatient, strain
anxiously for a sight of the procession. And then
it comes, aglitter with tiny colored lights, accompanied by some of the most tuneful music that
ever graced a parade, the "Baroque Hoedown,"
written by Gershon Kingsley and
Jean-Jacques Perrey. Heads
nod and feet tap. Windows and
eyeglasses reflect the sparkle of
the lights. One by one the floats
cruise by: Alice, atop her mushroom; Pinocchio, the marionette
without strings; Pete, atop his

dragon; and more. While the parade theme is
piped over the park's P.A. system, each float
carries radios that receive their own variations
from a transmitter atop Cinderella Castle, and the
floats' speakers broadcast these tunes. The combination creates a complex tapestry almost as
grin-inspiring as the spectacle of the lights.

Where to catch the parade: Of all the spots
along the route outlined in the first paragraph of
this section, the single best vantage point for
watching this stupendous procession is the very
center of the platform of the Walt Disney World
Railroad's depot. From there, it's possible to see
the floats circling Town Square, and then you can
get the effect of the whole stream of lights as the
parade continues down Main Street and around
the Hub. You're close enough to catch the glitter
but far enough away so that you don't see the
framework that holds it all together. Unfortunately
only a couple of seats here have views that are
not obstructed by trees.

The next-best viewing point is from the curb on
either side of Main Street. It's very crowded here,
and you must claim your foot of curb as much as
an hour before the parade (particularly for the
busier 9 P.M. running). But there's something
about seeing the show at its beginnings
on the edge of one of the quaintest avenues on earth, that enhances the experience enormously.

If you hate crowds, head for Pecos
Bill's; park yourself on one of the restaurant's stools right next to the parade route.
Note that the 9 P.M. parade is always
more crowded than the one at
11:30 P.M.

HOLIDAY DOINGS

EASTER SUNDAY: Everyone carries parasols and wears his Easter best and fancy hats. There are antique automobiles, comedians—and, of course, the Easter Bunny.

FOURTH OF JULY CELEBRATION: The busiest day of the summer—and with reason: there's a double-sized fireworks display, whose explosions light up the skies not only above Cinderella Castle, but those over the Seven Seas Lagoon.

CHRISTMAS: A Christmas tree—a real Douglas fir that is as perfect among trees as Main Street is among small-town thoroughfares—goes up in Town Square, and the entire Magic Kingdom is decked out as only Disney can do it. There are also special

Christmas parades and carolers. The crowds, of course, are thick. But the scenery is beautiful, and the weather is fine (if chilly)—so it's no wonder that some veteran Magic Kingdom lovers call this the very best time of year.

NEW YEAR'S EVE CELEBRATION: With nearly 93,000 people streaming through the gates of the theme park, New Year's Eve Day of 1980 hosted the biggest crowd in Magic Kingdom history. And though the visitation rate was a little higher than in years

past, it has always been true that on December 31 the throngs are practically body to body. For a celebration, that's fun. (On an introductory visit, it could be less delightful; first-timers take note.) There is a double-sized fireworks display, and the Main Street holiday decorations (including that almost surrealistically perfect Christmas tree presiding over Town Square) are still up. There's plenty of nip in the air as the evening wears on, so dress accordingly.

TENCENNIAL: WALT DISNEY WORLD THROWS A BIRTHDAY PARTY

Ten years old on October 1, 1981, Walt Disney World celebrates its first happy decade with some of the most dazzling festivities to date. Through September 30, 1982, visitors will find the following:

THE TENCENNIAL PARADE: One of the largest parades that Disney has ever staged, with some 250 performers singing and dancing and creating musical magic, plus six prizewinning Percherons pulling an antique circus calliope and miniature white ponies with Cinderella's glass coach, this procession saluting each of the lands will get under way every day at 2 or 4 P.M., and during the Thanksgiving and Christmas holidays and at other especially busy times of the year, again at 9 P.M.

COME FOLLOW THE BAND: At noon and 6 P.M. every day, more than 100 dancers, Disney characters, and musicians will invite guests to get into the action and follow the parade from Town Square to the Cinderella Castle Forecourt at the Hub for more singing, dancing, and fun—and a grand balloon release that will make the Florida skies look a bit like a pointillist painting.

WALT DISNEY WORLD IS YOUR WORLD: The bubbly Kids of the Kingdom are at their most effervescent during this bouncy, 30-minute-long musical revue, featuring zany Disney characters (among them Donald Duck, as a ghost, and Goofy, playing bagpipes) and an eight-piece band. You can see this four or five times daily at the Tomorrowland Theater.

TIPS FROM WDW VETERANS

• Study up before you arrive in the Magic Kingdom so that you're familiar with the layout and the things to see and do before arrival. Special services are occasionally available to guests during slack seasons, so be sure to peruse any printed information you find in your room.

• Allow plenty of time, so that you can sample the Magic Kingdom in small bites. Trying to see it all in a day (or even just two) is like eating a rich ice-cream sundae too quickly.

• Try to visit the park on a weekend in summer—and any day but Monday, Tuesday, or Wednesday (the busiest days) year round.

• Start out early. Most people arrive between 9:30 and 11:30, when the roads approaching the Toll Plaza and the parking lots are jammed. If you're coming at Easter, Christmas, or in summer, plan to arrive before 8:30 A.M., or wait until nightfall, when things are less crowded. Arrive very early, so as to be at the gates to the Magic Kingdom when they open; have breakfast at the Town Square Cafe or the Crystal Palace, and then be at the end of Main Street when the rest of the park opens.

• Organize your visit so that you don't hop around from area to area, for that wastes time. Plan to eat before 11 A.M. or after 2 P.M., and before 5 P.M. or after 8 P.M.

• Break up your day. Buy a River Country ticket at the Transportation and Ticket Center on the way into the Magic Kingdom, and plan on heading for its beach when the crowds get thickest. Or take in Discovery Island. Or head back to your hotel, if it's not too far, for some swimming or other activities available there. Guests not staying at WDW's own resorts should be sure to have their hands stamped and hold on to their parking-ticket stubs, to avoid paying additional fees when returning.

• At busy times on busy days, take in the following not-so-packed attractions:

Main Street: Walt Disney World Railroad,
           Main Street Cinema
Adventureland: Pirates of the Caribbean
Liberty Square: Liberty Square Riverboats
Tomorrowland: Mission to Mars,
           WEDway PeopleMover, Carousel
            of Progress,
           If You Had Wings, Circle-Vision
            360 "Magic Carpet 'Round the
            World "
Fantasyland: It's A Small World (after 5 P.M.)

• Shop on Main Street in the early afternoon, not at day's end, when everybody else goes. Besides, the stores are good places to escape the afternoon heat.

• Many attractions have two lines. Before getting into the one on the right-hand side, look at the one to your left. Most of the time it will be less crowded, since most Magic Kingdom visitors automatically head for the one on the right.

• Wear your most comfortable shoes: you'll be spending a lot of time on your feet. (Note that no bare feet are permitted in the Magic Kingdom.)

• Don't take food into the Magic Kingdom. It isn't allowed because there are no picnic areas.

• If your party decides to split up, set a fixed meeting place and time that can't be confused.

• If you have arranged to meet members of your group somewhere, don't get into a queue as the meeting time approaches.

• If you've a limited amount of time remaining before meeting the rest of your group, don't hesitate to ask a Disney employee for suggestions about things to do.

USEFUL STOPS

Cash: The Sun Bank, located in Town Square next to City Hall. Open seven days a week, from 9 A.M. to 4 P.M.

Tobacco: The prime outlet is the Tobacconist on the west side of Main Street.

Baby care needs: The Magic Kingdom Baby Care Center, at the Hub end of Main Street, next to the Crystal Palace Restaurant, is the best source. But disposable diapers and other infant paraphernalia are also available on request at other shops. This is a good area for nursing mothers. Sponsored by Gerber.

Strollers: For rent at the Stroller Shop, located to the right in the souvenir area near the turnstiles at the entrance to the Magic Kingdom.

Haircuts and shaves: At the Harmony Barber Shop on Center Street, the flower-filled cul-de-sac off the west side of Main Street. The barber chairs are heavy, curlicued metal, like the cash register—the real McCoy.

Postcards and stamps: The Hallmark Card Shop on the west side of Main Street is the prime source.

Mailboxes: Located up and down Main Street, they're olive-drab. An elaborate polished brass one can be found next to the stamp machine at the Penny Arcade entrance to the Hallmark Card Shop. Postmarks read Lake Buena Vista, *not* Walt Disney World.

MAGIC KINGDOM SCHEDULES

On a first-time visit, it's hard to know just what to do first. These programs should help put you on the right track. In general, you should count on visiting seven or eight attractions per day. That leaves you time for shopping and stops in restaurants, as well as time for waiting in line. (In quieter seasons, you may have time for more attractions.) These schedules are meant for an energetic family with children aged ten and up; families with younger children will want to add more attractions in Fantasyland at the expense of slower-paced attractions. Be sure to stop at City Hall on your way into the park to get information about the times for various shows and parades. Slight modifications in your timing may be desirable in order to take in some of these.

ONE-DAY VISIT
Comment: There's so much to see that it's almost better not to come at all if you have only a day to spend. But it's possible to at least get the flavor of the Magic Kingdom in eight or ten hours, if the visit is properly planned.

During busy seasons, when the park is open late
Arrive at 7:30 to 8 A.M.
Breakfast at Town Square Cafe or Crystal Palace Buffeteria.
Circumnavigate park on Walt Disney World Railroad.
Leisurely stroll down Main Street.
Jungle Cruise, Adventureland.
Pirates of the Caribbean, Adventureland.
Country Bear Jamboree, Frontierland.
Hall of Presidents, Liberty Square.
Take a break. Leave the park for lunch at Golf Resort, Contemporary Resort Hotel, or Polynesian Village. Cruise to Discovery Island or River Country, or return to your hotel for rest.
Return to park between 5 and 6 P.M.; check City Hall for times of Michael Iceberg show at Tomorrowland Terrace.
Early dinner at Tomorrowland Terrace.
Magic Carpet 'Round the World, Tomorrowland.
If You Had Wings, Tomorrowland.
At 8 P.M., claim a stretch of Main Street curb for the Main Street Electrical Parade at 9 P.M. While adults are holding places, older children visit Penny Arcade. Watch Fantasy in the Sky fireworks after parade.
Haunted Mansion, Liberty Square.
Big Thunder Mountain Railroad, Frontierland.

The rest of the year
Arrive at 8 to 8:30 A.M.
Breakfast at Town Square Cafe or Crystal Palace Buffeteria.
Circumnavigate park on Walt Disney World Railroad.
Leisurely stroll down Main Street.
Jungle Cruise, Adventureland.
Pirates of the Caribbean, Adventureland.
Country Bear Jamboree, Frontierland.
Hall of Presidents, Liberty Square.
Lunch at Pinocchio Village Haus or Lancer's Inn (pizza), Fantasyland.
Peter Pan's Flight, Fantasyland.
Magic Carpet 'Round the World, Tomorrowland.
If You Had Wings, Tomorrowland.
Haunted Mansion, Liberty Square.
Big Thunder Mountain Railroad, Frontierland.
Dinner at Pecos Bill's.

TWO-DAY VISIT
Comment: Allows you to see more than the highlights.

First Day
Repeat first day as above.
Second Day
Arrive at 7:30 to 8 A.M.
Breakfast in the park on Main Street.
When park opens, head for Diamond Horseshoe Revue (Frontierland) to get reservations for lunchtime show.
Swiss Family Island Treehouse, Adventureland.
Enchanted Tiki Room, Adventureland.
It's a Small World, Fantasyland.
Snow White's Scary Adventures, Fantasyland.
Lunch at the Diamond Horseshoe.
Mr. Toad's Wild Ride, Fantasyland.
Grand Prix, Tomorrowland.
WEDway PeopleMover, Tomorrowland.

First Day
Repeat first day as above.
Second Day
Follow program for second day of two-day visit in busy seasons (opposite).

THREE-DAY VISIT
Comment: Allows you the time to see the park at a more leisurely pace; this is the optimal length for a visit, especially the first time around.

First Day
Repeat first day as above.

Second Day
Repeat second day as above.

Third Day
Arrive early to make reservation for lunch at King Stefan's.
Spend some time exploring the shops all around the Magic Kingdom.
Look closely at the surrounding landscaping and details of the Main Street buildings.
Visit the rides and attractions you may have missed during the first two days.
Leave the park after lunch for a visit to Walt Disney World Shopping Village.
Visit the Petting Farm at Fort Wilderness.
Dinner at one of the restaurants on the *Empress Lilly*, or in Walt Disney World Shopping Village.

First Day
Follow program for the first day of a two-day visit as outlined above, omitting Walt Disney World Railroad.
Second Day
Follow program for second day of two-day visit in busy seasons (opposite).
Third Day
Same as at left.

THE MAGIC KINGDOM'S BEST ATTRACTIONS

Everybody has his favorites, but there are a number that nobody disputes:

Adventureland	*Frontierland*	*Liberty Square*	*Tomorrowland*
Jungle Cruise	Country Bear Jamboree	Haunted Mansion	Space Mountain (for those with
Pirates of the Caribbean	Big Thunder Mountain Railroad	Hall of Presidents	strong constitutions)

EVERYTHING ELSE IN THE WORLD

The Magic Kingdom, that ultimate Land of Make Believe, is only the most famous feature of Walt Disney World. The *overall* World comprises 43 square miles, much of it crammed with all sorts of diverse and irresistible activities. These attractions are of a quantity and quality seldom found anywhere else on the globe.

There is superb golf and tennis; there are beaches for sunbathing; lakes for speedboating and sailing; canoes for rent and winding streams on which to paddle along; bicycles for hire; campfire sites; nature trails; and picnic grounds. And that list still doesn't include River Country, a Disney creation of the kind of old-fashioned swimming hole of which most people only dream; Walt Disney World Shopping Village, an assortment of shops seldom found outside the most cosmopolitan cities; and the nonpareil botanical garden and bird sanctuary that's called Discovery Island.

Among the other activities worth mentioning at WDW is the program known as the Wonders of Walt Disney World, in which youngsters attending grades five through ten are offered the opportunity to go behind the scenes—to meet the Disney entertainers and receive instructions from Disney cartoonists; to visit the World's extraordinary 7,500-acre conservation area; or to tour the WDW solar-powered office building (among other unique ecological operations). Developed in cooperation with educators from all over the country, this learning program has earned such widespread acclaim that many schools grant excused absences to those who participate.

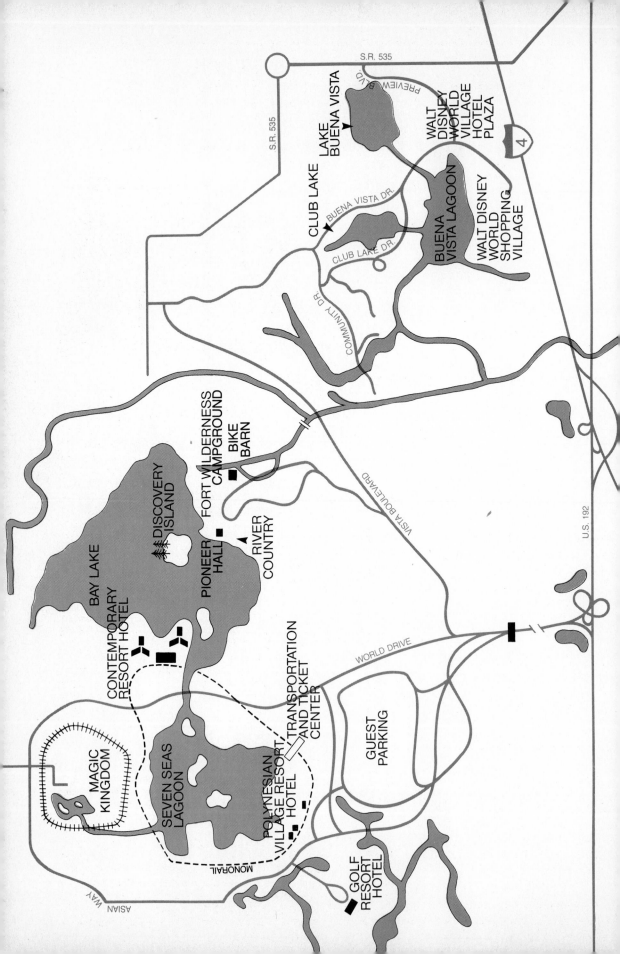

WALT DISNEY WORLD VILLAGE

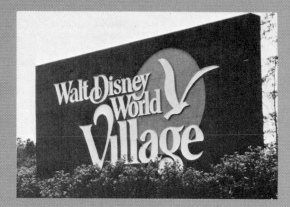

SHOPS

A visit to Walt Disney World Shopping Village can involve eating in a restaurant, meeting a film star, listening to first-rate jazz over some frothy cream-and-liqueur concoction, or just sitting on a bench by the water looking at the boats zipping back and forth across Buena Vista Lagoon. But for most people, those are the extra added attractions of a complex whose real raison d'être is shopping.

Arranged in eight low-lying, shingle-sided buildings flanking the hexagonal Captain's Tower on the shores of Buena Vista Lagoon, the Walt Disney World Shopping Village boutiques stock everything from baby bonnets to silk dresses, thousand-dollar bottles of wine to toy soldiers and stuffed animals—and then some. There is one store devoted exclusively to Disney merchandise, but that was added only because of popular demand; the merchandise in the other stores differs little from what might be found in any other fine shopping area in America.

The best way to take it all in is simply to wander at will. Stop for lunch or a snack after a couple of hours, then go out and stroll some more. The descriptions below suggest the types of merchandise that each store offers. Particular items may not be there when you are, but comparable goods should be available. Note that weekends are fairly busy, but even then the pace tends to be leisurely. Kids who get bored by their elders' browsing can be turned loose at the marina, or at an innovative playground near the Village Stage (where the annual Christmas pageants are presented).

CHRISTMAS CHALET: If anything can set a mind to dreaming of white Christmases when the mercury is hitting 95° outside (and the humidity is just about the same), this lovely little shop is it. In the first place, there's its immense white centerpiece, a vast bouquet of bare white birch branches, each one dripping with ornaments in white or silver, flashing with mirrors and spangled with fragile white lights. Arranged at the edges of the rooms there are small treasures in

Located about five miles from the Magic Kingdom, Walt Disney World Village comprises a number of hotel and villa-type accommodations (with and without kitchen facilities), the Lake Buena Vista Club, the Walt Disney World Conference Center, the Walt Disney World Shopping Village, several lakes, and a number of sports facilities—among other things. Because it is significantly removed from the Magic Kingdom, it is relatively quiet, and the pace is far more leisurely than exists around the Polynesian Village and Contemporary Resort hotels. In the Buena Vista Lagoon, along whose shores the shopping area was constructed, there are even a few alligators.

But the Village is still convenient to the main activities of the World and is easily accessible. It has its own exit off highway I-4, 4½ miles east of the Magic Kingdom exit. Red-flagged buses also make the trip to and from the Transportation and Ticket Center on a regular basis; holders of ID cards issued by WDW resorts and WDW Village Hotel Plaza establishments, as well as bearers of most types of two- and three-day passports, can ride them at no extra charge.

For details about WDW lodgings and about getting around, see *Transportation and Accommodations*.

traditional reds and greens—ornaments made of painted eggs, or covered with feathers, or made of wood, metal, glass, dough, felt, or calico. The selection is one of the best of its type anywhere.

In addition, there are Christmas mugs and plates, coffeepots, ice buckets, and wreaths of straw and dough, velvet and calico, and other more ingenious and occasionally truly startling combinations. You even may find a Santa squirt gun, or a special Christmas jump rope.

POTTERY CHALET: This large store adjoining the Christmas Chalet offers the kinds of kitchen utensils and tableware that otherwise might be found only in a good housewares-oriented department store. There are things with which to cook and things to put on the table, light fixtures and canisters, cut crystal and pressed glass, music boxes and wind chimes, aprons and place mats. The selection of cookie cutters is particularly excellent; they come in both metal and plastic, in geometric, animal, and human shapes. There are several just for cutting different styles of gingerbread men. In addition, there's a huge display of animal figurines—tigers and dogs, owls and cats (domesticated and otherwise), hippos, and even parrots. Jack Daniels square yardsticks, tin boxes emblazoned with old-fashioned advertisements, reproduction whiskey cases, and Coca-Cola cartons and the like, can also be found here. It's a shop for rambling, and lots of fun for lovers of knick-knacks.

CHALET CANDLE SHOP: The big deal in this small, sweetly scented shop (which actually seems a part of the adjoining Pottery Chalet) is the candle-maker who produces lacy, ornamental, hand-dipped and carved candles festooned with multicolored ribbonlike curls of wax. Not everyone may care for this product, but there are plenty of other items in wax and paraffin here, in all sizes and shapes.

CHINA, CRYSTAL & SILVER: The gleaming $30,000 Lalique crystal table at the center of this shop (next to the Pottery Chalet) may not be here forever, and some figures from the realistic set of *Wizard of Oz*-character figurines may have been sold by the time you arrive. But there always is plenty of fine, delicate merchandise on display, by such top makers as Wedgwood, Bing & Grøndahl, and Belleek, to say nothing of Disney characters crafted of pewter.

2 R'S READ'N & RITE'N: Party supplies, stationery, cards for all occasions, desk accessories, and assorted gift items are all for sale at this emporium near the Chalet Candle Shop and the Lite Bite Snack Spot. Bookworms, however, will be most grateful for its excellent selection of hardbound and paperback books, the best in all of WDW. There's something for the very serious-minded, something to tickle the funny bone, and tomes at all levels of literature in between.

CRISTAL ARTS: This shop sells roughly the same sort of cut-glass merchandise available at Main Street's Crystal Arts and Adventureland's La Princesa de Cristal in the Magic Kingdom. Large green, blue, or red cut-glass bowls and vases are available, along with clear-glass mugs and other items engraved to customers' specifications with initials, messages, or pictures. Note: If you bring a favorite photograph with you to this shop, the engraver can have it reproduced on a plate or other item.

TOLEDO ARTS: Adjoining Cristal Arts on the east, Toledo Arts offers leather items, porcelain figurines, swords and ships, carved olive-wood boxes, napkin rings, salt-and-pepper shakers, and statues; plus other items, many imported from Spain. Damascene work, which involves etching a metal surface with acid, then encrusting it with silver or gold, is also sold, and craftsmen are usually on hand to demonstrate the process.

GREAT SOUTHERN CRAFT COMPANY: More stitchery and needlepoint kits than even the most avid hobbyist could imagine, plus supplies for quilting, macrame, and latch hook. Located between Toledo Arts on the west and Port of Entry on the east.

LILLIE LANGTRY'S OLD-FASHIONED PHOTO STUDIO: Main Street in the Magic Kingdom has a photo studio in the Camera Center, and Adventureland has Laffite's Portrait Deck. Lillie Langtry's is the last-but-not-least of the trio of locations where guests can pose for Polaroid portraits in Edwardian suits or flounced-and-furbelowed gowns of a degree of frilliness rarely found outside a film studio's wardrobe department.

PORT OF ENTRY: If you were to shop your way around this planet, picking up local products in all the markets and souvenir shops as you went, you could open a store like this one when you returned home. Europe is represented by Delft knickknacks, small windmills, and piggy banks. From Mexico come pottery figurines, piñatas, copper kettles, and pots. The artisans of India are represented by carved bangles and boxes, clothing, and candleholders. From Guatemala come pots and a wealth of baskets. Straw and rattan items have been collected from all corners of the globe. And there are leather goods, carved marble items, necklaces, bracelets, and more from Africa and the Orient. Not far from the Captain's Tower and the Village marina.

BATH PARLOR: This is the place for elegant bath towels, fancy toilet seats, bathroom rugs, laundry bags, bath brushes, and all sorts of other appurtenances for the perfect toilette. A few gag items (striped, polka-dotted, or initialed toilet paper, for instance) are also available, along with designer sheets and other bed clothes.

SACHET IN: Located alongside the Bath Parlor, this boutique is devoted to things fragrant—not just sweet-smelling sachets for drawers and closets, but also fancy soaps, of which the shop has Orlando's widest selection.

SIR EDWARD'S HABERDASHER: Named after Edward Moriarity, a Disney executive, this shop, full of good-quality clothing for men and boys, is an oasis of traditional masculinity in a bustling village otherwise filled with trifles and treasures that seem to appeal most to the feminine heart. Located near Sachet In, close to the parking lot.

GOURMET PANTRY: Not long ago, one vacationer searching for coffee and orange juice for the next day's breakfast passed up this store on the assumption that he'd find only escargots and smoked oysters. Wrong! These things can be found here, but there also are breads and pastries, meats and cheeses, cereals, yogurt, beer and soft drinks, and many more items—both mundane and exotic. Unusual teas and specially blended, freshly ground coffees are also available, and, occasionally, free tastes are offered to passersby. The coffee-and-pastry window opens for breakfast at 9 A.M. daily. Villa and Treehouse guests take note: purchases will be delivered to your room at no extra charge; if you aren't going to be home, the delivery person will even stash perishables in your refrigerator. To order by phone, touch "1" on your room telephone, or, when calling from outside, dial 824-6993.

POOH'S PLACE: When the Walt Disney World Shopping Village was first planned, no provision was made for a store selling Disney souvenirs. Popular demand changed that, and Pooh's Place was the result. Dumbo, Jiminy Cricket, Minnie and Mickey, Chip and Dale, Tigger, Pooh, and Eeyore, Tramp and his Lady are all here—stuffed, in porcelain, and emblazoned on everything from T-shirts and back scratchers to pencils and carry-all bags. There even are windup toys, hats, visors, blue-and-white Alice-in-Wonderland dresses with pinafores, and white-polka-dotted red Minnie dresses (also sold at Tinkerbell's Toy Shop in Fantasyland in the Magic Kingdom). Be sure to look for the larger-than-life stuffed Mickey.

TOYS FANTASTIQUE: The rocking-horse sign outside is one of the Disney sign shop's most handsome efforts, and there are even greater delights inside, among the toys that are the products, some handmade, of both Europe and America. This is a toy shop to end all toy shops. The stuffed animals and dolls come in enough variety to make a collector of even the most staid grown-up. There are model kits, imported die-cast toys, and windup bath toys (sometimes displayed in a large tank, to give everyone a chance to see how they work), and electric trains with all the necessary fittings and accessories. Don't fail to inspect the doll's house, a miniature Victorian mansion complete with etched-glass windows, a crystal chandelier, and lights that really work. Built by an Orlando resident at a cost of some $5,000 (another $5,000 was put into its furnishings), it is not for sale, though reproductions can be specially ordered. Collectors come from all over the state to see it and to shop for hand-carved miniatures, another store offering. A must.

CANDY SHOPPE: Adjoining the Gourmet Pantry, this small, fragrant enclave sells Godiva chocolate, fudge, chocolate barks and creams, red licorice, peppermint sticks, hard candies, and just about everything else that ever made a sweet tooth ache.

IT'S A SMALL WORLD AFTER ALL: Doting aunts and uncles, not to mention fond grandparents, will find the children's clothing that crowds the racks and shelves here well-nigh irresistible. The prices are generally on the high side (relative to what Mom herself might spend at home), but business booms nonetheless. Adjoining Toys Fantastique.

COUNTRY ADDRESS: This very good woman's clothing store offers a range of merchandise from the middle-priced and polyester to the oh-so-chic, and terribly expensive, fashions by designers such as Anne Klein. Active and spectator sportswear and separates are offered in addition to dresses and evening wear. Next to It's A Small World.

24KT PRECIOUS ADORNMENTS: One Christmas not long ago, mink teddy bears joined the elegant gold and silver jewelry offered here; at last look, there were still a few available, at a mere $800 each. Located in the same building as the Village Restaurant and Lounge, at the north end of the Shopping Village, near Country Address.

VILLAGE GIFTS AND SUNDRIES: When you run out of shampoo or film, or want to stock up on cosmetics or buy a magazine, or if you run out of any number of other necessities, this is the place to look. If you need something that nobody else seems to carry, Village Gifts and Sundries might have it. Polaroid OneStep cameras are available on loan here, as well as rental wheelchairs. Occupies the west end of the building next to the Village Restaurant and Lounge, near 24KT.

VILLAGE SPIRITS: Spirits, liqueurs, ales, and other alcoholic products from all around the world are stocked at this shop next door to Village Gifts and Sundries. Inexpensive wines from California and New York keep company with vintages priced at $100 and more a bottle, plus a few very rare (and expensive) foreign wines bought at London auction houses. Some very good values. Decanters, glasses, serving trays, and other bar items in abundance are also on sale, as well as the strawberry tequila served in Cap'n Jack's popular margaritas.

SHOE TIME: In these days of ever-climbing prices, the store buyer here has managed to put together a selection of stylish, high-quality, casual-to-dressy footwear that won't break the bank. Handbags and other accessories are also available, as well as Etienne Aigner designs. Next to Heidelberger's Deli and opposite Village Spirits.

PLUS YOU: Accessories in all price ranges for teeny-boppers and female executives alike can be found here; worth a look. Adjoins Shoe Time.

MISS MERRILY'S FASHIONS: Kicky dresses, shorts and trousers, flowing skirts and blouses to match, with a supporting cast of French-cut jeans, swimsuits, and other junior-sized clothing in trendy styles, jam this lively shop (once aptly named Miss Merrily's Madness). Opposite Village Gifts and Sundries.

SASSY'S: This boutique, next door to Miss Merrily's, stocks preteen clothing from shoes to lingerie, accessories, school clothes, and designer jeans.

WINDJAMMER DOCK SHOP: You go through this shop on the way to Cap'n Jack's Oyster Bar. The first section is devoted to women's fashions—Javanese batik shorts; swimsuits and cover-ups; skirts and tops; cool, crinkly cotton sundresses; and shorts in a paint store's worth of colors, and just about any style imaginable. In another area, closer to Cap'n Jack's, are nautically flavored gifts—ships in bottles, books about ships, brass goods, wall plaques, and other gift items.

RESTAURANTS

For a complete listing of all Walt Disney World Village restaurants, bars, and snack shops, see *Good Meals, Great Times.*

LAKESIDE ACTIVITIES

The 35-acre Buena Vista Lagoon that borders this village of cedar-shingled shops also gives it much of its atmosphere: When the sidewalks radiate heat, the water looks cool and inviting; in the slanting rays of the late afternoon sun, it glistens like a sheet of silver.

And there's always something going on. Little Water Sprites zip to and fro, speeding to the dock from feeder canals to the west, while more laid-back folk float gently along in pedal boats or V-hulled, tent-topped, metal canopy boats.

It's pleasant to sit and watch all this activity—from the benches at the Buena Vista Lagoon marina, centrally located in Walt Disney World Shopping Village; over mammoth salads and gooey ice cream sundaes at the Verandah Restaurant on the lake's west shore; or over frozen fresh strawberry margaritas at Cap'n Jack's Oyster Bar. Those who opt to participate need walk only a few steps to the marina, where boats can be rented from morning until dusk. Opening and closing hours change from season to

season; call 824-4321 for details. No swimming is allowed.

WATER SPRITES: These tiny craft are very popular: Though they don't really move very fast, they feel as if they do; and, in any event, they get up enough speed to cover quite a lot of territory on Buena Vista Lagoon and along the winding, tree-lined canals behind the villas and the Lake Buena Vista Golf Course. Half-hour rentals cost $7.50. There are usually lines of people waiting for boats between 11 A.M. and 4 P.M.; plan accordingly. The minimum age to rent or drive one of these boats (even with an accompanying adult) is 12.

CANOPY BOATS: These metal, V-hulled, 16-foot craft can accommodate up to ten adults; some people stock up on picnic supplies at the Shopping Village's Gourmet Pantry and turn an afternoon sail into a party. Cost is $10 per half hour.

PEDAL BOATS: These craft can be rented for $3 per half hour.

CELEBRATIONS & SPECIAL EVENTS

There's nearly always something going on under the Captain's Tower in Walt Disney World Shopping Village. Some weeks the place might be stacked high with shiny new hardcover books; on another day, it might be cool and green, with an array of plants for sale. Crafts demonstrations and art shows are staged now and again, along with occasional manufacturers' promotions. In the past, these have included a fabulous exhibition of creations made with Lego blocks (among them a gigantic globe) and numerous guest appearances, including the father-and-son racing team of Richard and Kyle Petty; Shelley Duvall, appearing in conjunction with the opening of *Popeye*; and the dollmaker Madame Alexander, who was introducing a new line that had collectors lining up in the wee hours of the morning.

In addition, there are a number of annual events—some in celebration of holidays. And all of these are free.

CENTRAL FLORIDA BOAT SHOW (OCTOBER): Because this Central Florida region has no ocean beaches, most events of this type are staged in shopping malls and exhibition halls. Here, however, boats are displayed not only throughout the Shopping Village, but also in the water; and with over 120 boats from all manufacturers, this is the area's biggest in-the-water boat show. Demonstration rides are part of the fun.

HALLOWEEN: The Captain's Tower, made to look as spooky as a contemporary structure can be, with festoons of cobwebs and displays of Halloween merchandise, is the centerpiece of a number of activities around the Shopping Village. There's a Halloween Parade that allows local children (and vacationing youngsters with the foresight to bring an outfit) to join assorted costumed witches, ghosts, goblins, and Disney villains—*Sleeping Beauty*'s Maleficent and *Snow White*'s Wicked Witch—in a grand march down Preview Boulevard. On the Village Stage, Disney entertainers present a show, *Ghosts, Goblins, and Ghouls*, which features some decidedly evil-looking characters.

FESTIVAL OF THE MASTERS: This art show, which takes place in November of each year, is generally considered one of the state's best, thanks to the careful screening of applicants.

CHRISTMASTIME: Thanksgiving marks the beginning of the Christmas season here, as Disney entertainers present a fairly lighthearted Christmas show twice nightly until mid-month. Then the more serious *Glory and Pageantry of Christmas*, a reenactment of a nativity play fashioned after a thirteenth-century pageant whose origins are in southern France, makes its annual debut. In all, there are appearances by some three dozen characters garbed in period costumes made from brocades, satins, silks, velvets, wool, rough homespun, and monk's cloth—a baker, butcher, candlemaker, flower seller, fruit and vegetable peddler, weaver, and others. A concert of carols precedes each evening's tableau.

USEFUL STOPS

LOANER CAMERAS: Polaroid One-Steps are available at Village Gifts and Sundries. A refundable $50 deposit is required.

RENTAL WHEELCHAIRS: Available at Village Gifts and Sundries. Cost is $1 per day; a refundable $10 deposit and a driver's license are required.

BUS TRANSPORTATION: The WDW Shopping Village bus stop and shelter is located next to Sir Edward's Haberdasher. From there, you can get green-and-gold-flagged buses to the Lake Buena Vista Club and the Villas and Treehouses; blue-and-white-flagged buses to Walt Disney World Village Hotel Plaza; and red-flagged buses to the Transportation and Ticket Center. (From there, monorails and ferries go to the Magic Kingdom, gold-flagged buses to the Contemporary Resort, green-flagged buses to the Golf Resort and the Polynesian Village, and blue-flagged buses to Fort Wilderness.) For more information on transportation within the World, see *Transportation and Accommodations*.

STAMPS: The Walt Disney World Village Office Plaza, the sleek mirrored structure opposite the Shopping Village, has a U.S. Post Office where you can buy stamps, register letters, and obtain other postal services.

FOREIGN CURRENCY EXCHANGE: This can be done at the Sun Bank in the Walt Disney World Village Office Plaza building during regular banking hours. See *Getting Ready To Go*.

TRAVELER'S CHECKS: These can be purchased at the Sun Bank (see above); outside the bank, there is an American Express Cardmembers Cheque Dispenser, which cardholders (who have previously obtained a special number) may use to purchase traveler's checks.

FORT WILDERNESS

In a part of the state where campgrounds tend to look like a pasture—barren and very hot—the Fort Wilderness Campground, located almost due east of the Contemporary Resort Hotel, is an anomaly—a forested 650-acre wonder of tall slash pines, white-flowering bay trees, and ancient cypress hung with streamers of gray-green Spanish moss. Seminole Indians once hunted and fished here.

In all, there are some 825 woodsy campsites arranged in several campground loops; along some of them, close to 175 Fleetwood trailers are available for rent, completely furnished and fitted out with all the comforts of home. For information about these campsites, see *Transportation and Accommodations*.

Scattered throughout the campground loops, there are a number of sporting facilities—tetherball, horseshoe and volleyball courts, and, among other conveniences, large playing fields. Fort Wilderness has riding stables, a marina full of boats, a canoe livery, a beach, a jogging-and-exercise trail, bikes for rent, and a nature trail. Some of these facilities are available for the use of campground guests only; some are limited to guests at WDW-owned resort hotels and villas as well; and some can also be enjoyed by guests lodging at the establishments at the Walt Disney World Village Hotel Plaza and off the property.

There's also a petting farm where goats and ducks and other farm animals run free inside a white rail fence, and it's fun to walk through the barn that houses the large, sleek horses that pull the Magic Kingdom's Main Street trolleys.

Two stores, the Settlement and Meadow Trading Posts, stock campers' necessities and some Disney souvenirs. And then there's Pioneer Hall, widely known as the home of the Hoop-Dee-Doo Revue (described in *Good Meals, Great Times*). This rustic structure (made of western white pine shipped all the way from Montana) also encompasses a cafeteria and game room.

Last but not least in the Fort Wilderness catalogue, there's River Country. This eight-acre expanse of water-oriented recreational facilities embodies everyone's idea of what the perfect old-fashioned swimming hole should be like. It's a separate attraction, with its own hours and admission fees.

HOW TO GET TO FORT WILDERNESS

BY CAR: From outside WDW, take the Disney World exit off I-4, go through the Toll Plaza, and, bearing to your right, follow the Fort Wilderness or River Country signs. This is probably the most expeditious way to go, even for WDW resort guests coming from other parts of the World.

BY BUS: Take the gold-flagged bus from the Contemporary Resort, the green-flagged bus from the Polynesian Village, the red-flagged bus from

WDW Shopping Village, or the red-and-white-flagged bus from Walt Disney World Village Hotel Plaza establishments to the Transportation and Ticket Center. Change there to the blue-flagged bus to Fort Wilderness. Count on 30 to 45 minutes in transit. To ride the red- and red-and-white-flagged buses, you must show an ID card from one of the WDW-owned properties or a Hotel Plaza establishment, or a two- or three-day passport. No ID is necessary to ride blue-, gold-, or green-flagged buses.

In addition, special black-flagged buses make the trip to Pioneer Hall from the Polynesian Village and the Golf Resort in time for the Hoop-Dee-Doo Revue.

BY BOAT: Guests at WDW-owned properties, and those with admission tickets to River Country or Discovery Island, also can go by boat from marinas in the Magic Kingdom (green-flagged; about 30 minutes' ride); from the Polynesian Village (yellow-flagged; about 15 minutes' ride); and from the Contemporary Resort (blue-flagged; about 25 minutes' ride).

SOUVENIRS AND SUPPLIES

Staple food items and all sorts of other necessities of the camping life are available, along with souvenirs, at Fort Wilderness's two stores—the **Settlement Trading Post**, located not far from the beach at the north end of the campground; and the **Meadow Trading Post**, located near the playing fields and the campfire area near the center of Fort Wilderness.

The trading posts' deli counters will also make up sandwiches to go, for picnics on the beach or at River Country.

For a complete list of places to eat in Fort Wilderness, see *Good Meals, Great Times*.

HOOP-DEE-DOO REVUE

Sturdy, porch-rimmed Pioneer Hall is best-known Worldwide as the home of the Pioneer Hall Players, an energetic troupe of singing-and-dancing-and-wisecracking entertainers who keep audiences chuckling and grinning and whooping it up for two hours, during a procession of barbecued ribs, fried chicken, corn on the cob, strawberry shortcake, and other stomach-stretching viands. If you have time for only one of the Disney dinner shows, make it this one (for more details, see *Good Meals, Great Times*).

RIVER COUNTRY

THE PERFECT SWIMMING HOLE

It's next to impossible to go through childhood reading such classics as *Huck Finn* and *Tom Sawyer* (and other such great tales of growing up) without developing a few fantasies about what it would be like to swim in a perfect swimming hole. A group of Disney imagineers (who actually knew a commercial re-creation of such a place as kids) have concocted a Disney version on a somewhat larger scale at River Country, a water-oriented playground that occupies a corner of Bay Lake near Cypress Point at Fort Wilderness Campground.

Fred Joerger—the same Disney rock-builder who created Big Thunder Mountain, Schweitzer Falls at the Jungle Cruise, and the caves of Tom Sawyer Island (among other things) in the Magic Kingdom—has helped design scores of rocks used to landscape one of the largest swimming pools in the state; more have been piled into a small mountain for guests to climb up—and then slide down. The rocks, scattered with pebbles acquired from stream beds in Georgia and the Carolinas, look so real that it's hard to believe they aren't.

More to the point, the place is great fun. Slipping and sliding down the curvy water chutes at top speed; getting tangled up, all arms and legs, in the whirlpools of Raft River Ridge; and whamming into the water from the swimming pool's high slides makes even careworn grown-ups smile, grin, giggle, chortle, and roar with delight. People who climb to the top with trepidation embark on the lightning-fast journey to the bottom only because it seems too late to back out; at the bottom they rush back for more. Line-haters queue up—over and over gain. Those who associate lakes with muck and weeds go into ecstasies over the way the soft sand on the River Country bottom squiggles between their toes.

WHAT TO DO: There are several basic sections of River Country—the 330,000-gallon swimming pool, the largest in Florida's Orange County; Bay Cove (aka the "Ol' Swimmin' Hole"), the big walled-off section of Bay Lake that most people consider the main (and best) part of River Country; an adjoining junior version of the above for small children, with its own beach; and the grassy grounds, with picnic tables and a squirting fountain in which to play. On the edge of the lake, there's also a boardwalk-nature trail through a lovely cypress swamp, and a wide (if not terribly long) white-sand beach.

Heated in winter, the oversized swimming pool has two sets of diving rocks (in graduated sizes) at one end. On the other side of the pool is the pair of water slides that begin high enough above the water to make an acrophobe climb right down again. They plunge at such an angle that it's impossible to see the bottom of the slide from the top. Daredevils who don't chicken out are shot into the water from a height of about seven feet—hard enough, as one commentator observed, to "slap your stomach up against the roof of your mouth." Gutsy kids adore the experience; those who like their thrills a bit tamer might prefer to watch.

The heart of River Country, Bay Cove—actually a part of Bay Lake—is fitted out with rope swings, a ship's boom for swooping and plunging, and assorted other constructions designed to put hearts into throats as swimmers plunge from air to water. The big deals, however, are the two flume rides—one 260 feet long (accessible by a boardwalk and stairway to the far right of the swimming hole as you face it) and a smaller one, 100 feet shorter (accessible by a stairway to the left of that) and the white-water raft ride.

The flumes, which are like overgrown, steep-sided waterslides, corkscrew through the greenery at the top of the ridge known as Whoop-'N-Holler Hollow, sending even the most stalwart shooting into the water, usually like greased lightning. Timid folk will find it easy to control speed, however. The rule of thumb is to sit up to slow down, and lie back to speed up. Be warned that once you lie down to accelerate, getting up is virtually impossible. Reclining with arms at sides guarantees a slower ride than lying back with hands above the head. Arching your back so that only shoulders and heels are on the flume's surface increases the pace still further. Combining positions allows for braking and accelerating at will.

White Water Rapids, as the white-water raft ride mentioned above is known, involves a more leisurely trip through a series of chutes and pools in an inner tube, from the crest of Raft Rider Ridge (adjoining Whoop-'N-Holler Hollow) into Bay Cove. It's not a high-speed affair like the flumes, but some people like it better. The pools are contoured so that the water swirls through them in whirlpool fashion. You tend to get caught in the slow circling water, and when other tubers come sliding down the chutes at you, bare arms and legs get all tangled up.

ADMISSION: River Country is an attraction in its own right, with a separate admission charge that includes transportation to the site and use of all the facilities. A River Country and Discovery Island combination ticket, which includes transportation and admission to both, is also available. Some three-day passports (described in *An Essential Guide to the Magic Kingdom*) include admission to both River Country and Discovery Island, as well as the necessary transportation.

	Guests at WDW-owned resorts / children 3 through 11	Guests at establishments in Walt Disney World Village Hotel Plaza / children 3 through 11	Guests at hotels outside WDW and other day guests / children 3 through 11
River Country admission ($1 off after 6 P.M.)	$5.75/$3.50	$6/$3.75	$6.50/$4.25
River Country/ Discovery Island combination ticket	$8/$4.50	$8.25/$4.75	$8.75/$5.25

NOTE: Children under ten must be accompanied by an adult. Some of the River Country adventures require swimming ability.

WHEN TO GO: Daytime temperatures in Orlando are such that it's possible to enjoy River Country almost all year round, though it is perhaps most pleasant in spring—when the weather is getting hot but the water is still cool. In summer, the place can be very busy indeed.

Ticket windows close as the crowd approaches capacity. During WDW's busiest times of year, that may happen as early as 11:30 A.M. It's worth noting, however, that those who already have tickets will be admitted anyway. Consequently, if you plan to visit River Country in the afternoon of a summer day, it's smart to buy your tickets at the Transportation and Ticket Center on your way *into* the Magic Kingdom.

One of the World's best-kept secrets is the joy of River Country after 5 P.M. in the summer. Crowds begin to thin out dramatically then, but usually not so much that the place is empty; and a special reduced admission ticket is offered after 6 P.M. After dark, the surroundings are lighted and it's possible to watch the Electrical Water Pageant from the beach as it passes by around 9:35 P.M.

HOW TO GET THERE: From the Transportation and Ticket Center, blue-flagged buses (no IDs required) drop passengers off within walking distance of River Country. It's also possible to go by boat. Launches leave regularly from the dock near the gates of the Magic Kingdom. River Country tickets or IDs from WDW resorts are required.

TOWELS, DRESSING ROOMS, SUPPLIES: Men's and women's dressing rooms, and coin-operated lockers are available. Quarters for these can be obtained at the concession window, but to avoid waiting in line for change, it's best to bring your own.

Towels are available for rent at 25¢ each at the concession window, but they're small, so you'll probably want to bring at least one beach towel.

FOOD: Pop's Place, the main snack stand, sells quarter-pound burgers, hot dogs, beer and soda, hot pretzels, and the like. The Waterin' Hole, a smaller stand nearby, offers a more limited selection.

Picnicking is permitted. You can eat on the beach or seek out a table on the shady lawns.

MORE

Fort Wilderness Campground is one of the liveliest spots in the World.

BEACHES: The campground does not have its own swimming pool (and to use the one at River Country it's necessary to pay the River Country admission), but the clear waters of Bay Lake, which lap the 315-foot-long, 175-foot-wide, white-sand beach at the north end of the campground, are delightful, and swimming is allowed inside the roped-off areas. Open to guests at WDW-owned properties only.

BIKE RENTALS: Tandems, Sting Rays, and assorted other two-wheelers can be hired at the Bike Barn for trips along Fort Wilderness's bike paths and circuitous roadways—or just for getting around. Cost is about $1 to $2 per hour, or $4 to $6 per day.

BLACKSMITH SHOP: The pleasant fellow who shoes the big Belgians that pull the trolleys down Main Street in the Magic Kingdom is on hand at some time every day to answer questions and talk about what he does; occasionally guests can watch him at work, fitting the big animals with the special fiber-glass-covered, steel-cored horseshoes that are used here to protect the horses' hooves.

BOAT RENTALS ON BAY LAKE: Zippy little Water Sprites, sailboats, pontoon boats, and pedal boats (described in *Sports*) are available for rent at the Fort Wilderness marina, at the north end of the campground.

CAMPFIRE PROGRAM: Held nightly near the Meadow Trading Post near the center of the campground, it features Disney movies, a sing-along, cartoons. It's free for Walt Disney World resort guests only. Chip and Dale usually put in an appearance.

CANOE RENTALS: Fort Wilderness is ribboned with tranquil canals, sometimes in full sun and sometimes canopied by tall trees, which make for delightful canoe trips of one to three hours—or longer if you take fishing gear and elect to wet your line. Rentals are available at the Bike Barn ($2 per hour, $6 per day).

CHECKERS: Boards are set up in the Settlement Trading Post.

ELECTRIC CART RENTALS: Available at the Bike Barn for sight-seeing or transportation around the campground.

ELECTRICAL WATER PAGEANT: This twinkling cavalcade-of-lights (described in more detail in *Good Meals, Great Times*) can be seen from the beach here nightly at 9:45 P.M., and, during the hours that the Magic Kingdom is open late, at 9:35 P.M., from River Country.

FISHING EXCURSIONS ON BAY LAKE: WDW's restrictive fishing policy means plenty of angling action—largemouth bass weighing two or three pounds, mainly—for those who sign up for the special 8 A.M. and 3 P.M. fishing excursions offered to guests at WDW-owned properties. The fee is $50, and includes gear, driver/guide, and refreshments; no license is required. Guests whose accommodations have kitchens may keep their catch; for everyone else, it's catch-and-release.

FISHING IN THE CANALS: Largemouth bass can be caught here as well. Those without their own gear will find cane poles and lures for sale at the trading posts. No license is required.

HORSE BARN: The massive Belgian draft horses that pull the trolleys down Main Street in the Magic Kingdom call this corner of Fort Wilderness home. You can watch them chomping placidly on their food, and occasionally see young colts and fillies as well—offspring not of the draft animals, but of the horses used on trail rides (described below), most of them destined to be sold. The Tri Circle D insignia above the barn door is also the WDW brand: two small

FORT WILDERNESS FUN

circles, Mouse ears–style, atop one large one with the letter *D* inside.

JOGGING AND EXERCISE TRAILS: This 2.3-mile course, punctuated by exercise stations every quarter mile or so, is one of the Fort Wilderness attractions that draws WDW resort guests from all over the property. The weather is often steamy, but things are pleasant in the early morning—especially because most of the running trail is in the shade. You may just jog the whole length; or you can stop periodically to do the chin-ups, sit-ups, and other exercises outlined on nearby signs.

LAWN MOWER TREE: The tree that somehow, mysteriously, grew around a lawn mower is a Fort Wilderness point of interest, worth hunting down. It's just off the sidewalk leading to the marina.

MARSHMALLOW MARSH EXCURSION: A nightly marshmallow roast and sing-along follows a canoe trip and a short hike to the northern end of the campground, where a handful of big split logs is arranged around a fire ring. The Electrical Water Pageant, which can be seen just offshore, is part of the entertainment. Bring mosquito repellent. For Walt Disney World resort guests only; cost is $3 for adults, $2 for children (3 to 11).

PETTING FARM: This fenced-in enclave just behind Pioneer Hall is now home to some extra-friendly goats, a fully grown brahma bull, some sheep, a few rabbits, exotic chickens and pigeons, and a goose—the sole remaining member of an original trio, two thirds of which were promptly dispatched elsewhere when they developed the decidedly unamiable habit of chasing youngsters; the nasty twosome once trapped a woman in her trailer for four hours. (The colony of prairie dogs didn't work out either, because members persisted in burrowing out of their compound; no sooner would their Disney caretakers try to thwart them—by digging a bigger hole and installing a below-ground-level wire fence—than the little creatures would gnaw right through it.) Though mainly designed for youngsters, the Petting Farm is also a lot of fun for the adult crowd, and it's a good place to pass the time while waiting for seating at the Hoop-Dee-Doo Revue in nearby Pioneer Hall.

SOFTBALL AND BASEBALL DIAMONDS: Located in the meadow near the Bike Barn, these can be used by guests at WDW-owned properties. No balls and bats are available; bring your own. Free.

TRAIL RIDES: Offered from the corral at the kennel and livery area near the River Country parking lot, at 9 and 10:30 A.M., noon, and 2 P.M. daily, these trips take riders past an Indian village, some Western wagons, and assorted other frontier-type props.

These add a bit of atmosphere—but not nearly so much as the occasional sight of a real cougar or bobcat (extremely rare, but not totally nonexistent either) and deer (which are abundant here). Galloping is not part of the game, so you don't need riding know-how to sign up. Cost is $5 per person for both day visitors and for guests at WDW-owned properties. No children under 9 are allowed. Reservations are necessary; phone 828-2734.

VOLLEYBALL, TETHERBALL, BASKETBALL, AND HORSESHOE COURTS: Open only to guests at WDW-owned properties, these are scattered throughout the camping loops. No charge.

WATER-SKI TRIPS: Ski boats with driver and equipment can be hired at $35 an hour at the marina. Includes instruction. Reservations should be made two to three days in advance. Call the Contemporary Resort (824-1000; ask for the marina).

WILDERNESS SWAMP TRAIL: A mile-and-a-half long, this smooth footpath into the woods skirts the marshes along the shore of Bay Lake, then plunges into a forest full of tall, straight-standing cypress trees. Near Marshmallow Marsh, at the northern end of the campground.

DISCOVERY ISLAND

This 11½-acre landfall on the southeast shore of Bay Lake, a natural marvel full of exotic birds and a whole United Nations of plants, is a delightful place to go for a change of pace from the Magic Kingdom. Here you're in the domain of the animals and man is just a visitor. The mood is different from anywhere else in the World, and the scenery is remarkably lush.

Before the World began, this island was flat and scrubby, just a tangle of vines. But Disney planners, thinking of Robert Louis Stevenson's classic *Treasure Island*, decided to turn it into a horticultural and zoological paradise. They cleared the vegetation, brought in 15,000 cubic yards of sandy soil, and added 500 tons each of boulders and trees. They built hills, carved out lagoons, sowed grass seed, and planted 20 types of palm trees, 10 species of bamboo, and dozens upon dozens of other plants from Argentina, Bolivia, the Canary Islands, China, Costa Rica, Formosa, the Himalayas, India, Japan, Peru, South Africa, Trinidad, and other nations around the world. Then they added winding paths, built aviaries and filled them with birds, and added a few props to carry through the Treasure Island theme. A wrecked ship salvaged from off the coast of Florida was installed on the beach, and a Jolly Roger waved from the lookout post. The creation was dubbed Treasure Island.

Since then, that theme has been abandoned and the island's name changed. But the ship is still there, as is the vegetation (lusher than ever). And the avian population is flourishing so well that the droning of the motors of the Water Sprites on Bay Lake is almost drowned out by chirps and tweets, crows and hoarse caws, cries and squeaks, and the lonely-sounding squawks of peacocks.

Now nobody makes any bones about the fact that the birds and the extraordinary vegetation constitute the island's chief attraction. Far from taking a backseat to the man-made, nature is the big deal on Discovery Island. The sweet-smelling flowers in pinks and reds and yellows that polka-dot the billowing greenery, the ferns that hang in the forests, the trees that canopy the footpaths, the butterflies, the dense thickets of bamboo, and the graceful palms—not to mention the birds themselves—are all very real; during Discovery Island hours—that is, from 10 A.M. to 5 P.M. every day—visitors provide (as curator Charlie Cook tells it) a good show for the birds and animals.

WHAT TO SEE: It's possible to walk the length of the paths and boardwalks that wind through the island in 45 minutes or so. But spending the better part of a day—or at least several hours—is a far better idea, since there is so much to see that it warrants more than just a rushed look. This is especially true in spring, when the birds are in breeding condition—looking their best, putting on courting displays, and sometimes collecting materials for nests. Even dur-

ing other seasons, however, each stop yields rewards. An ibis might be spotted building its nest. A sleeping tortoise—dinosaur-like, with the papery, wrinkled skin of an old woman's neck—suddenly rouses himself and creeps forward to join a clump of rocks that turn out to be other tortoises.

Many animals run free. Peacocks trail their spotted trains of iridescent green, blue, and gold around the grounds. They lose their tail feathers every September, and spend the winter growing new plumage in preparation for their springtime mating dance—a slow turning to and fro, sometimes punctuated by a quiver and a shudder of their graceful fans. A type of chicken developed in Poland, where chicken breeding is a popular hobby, occasionally chases the peacocks. The large rabbit-like animals are Patagonian cavies, members of the guinea pig family, who in the wild live in burrows to escape predators. Keeping quite calm, you can approach them slowly to examine them at close range.

In addition, there are a number of special points of interest, which are marked on maps available on the island:

COOCOO CABANA: The macaws, cockatoos, and other trained birds that comprise the Jose Carioca Flyers make their home here and at a small enclosure dotted with perches nearby. One six-year-old bird can stand on his head. Little green ones named Moe, Larry (the greenest; actually a female), and Curly (the shyest) know how to roll over. Andrew waves good-bye. Each one has his own trick, and you can stand and watch the caretakers putting them through their paces for hours. One of these clowns, a gray rhea named Ringo, once demonstrated a mind of his own by snatching—then swallowing—a guest's ring, which finally was retrieved by doctors in Tampa who used a device called an indescope.

TRUMPETER SPRINGS: The trumpeter swans who live here, the largest members of the waterfowl family, belong to a species that once was nearly extinct—as a result of hunting in the early part of the century.

BAMBOO HOLLOW: The sturdy bamboo here was planted on the island's windward side as protection against occasional harsh weather and wind.

CRANE'S ROOST: The large, red-banded Sarus cranes, the small Demoiselle cranes, and the striking gold-crested African Crowned cranes engage in wonderfully elaborate courting dances every spring.

AVIAN WAY: One of the largest walk-through aviaries in the world, this large enclosure, occupying close to an acre, is the home of the United States' most extensive breeding colony of Scarlet ibis. Their incredible color, even richer than that of ibis in the wild, derives from a diet that is especially rich in carotenes. Even those in the forest are striking. The early South American explorers who first saw them thought that the trees were covered with blood.

Also in the aviary are white peacocks, albino animals with tails that look like the train of a lacy wedding gown, and elegant African Crowned cranes, almost as common in Africa as cats and dogs are in the United States; they have a voracious appetite for insects that aids in controlling insect pests, and farmers keep them for that purpose.

PELICAN BAY: Brown pelicans became almost extinct because the chemical DDT, washed into rivers and absorbed by fish that the birds subsequently ate, caused their eggs to have such thin shells that even the weight of the mother pelican nesting on them broke them before hatching. It only has been since Florida's 1965 ban on the chemical that the population has grown again. The Discovery Island birds, though now healthy, have suffered injuries that have left them crippled in ways that would make it impossible for them to survive in the wild.

FLAMINGO LAGOON: Native flamingos—which nested in colonies some 20,000 strong when John James Audubon visited Florida in the early part of the 19th century—have not lived in the wild here since around 1920. The Discovery Island birds are Caribbean flamingos. They have grown accustomed to man's presence, as the early Florida flamingos could not, and are breeding.

TURTLE BEACH: Early explorers used to lead Galapagos tortoises, now rare and endangered, onto their ships; because the animals can live for some time without food or water, they provided the crews with fresh meat for the duration of a trip. There are 11 here; the largest weighs some 500 pounds.

EAGLE'S WATCH: The pair of southern bald eagles here belong to a species that nests in the wild only in Florida. Sharp-eyed and white-headed, the birds seen here are on loan from the U.S. Department of the Interior.

HOW TO GET THERE: Watercraft from the Magic Kingdom, the Polynesian Village, and the Contemporary Resort, Fort Wilderness, and River Country all call regularly at Discovery Island; to ride these, you must show a Discovery Island admission ticket or a WDW resort ID. Alternatively, you can board one of the big paddlewheelers that dock at the Magic Kingdom for the narrated World Cruise, which calls at the island ($4 for adults; $2.50 for children aged 3 to 11). If you elect to sail on the narrated World Cruise, there is no additional admission charge for Discovery Island.

ADMISSION: Cost is $3 ($1.50 for children 3 through 11); combination tickets that include River Country admission as well are also available (described in this chapter's River Country section). Some three-day Passports, available to the guests at WDW-owned resorts as well as to vacationers on some Eastern Airlines packages (and described in *An Essential Guide to the Magic Kingdom*), include admission to both Discovery Island and River Country.

PHOTOS: The birds on Discovery Island offer wonderful photographic possibilities. Don't forget your camera. Film is available on the island.

BEACH: Swimming isn't allowed, but the peaceful strand flanking the shipwreck is great for sunbathing and sandcastle building—or just for sitting and watching the brightly colored sails of the Hobie Cats (from the Fort Wilderness marina) go by.

FOOD: It's fun to pack a picnic, with supplies from the Gourmet Pantry at Walt Disney World Shopping Village or one of the Fort Wilderness Campground's trading posts, for lunch on the beach near the handsome old wreck (which is still aging gracefully along the Bay Lake shore). Ice cream sandwiches and bars, frozen juice bars, frozen chocolate-covered bananas, and beer and soft drinks are also available at the island snack bar, the Thirsty Perch. Those who come to Discovery Island as part of the World Cruise can get light sandwiches on board.

WONDERS OF THE WORLD

BEHIND THE SCENES

There isn't a Magic Kingdom visitor around who wouldn't like to see Disney character costumes being made, or to go backstage at the Diamond Horseshoe and ask the dancers how they make it look so easy, or to talk to a Disney character artist in person and watch him draw Donald Duck. Outdoor lovers who hear of wildlife-rich WDW's 7,500-acre nature preserve, not normally open to the public, would give their eyeteeth to explore its glass-smooth waterways.

Wonders of Walt Disney World, a program offered to students in the fifth through tenth grades, shows off these aspects of WDW (and more) in four special courses devoted to the creative arts, ecology, energy, and entertainment The inside look at parts of this 43-square-mile complex is one that any adult would envy. The Wonders of Walt Disney World program is even more enriching because the on-property experience is augmented by excellently produced books designed to prepare kids for what they'll be learning before they arrive, and to help them follow through on the knowledge they've acquired once they're back home again. Developed in cooperation with educators from the Orlando area and from out of state, the program has won accolades from teachers and state school superintendents all over the country; many educational institutions give students credit for their participation and grant excused absences to those who complete the course. (Therein lies the other positive aspect of the program: it allows families to vacation at Walt Disney World during spring, winter, and fall—when crowds are smaller and things are generally more manageable.)

ALL ABOUT THE PROGRAMS: The WDW section of the program, as distinct from the pre- and post-trip work that each participant completes, lasts about six hours. Each student is given a Polaroid OneStep camera to use during the session to record his or her impressions; the cost of the film, as well as the cost of lunch and the pre- and post-trip materials, is included in the $40 fee. Only one program may be chosen by each participant.

CREATIVE ARTS: A visit by a Disney artist, who shows students how to draw a character or two and then critiques them as they execute their own versions, is the highlight of the *Disney Creative Arts* course. There's also a walk through the Magic Kingdom, during which the Wonders program instructor points out some of the park's design elements—the careful painting of signs and buildings to make them look antique (though they're really not), the scaling of the buildings on Main Street so that they look bigger than they are, and instances of the use of colors, shapes, and texture to produce effects.

ECOLOGY: *The Wonder and Beauty of Our World* course begins with a film describing Floridian ecosystems in general; then proceeds with tours of 11½-acre Discovery Island and the 7,500-acre conservation area, where students look for air plants and orchids, ospreys and egrets, alligators, and bald cypress. Each youngster is given not only a camera and binoculars to use during the session, but also a nature log in which to record his or her observations. There's talk of the interrelationships of soil and water and plant and animal life, and of the ways in which the destruction of one of these elements can mean the ruin of the whole community; there's no development-is-bad message here, just a caution, and adult bird watchers and other nature lovers (as well as photographers who normally wouldn't be interested in demurring to their kids' pleas for a trip to WDW) usually look more favorably on the idea when this course comes to their attention.

ENERGY: During *The Energy That Runs Our World* course, students learn how energy is produced, distributed, used, and conserved, and talk about transportation systems from the steam-powered motors of the past to the linear induction motors that power the WEDway PeopleMover, a Disney-developed prototype for mass transit. On a trip through the Magic Kingdom, youngsters discuss the ways in which energy is used there; and at the Walt Disney World Central Energy Plant—a facility that few outsiders ever see—they learn about the World's computerized energy distribution system and see how its prototype solar-powered office building actually works.

ENTERTAINMENT: *The Walt Disney World of Entertainment* course has students looking not just at the onstage performers, but also at the people backstage and the audience. Lighting, music, pacing, sets, and timing are all discussed as well. Students meet a Disney character (and practice walking and communicating like that character) and talk to the performers at the Diamond Horseshoe and other Disney showfolk. Youngsters aspiring to show business careers (or those interested in becoming a better audience) can learn a lot; and everyone has a great time.

MORE INFORMATION: To find out more and make reservations, write Wonders of Walt Disney World; Box 40; Lake Buena Vista, FL 32830. The Wonders program is also available to purchasers of Eastern Airlines packages.

SPORTS

Many first-time visitors don't realize that Walt Disney World is much more than just the amusement area called the Magic Kingdom. Within WDW's 27,000-odd acres there are more tennis courts than at many tennis resorts, more holes of championship-caliber golf than at most golf centers, and so many acres of other diversions—from fishing and bicycling to boating and swimming—that the quantity and variety are matched by very few other vacation destinations.

So while the golfers in the family are earnestly pursuing a perfect swing on one of the trio of first-class layouts, tennis buffs can be wearing themselves out on the courts, sailors can be sailing, water skiers can be skimming back and forth across powerboat wakes, and anglers can be dangling a cane pole in a canal—in the hopes of bringing in a big bream for dinner.

Instruction (formal or impromptu), as well as guides, drivers, and assorted leaders and supervisors (as required), make each sports offering as much fun for rank beginners as for hard-core aficionados. Moreover, the ready accessibility of all these WDW sporting activities—via an excellent system of public transportation (see *Transportation and Accommodations*)—means that no member of a visiting family or group need give up play time to chauffeur others around. By the same token, excellent supervision in all sports areas keeps to a minimum any parental fears that youngsters might get into trouble the moment they stray off to play without accompaniment.

Finally, staying in one of the WDW-owned hotels, in the villa complex, or in the WDW Fort Wilderness campground is quite different from lodging off the property and visiting the World by the day, for certain sporting activities that are available to WDW resort guests are off limits to day visitors. However, most sports facilities are available to all, and except for the potential logistical problem of coordinating a day's-end rendezvous back at the car, the functional design and convenient placement of WDW sports and recreational facilities make them as compelling for off-property lodgers as for guests at WDW's own resorts.

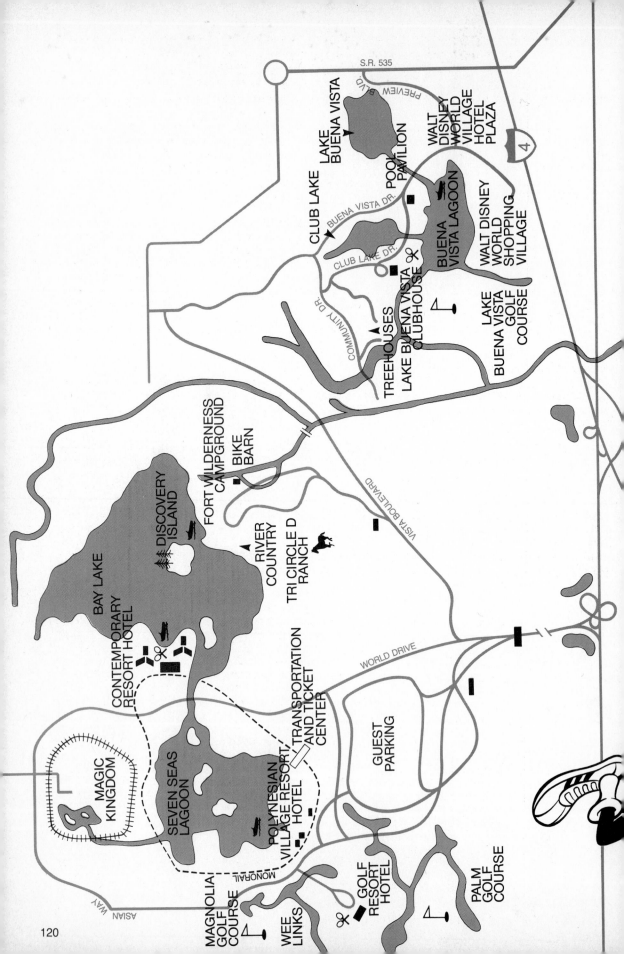

S.R. 535

PREVIEW BLVD.

LAKE BUENA VISTA

CLUB LAKE

BUENA VISTA DR.

POOL PAVILION

WALT DISNEY WORLD VILLAGE HOTEL PLAZA

4

CLUB LAKE DR.

COMMUNITY DR.

BUENA VISTA LAGOON

WALT DISNEY WORLD SHOPPING VILLAGE

TREEHOUSES

LAKE BUENA VISTA CLUBHOUSE

LAKE BUENA VISTA GOLF COURSE

FORT WILDERNESS CAMPGROUND

BIKE BARN

DISCOVERY ISLAND

RIVER COUNTRY

VISTA BOULEVARD

TRI CIRCLE D RANCH

BAY LAKE

CONTEMPORARY RESORT HOTEL

WORLD DRIVE

TRANSPORTATION AND TICKET CENTER

MAGIC KINGDOM

MAGNOLIA GOLF COURSE

SEVEN SEAS LAGOON

POLYNESIAN VILLAGE RESORT HOTEL

GUEST PARKING

ASIAN WAY

MONORAIL

WEE LINKS

GOLF RESORT HOTEL

PALM GOLF COURSE

TENNIS EVERYONE

No one comes to Walt Disney World just for a tennis vacation; there just isn't the country-club ambience of a tennis resort where everyone is totally immersed in the game. But the facilities and instruction program at WDW are extensive enough that such holidays are certainly within the realm of possibility. And at the very least, a game of tennis on one of the World's 11 courts is a good way to rest up from a mad morning in the Magic Kingdom, for there's seldom a problem arranging court time.

Only in February, March, and April do the courts at the three separate tennis locations enjoy fairly heavy usage, but even then there is usually a lull between noon and 3 P.M., and again from dinnertime until 10 P.M. Even in these busy months, however, it's usually possible to get a reservation. Of the three sets of courts, those at the Lake Buena Vista Club are usually the least crowded, with those at the Golf Resort also available for play most of the time.

WHERE TO FIND THE COURTS: There are six tennis courts at the **Contemporary Resort Hotel**, just beyond the garden wings to the north of the Tower. This is WDW's major tennis facility. It boasts a backboard, plus two practice "lanes" (about half as long and wide as a normal court) with automatic ball machines which shoot out about 400 balls per half hour to backhands or forehands, or both. There are two additional courts tucked away behind the **Golf Resort**, and three, cradled by adjacent woods and a section of the golf course, at the **Lake Buena Vista Club**. All WDW tennis facilities are hard courts and are open from 8 A.M. to 10 P.M. daily. All are lighted for play after dark.

COURT FEES: To WDW resort guests, the cost is $3 an hour for singles, $5 for doubles; day visitors pay an extra $1. Use of the backboard is free, except during busy periods, when the regular court fees are charged. Guests pay $5 per half hour to use practice lanes.

RESERVATIONS: Courts can be reserved 24 hours in advance. Call 824-1000, ext. 3578, to play at the **Contemporary Resort**; 824-2200 for the **Golf Resort**; 828-3741 for the **Lake Buena Vista Club**. The limit on the number of hours a day any single group of players can occupy a court—a restriction in effect only during very busy periods—is two hours for any single morning, afternoon, or evening. But that still means that you can spend up to six hours a day on any given court even at the busiest times, and the fact is that these restrictions on court time have never yet been imposed.

For players without partners, the "Tennis Anyone?" program will help find an opponent. Just call the Pro Shop at the Contemporary Resort to get your name posted.

INSTRUCTION: The tennis program at the Contemporary Resort offers **adult clinics** every morning ($15) and **junior development lessons** for players aged 4 through 16 every afternoon ($8). Video cameras are used to record players' on-court efforts for subsequent review at both clinics; children as young as 3 and adults as old as 80 have participated. Nobody will try to radically change your game; the idea is to help you play better with what you have.

Private lessons are also available, by appointment at the Lake Buena Vista Club and at the Contemporary Resort; the cost is $10 per half hour with a staff professional, $12 per half hour with head pro Steve Babb, who supervises the entire WDW tennis program and is one of the rare players in the world who plays equally well with either hand. Videotape reviews are included as part of hour-long lessons at the Contemporary Resort for an additional $5.

For more information about private lessons and group development sessions, call 824-1000, ext. 3578.

TOURNAMENTS: Individual tournaments may be arranged by calling the Pro Shop at the Contemporary. The fee for running such a tournament is $50.

RACQUET RENTAL: Good-quality racquets are available for rent for $1 an hour. Balls must be purchased (for about $4 per can of three). And some boast a Micky Mouse logo.

LOCKERS: Locker facilities are available at all tennis court areas. There is no charge for the use of a locker.

Most people probably don't think of Walt Disney World immediately when they contemplate a golf vacation. Yet there are three superb courses right in the Vacation Kingdom: the **Magnolia** and the **Palm** flank the hotel named for the sport, the Golf Resort, and extend practically to the borders of the Magic Kingdom. In addition, just a short drive away, there's the **Lake Buena Vista Golf Course**, whose borders are punctuated by the units of yet another lodging facility christened in honor of the game, the Fairway Villas.

None of these three Joe Lee-designed courses will set anyone's knees to knocking in terror, though all three courses are demanding enough to provide the site for an annual stop on the PGA Tour tournament trail. Depending on the tee from which a golfer chooses to play, the Disney courses are challenging and/or fun, and they are constructed to be especially forgiving for the mid-handicap player. What's more, they're remarkably interesting topographically, considering that the land on which Lee started was about as hilly as a formica tabletop.

At all three, the green fees (including the required cart), are $20 for WDW resort guests, $26 for day visitors, and $24 for guests at the several area hotels that offer a special Vacationer's Golf Membership card; twilight rates, in effect beginning at 3 P.M., are $12 for both resort guests and day visitors.

For tee-off times on any of the three courses, just phone the Master Starter at 824-3625. Especially from February through April, it's a good idea to reserve starting times well in advance for play in the morning and early afternoon (though starting times after 3 P.M. are almost always available at the last minute). Those with confirmed reservations at a WDW resort can reserve as far in advance as desired the year round. Day visitors (which include guests at Walt Disney World Village Hotel Plaza) can reserve only seven days ahead for play between January 1 and April 30.

THE GOLF COURSES

AT THE GOLF RESORT: The wide-open, tree-dotted **Magnolia**, which flanks the hotel to the north, plays from 5,903 (ladies) to 7,253 (championship) yards at par 72. The par-72 **Palm** to the south—shorter and tighter, with more wooded fairways and nine water hazards—plays from 5,785 to 6,951 yards; it was ranked by *Golf Digest* magazine among the nation's top hundred courses. Together, this pair (and the Lake Buena Vista Club course) hosts the big Walt Disney World National Team Championship Golf Classic every year, a good indication of the quality of the play to be found. Driving ranges are located near the Magnolia and Palm courses.

The Wee Links: This six-hole, 1,525-yard experimental beginners layout—a championship-course-in-miniature nestled on a 25-acre corner of the Magnolia—was designed especially with the young beginner in mind. The design incorporates sand and water traps, tees and greens, just like an adult layout. But the traps are small and flat, and the water hazards are shallow enough to allow easy ball retrieval. The yardage is measured in "junior yards"—that is, only two feet to the yard; and the greens are made of a special low-maintenance artificial turf called Mod Sod (which can be top-dressed to allow greater control of roll speed) instead of more-difficult-to-care-for grass. The PGA Tour, which funded the course, hopes that its ease of maintenance and low cost will encourage other communities around the country to establish similar layouts—and eventually lead to "little leagues" for young duffers.

The $2 fee for juniors (under 18) includes Spalding junior clubs and a Wee Links Lesson covering the fundamentals of the swing, golf etiquette, and the rules of the game (offered daily at 8:30 and 11:00 A.M. and 2:00 and 4:00 P.M., mainly for rank beginners). The $2 fee covers 12 holes of play (2 rounds). Adults pay $5 to play on the Wee Links, and it should be noted that this is a walking course only.

COURSES

AT THE LAKE BUENA VISTA CLUB: Located to the south of the clubhouse and the Buena Vista Lagoon, this par-72 layout plays from 6,002 to 6,540 yards. The shortest of the trio, with the narrowest fairways, it bears less resemblance to the Magnolia than to the Palm, but lacks the water hazards that characterize the latter.

INSTRUCTION: The **Walt Disney World Golf Studio** is the most compelling aspect of the golf instruction available at WDW. Using a program developed by WDW's Director of Golf, South African Phil Ritson (whom student Gary Player rates among the top golf instructors in the world), each Golf Studio instructor works to help golfers develop their own styles by building on what skills they already possess. Instruction is provided via small classes with a high teacher-student ratio. Part of each lesson is recorded on videotape and then, back in the Pro Shop, given a thorough viewing and critique. Then, to hammer in what has just been learned, the instructor repeats his suggestions and admonitions on an audio cassette tape that students can take home. (The first half of this tape is prerecorded with general commentary by Ritson himself.)

The studios, which last about two hours each, are offered at 9 and 11:30 A.M. and 2:30 P.M. Monday through Friday, and at 9 and 11:30 A.M. on Saturday at the Magnolia driving range. Call the Master Starter at 824-3625 for reservations. The fee is $30 (or, including nine holes of post-studio golf, $34 for WDW resort guests and $35 for everyone else).

Private Lessons: These are available at both the Golf Resort and at the Lake Buena Vista Club at $15 per half hour ($20 with Golf Resort head pro Eric Frederickson or LBV head pro Rina Ritson, Phil's wife, the first woman golf pro ever to hold the top position at a major golf club). Lessons with Phil Ritson himself—who has taught PGA Tour star Andy Bean and top LPGA pro Sally Little and over 50 other PGA Tour players during his busy career—cost $30 per half hour.

Playing lessons with Phil Ritson are also available ($50 for nine holes, $75 for eighteen).

Call 824-3628 to book private lessons at the Golf Resort, 828-3748 to arrange instruction at Lake Buena Vista.

EQUIPMENT RENTAL: Spalding Executive and Top-flight rental clubs ($8), buckets of range balls ($1.95 each), and shoes ($2.50) are all available at the Pro Shop—what you rent here may be better than your own gear.

TOURNAMENTS

The $450,000 Walt Disney World National Team Championship Golf Classic, a popular spectator event that ranks as the most important on WDW's sports calendar, takes place in the fall, usually in October, and features most of the pro tour's top players. So guests who plan to play golf during their WDW vacation are advised *not* to schedule a visit for tournament week.

You can play alongside the pros if you pay for it: $2,750 is the price of a one-year membership in the **Classic Club**. As a tourney sponsor, each member plays with two of the competing pros daily, for three of the four days of the tourney. While the pros are competing for cash prizes, the amateurs vie for trophies and plaques in a separate but simultaneous competition. The $2,750 fee also includes six nights' lodging during the tournament, and the waiver of green fees for a year, and admission to the Magic Kingdom for a week. For details, phone 828-3692.

At other times of year, smaller private competitions are held for civic, corporate, and social groups; to arrange for one (at no charge beyond the green fees), contact the Tournament Coordinator at 824-4602.

BOATING

Walt Disney World is the home of the country's largest fleet of pleasure boats. Most of the action is centered on two lakes—the 200-acre **Seven Seas Lagoon**, the body of water that the ferries cross and the monorails circle as they carry guests between the Transportation and Ticket Center and the Magic Kingdom; and 450-acre **Bay Lake**, which is connected to the Seven Seas Lagoon by the Water Bridge.

Cruising on Bay Lake and the Seven Seas Lagoon can be excellent sport, and a variety of boats are available for rent at the **marinas** at the **Contemporary Resort**, on the eastern shore of Bay Lake; at **Fort Wilderness**, to the southwest beyond Discovery Island; and at the **Polynesian Village**, which occupies the southern edge of the Seven Seas Lagoon.

In addition, boaters can explore the lakes of Walt Disney World Village—11-acre **Club Lake**, 13-acre **Lake Buena Vista**, and 35-acre **Buena Vista Lagoon**, which all are connected by canal.

To rent, day visitors and resort guests alike must show a resort ID, a driver's license, or a passport. Rental of certain craft may carry other special requirements (described below).

Note that no privately owned boats are permitted on any of the WDW waters.

SPEEDBOATS: Particularly when the weather is warm, there are always dozens of small boats zipping back and forth across the surface of Bay Lake, the Seven Seas Lagoon, and the lakes at Walt Disney World Village. These are called *Water Sprites,* and they are just as much fun as they look. Though they don't go too fast, they're so small that a rider feels every bit of speed, and they get you around quickly enough so that a lot of watery terrain can be covered in a half-hour rental period ($7).

You can rent them at the **Contemporary Resort, Polynesian Village, Fort Wilderness,** and **WDW Village marinas.** During warm weather, lines of people waiting to rent these zippy little craft usually form at about 11 A.M. and remain fairly constant until about 4 P.M. The minimum rental age is 12. Even with an accompanying parent or adult, children under 12 are not allowed to drive.

SAILBOATS: The size of Bay Lake and the Seven Seas Lagoon—and their usually reliable winds—make for good sailing, and the **Contemporary Resort, Polynesian Village,** and **Fort Wilderness marinas** rent a variety of sail craft. *Sunfish,* which can hold two, go for $5 an hour. *Capris,* accommodating from one to six—more stable because of their leaded keel, wider beam, and greater weight, and consequently better for beginners—cost $7 an hour. *Hobie Cat 14*s and *16*s cost $7 and $9 an hour respectively; catamaran experience is required. The Hobie 16, which has a main and a jib, requires two to sail, but cannot accommodate more than three. Sailing conditions are usually best in March and April and before afternoon thundershowers in the summer—and that's when demand is greatest. So don't tarry. Get to the marina when the urge to sail strikes.

PONTOON BOATS: *Flote Botes*—motor-powered, canopied platforms-on-pontoons, really—are perfect for families, for water lovers who aren't experienced sailors, and for older visitors more interested in serenity than thrills. They're available at the **resort marinas** ($20 an hour).

CANOPY BOATS: These 16-foot, V-hulled, motorized boats-with-canopies are also good for slow cruises, and can accommodate up to ten adults. They can be rented for $8 per half hour at the **WDW Village Marina.**

PEDAL BOATS: These craft are for rent, for $2 per half hour at **all WDW lakeside marinas,** for excursions on the WDW lakes. They're also available at **Fort Wilderness's Bike Barn** for trips onto the placid canals that loop through the campground.

CANOEING: A long paddle down the glass-smooth, wooded Fort Wilderness canals is such a tranquil way to pass a misty morning that it's hard to remember that the bustle of the Magic Kingdom is just a launch ride away. Canoes are for rent (from 9 A.M. to 7 P.M.) at **Fort Wilderness's Bike Barn** ($2 per hour, $6 per day). Most trips last from one to three hours; those who take fishing gear can easily stay out longer. Canoes are restricted to the canals of WDW.

OUTRIGGER CANOES: It takes eight to paddle one of these long, skinny Polynesian-style canoes. They're available at the **Polynesian Village Marina** ($1 per guest per hour), and are permitted on the Seven Seas Lagoon.

WATER SKIING: Ski boats with driver and full equipment ($30 an hour) are available at the **Fort Wilderness** and **Contemporary Resort marinas.** Anyone is allowed to water ski, but there is no discount on the posted price even if you bring along your own skis and other gear.

SWIMMING

Between Bay Lake and the Seven Seas Lagoon, Walt Disney World resort guests have five miles of powdery white sand beach at their disposal. And that doesn't include the nine swimming pools that come in all shapes and sizes. River Country (see *Everything Else in the World*) may be the ultimate "swimming hole," but each pool has charms of its own.

BEACHES: When Walt Disney World was under construction in the mid-1960s, Bay Lake, with an eight-foot layer of muck on its bottom, was found to be unpolluted, though murky. It was drained and cleaned, and below the muck, engineers unearthed the pure white sand that now edges parts of the shore, most notably behind the Contemporary Resort and across from it on the lake's Fort Wilderness shore. These two sections of beach, plus the one at the Polynesian Village, make up WDW's principal sandy areas. They aren't the walk-forever strands found on Florida's east and west coasts, but they are long enough that most people never bother to go all the way to the end.

POOLS: There are two each at the **Contemporary Resort Hotel**, the **Polynesian Village**, and the **Walt Disney World Village area Vacation Villas**; plus one each at the **Lake Buena Vista Club**, the **Golf Resort Hotel**, and at **River Country**. There's no charge for admission, towels, or chairs anywhere, except for the admission charge at River Country. One of the pair of pools at the Polynesian Village has a water slide built into great Disney-made boulders that are part of the landscaping; to get to the carved-out stairway that leads to the top, duck under a waterfall. River Country's pool has two similar (but scarier) slides that end abruptly seven feet above the water. For lap-swimming, the best is the big 20-by-25-meter pool at the Contemporary Resort. When it isn't crowded (early in the morning and around dinnertime), the lifeguard is usually happy to haul in the rope that separates the deep and shallow ends. There are no diving boards at any of the pools; to practice cannonballs, head for River Country, where there are large boulders made especially for leaping.

Lifeguards are on duty during most daylight hours, and thereafter a sign warns that swimming is at the guest's own risk. Swimming after dark is permitted on this own-risk basis. There is no formal swimming instruction at WDW.

In addition, all four of the establishments at Walt Disney World Village Hotel Plaza have pools for their own guests' use; the biggest is at the Royal Plaza.

DAY VISITORS: Pools and beaches at the resort hotels are not open to day guests (or to guests staying at the hotels at Walt Disney World Village Hotel Plaza). If you're just at WDW for the day and want to take a break from the afternoon heat, head for River Country (see *Everything Else in the World*).

FISHING

The 70,000 bass with which Bay Lake was stocked in the mid-1960s have grown and multiplied as a result of WDW's restrictive fishing policy. No angling is permitted on Bay Lake or the Seven Seas Lagoon except on the two-hour **Fort Wilderness fishing expeditions** (for WDW resort guests only). There's one leaving the campground marina each morning at around 8 A.M. and one each afternoon at around 3 P.M.; a maximum of five fishing persons can be accommodated on each. The fee is $50, and includes gear, driver/guide, and coffee and pastries (in the morning) or soft drinks (in the afternoon). No license is required. Largemouth bass weighing two to three pounds each are the most common catch, though occasionally someone will reel in a bream or a bigger largemouth. Bass up to nine pounds have been recorded.

Guests at WDW accommodations with kitchens may keep the contents of their creel; for everyone else, it's catch-and-release. By the way, there are no official WDW facilities for cleaning fish you catch. **Fishing on your own** is permitted in the canals in the Walt Disney World Village area and at Fort Wilderness. Fort Wilderness campers can toss in their lines from any shore; villa guests can cast from the banks of the nearest canal or rent a canopy boat and chug back into remoter waters for their sport. (The waters around the Treehouses are particularly productive.) Licenses are not required. No gear is available for rent, but cane poles and lures are for sale at the Fort Wilderness trading posts.

MORE FUN STUFF

JOGGING: Except in winter, late fall, and very early spring, the weather is just too steamy in central Florida to make for the exhilarating jogging found in cooler climes. If you run early in the morning in warm seasons, the heat is somewhat less daunting. (The scenery is also usually good enough to take your mind off the perspiration.) Guests staying at **Walt Disney World Village** accommodations can just head out the door and run as they please along the winding drives where everything is green and blessedly quiet. **Fort Wilderness** offers a 2.3-mile course (partially paved) punctuated by exercise stations.

Jogging maps that outline the Fort Wilderness route, as well as the best courses from the **Contemporary Resort**, the **Polynesian Village**, the **Golf Resort**, and around Walt Disney World Village, are available at Guest Services desks in hotels and villa check-in areas; mileages range from 3.4 to 4.2 miles round-trip.

FORT WILDERNESS'S EXERCISE TRAIL: This 2.3-mile course gives joggers the chance to do chin-ups, sit-ups, and other exercises on special apparatus. Signs explain all the maneuvers—and it's almost all in the shade. There is no charge.

HORSEBACK RIDING: Trail rides into the pine woods and scrubby palmetto country—past an Indian village, some Western wagons, and assorted other western-style props—leave from the corral at **Fort Wilderness's Tri Circle D Ranch** (near the River Country parking lot) at 9 and 10:30 A.M., noon, and 2 P.M. daily. This is not for big time gallopers—you can't ride off on your own—and the horses have been culled for gentleness so that the trips are suitable even for nonriders. Cost is $5 a person for both day visitors and resort guests (no children under nine are accepted). For advance reservations, which are necessary, phone 828-2734.

WALKS: There are lovely nature trails through the moss-hung remains of a cypress swamp near **River Country** (about ¼ mile), and near **Marshmallow Marsh** at **Fort Wilderness**. The latter, about a mile long, leads along the reedy, sunny shores of Bay Lake, then heads into the cool woods before looping back to the starting point.

BIKING: Pedaling along the eight miles of bike paths at **Walt Disney World Village** and the lightly trafficked roads there and at **Fort Wilderness** can be a pleasant way to spend a couple of hours—especially in the winter or in the mornings and late afternoons during the rest of the year, when it's not too hot. Both areas are sufficiently spread out that two-wheelers are a practical means of getting around in general as well. If you don't bring your own bike, you can rent one at **Fort Wilderness's Bike Barn** or at the **Pool Pavilion** near the Vacation Villas at Walt Disney World Village for $1 an hour or $4 a day. Tandems are available at the Bike Barn and the Pool Pavilion ($2 an hour or $6 a day). Anyone is allowed to ride bikes on the property, though no motorbikes are permitted.

THE SPA: The **Contemporary Resort's Olympiad Health Club** (located on the hotel's third floor) has a back presser, wall pulleys, a sit-up bench, stationary bicycle, 5- to 35-pound dumbbells, a vibrating belt, and a leg bar to remove what get-up-and-go remains after a day in the Magic Kingdom. Afterward, it's almost not necessary—though it's decidedly pleasant—to relax in the sauna or in individual whirlpools; or to indulge yourself in a massage—45 minutes to an hour of sheer heaven at the hands of the Spa's U.S. Air Force–trained masseur (also a licensed RN and respiratory therapist). For use of the facilities, the cost is $2; whirlpools are an additional $3, and massages an extra $15. Appointments for massages must be made in advance; call 824-1000, ext. 3410. The health club is open to women from 9 A.M. to noon on Mon., Wed., and Fri.; from 9 A.M. to 1 P.M. on Tues., Thurs., and Sat. Men may use the facilities from 1 P.M. to 6 P.M. on Mon., Wed., and Fri.; from 2 P.M. to 6 P.M. on Tues., Thurs., and Sat.

VOLLEYBALL, TETHERBALL, AND HORSE-SHOES: Courts are scattered throughout the **Fort Wilderness** camping loops. But they're open to WDW resort guests only.

SOFTBALL AND BASEBALL: Diamonds, complete with backstop, are located in the meadow near **Fort Wilderness's Bike Barn**, and are available for the use of WDW resort guests. But bring your own balls and bats.

GOOD MEALS, GREAT TIMES

In the Magic Kingdom, fast food is king: even machines that broil 3,500 hamburgers an hour can't keep up with the demand, and in the course of just a single year, enough burgers are served to allow an individual to eat one for every inch of the 400 miles from Orlando to Atlanta. And that's in addition to enough French fries to fill ten boxcars, and a quantity of ice cream sufficient to build a minor mountain in an Olympic-size swimming pool.

But by no means is that all of the Walt Disney World food story. For breakfast, it's possible to sample some of the country's most unusually delectable French toast; for lunch, it's de rigueur to eat quiche and salad or seafood-stuffed crepes, or a fruit-and-cottage cheese platter. For dinner, there's fried chicken or roast beef, or more ambitious meals that end with a flambéed hot fudge sundae or an elegant amaretto-flavored soufflé. Restaurants at WDW run the gamut from a simple snack shop to an elegant salon.

In the following pages, we'll describe many meals worth a detour at any time of day. Specialties do change from time to time, though the basic types of food available remain the same. Hours at most establishments also vary from one season to the next; those given here are the ones that remain fairly stable year round. Prices are comparable to those for similar meals elsewhere in the United States (and they move upward as relentlessly); children's menus, or special rates for youngsters at buffets, are widely available. Occasionally, a restaurant will close for a few weeks for refurbishing. So consult bulletin boards in the individual resort hotels, or call Guest Services at your hotel for up-to-the-minute details.

A DIRECTORY TO THE
RESTAURANTS
OF WALT DISNEY WORLD

HOW TO USE THIS CHAPTER

Because the number of restaurants, snack shops, cafeterias, and other miscellaneous eateries around the World is so large and so varied, this chapter offers meal information in three different ways. To find a specific restaurant, we've provided an alphabetized directory to all restaurants on the property—with their exact locations. So if you know the name of a desired dining place, this directory will tell you where to find it.

If you are getting hungry in a particular area of the World, and want to know what's available in the immediate vicinity, the second section of this chapter offers an area-by-area rundown of nearly all operative eateries. Detailed data on each restaurant's atmosphere, decor, and menu specialties are also included.

Finally, to help in the planning of systematic programs for eating a broad swath across the World, this chapter also contains a meal-by-meal selection of eating places. These restaurants are organized by breakfast, lunch, and dinner specialties, and we've indicated certain entries for which we think it's worth going a bit out of your way.

This chapter contains eating places within the boundaries of Walt Disney World only. For recommendations of restaurants *outside* the World, refer to the "Where To Eat" section of the *Orlando* chapter.

WHERE TO FIND THEM

The list below includes all the restaurants and snack spots currently operating in Walt Disney World—at the hotels, at Fort Wilderness Campground, at Walt Disney World Village, and in the Magic Kingdom.

Adventureland Veranda: Magic Kingdom; at the east edge of Adventureland, between the bridge to the Hub and the Swiss Family Island Treehouse

Aunt Polly's: Magic Kingdom; in Frontierland, on Tom Sawyer Island

Barefoot Bar: Polynesian Village; near the Swimming Pool Lagoon

Barefoot Snack Bar: Polynesian Village; on the lobby level of the Great Ceremonial House

Baton Rouge Lounge: WDW Shopping Village; on the main deck of the *Empress Lilly* riverboat restaurant

Beach Shack: Fort Wilderness Campground; near the beach

Campfire Snack Bar: Fort Wilderness Campground; inside Pioneer Hall

Cap'n Jack's Oyster Bar: WDW Shopping Village; on the edge of Buena Vista Lagoon

Captain Cook's Hideaway: Polynesian Village; on the first floor, adjoining the Polynesian Princess boutique

Coconino Cove: Contemporary Resort; at the south end of the Grand Canyon Concourse (fourth floor), near the Pueblo Room

Columbia Harbour House: Magic Kingdom; in Liberty Square near the entrance to Fantasyland

Coral Isle Cafe: Polynesian Village; on the second floor of the Great Ceremonial House, around the corner from Papeete Bay

Crystal Palace: Magic Kingdom; near the Adventureland Bridge, at the north end of Main Street

Diamond Horseshoe: Magic Kingdom; in Frontierland at the edge of Liberty Square

Dock Inn: Contemporary Resort; in the Marina Pavilion near the beach

El Pirata Y el Perico: Magic Kingdom; in Adventureland, opposite Pirates of the Caribbean

Empress Lounge: WDW Shopping Village; aboard the *Empress Lilly*

Empress Room: WDW Shopping Village; aboard the *Empress Lilly*

Fiesta Fun Center Snack Bar: Contemporary Resort; first floor

Fife and Drum: Magic Kingdom; in Liberty Square, behind the Silversmith Shop

Fisherman's Deck: WDW Shopping Village; aboard the *Empress Lilly*

Fort Sam Clemens Snack Bar: Magic Kingdom; in Fort Sam Clemens on Tom Sawyer Island, in Frontierland

Gulf Coast Room: Contemporary Resort; on the second floor near the escalators

Heidelberger's Deli: WDW Shopping Village; near the edge of the parking lot

Ice Cream Parlor: Magic Kingdom; on the east side of Main Street opposite Refreshment Corner

King Stefan's: Magic Kingdom; in Cinderella Castle

Lake Buena Vista Club: WDW Village

Lake Buena Vista Club Snack Bar: WDW Village; at the Lake Buena Vista Club, downstairs from the dining room, near the Pro Shop

Lancer's Inn: Magic Kingdom; in Fantasyland, near The Royal Candy Shoppe

Liberty Tree Tavern: Magic Kingdom; in Liberty Square

Lite Bite: WDW Shopping Village; near Crystal Arts and Toledo Arts

Lunching Pad: Magic Kingdom; in Tomorrowland between the Space Port and Mickey's Mart, opposite the Ticket and Information Booth

Main Street Bakery: Magic Kingdom; on the east

side of Main Street, halfway between the Hub and Town Square

Meadow Trading Post: Fort Wilderness Campground; near the playing fields

The Mile Long Bar: Magic Kingdom; in Frontierland, between Pecos Bill's and the Country Bear Jamboree

Monorail Club Car: Contemporary Resort; on the east side of the Grand Canyon Concourse (fourth floor), near the elevators

Outer Rim: Contemporary Resort; on the east side of the Grand Canyon Concourse (fourth floor)

Papeete Bay Verandah: Polynesian Village; second floor of the Great Ceremonial House

Pecos Bill's Cafe: Magic Kingdom; near the Walt Disney World Railroad's Frontierland depot

Pinocchio Village Haus: Magic Kingdom; in Fantasyland, adjoining It's A Small World

Player's Gallery: Golf Resort; adjacent to the Trophy Room on the main floor

Plaza Pavilion: Magic Kingdom; east of the Plaza Restaurant, on the edge of Tomorrowland (considered part of Main Street)

Plaza Restaurant: Magic Kingdom; on Main Street around the corner from Ice Cream Parlor

Pop's Place: Fort Wilderness Campground; inside River Country

Promenade Lounge: WDW Shopping Village; on the Promenade Deck of the *Empress Lilly*

Pueblo Room: Contemporary Resort; south end of the Grand Canyon Concourse (fourth floor)

Refreshment Corner: Magic Kingdom; on the west side of Main Street, opposite Ice Cream Parlor

Round Table: Magic Kingdom; in Fantasyland near Cinderella's Golden Carrousel

Sand Bar: Contemporary Resort; in the Marina Pavilion near the beach

Sand Trap: Golf Resort; downstairs next to the Pro Shop

Settlement Trading Post: Fort Wilderness Campground; near the Fort Wilderness marina and Pioneer Hall

Sleepy Hollow: Magic Kingdom; in Liberty Square, opposite Olde World Antiques

South Seas Dining Room: Polynesian Village; on the west side of the second floor of the Great Ceremonial House

Space Bar: Magic Kingdom; at the base of the StarJets in the center of Tomorrowland

Starboard Lounge: WDW Shopping Village; on the Main Deck of the *Empress Lilly*

Station Break: Magic Kingdom; underneath the Walt Disney World Railroad's Main Street depot

Steerman's Quarters: WDW Shopping Village; aboard the *Empress Lilly*

Sunshine Tree Terrace: Magic Kingdom; in Adventureland, adjoining the Enchanted Tiki Room

Tambu Lounge: Polynesian Village; adjoining Papeete Bay, on the second floor of the Great Ceremonial House

Tangaroa Snack Isle: Polynesian Village; in a separate building near the east swimming pool

Tangaroa Terrace: Polynesian Village; in a separate building on the eastern edge of the property

Terrace Buffeteria: Contemporary Resort; on the Grand Canyon Concourse (fourth floor) immediately to the right of the elevators

Terrace Cafe: Contemporary Resort; adjoining the Terrace Buffeteria

Tomorrowland Terrace: Magic Kingdom; at the Fantasyland edge of Tomorrowland, opposite the Grand Prix Raceway

Top of the World: Contemporary Resort; on the 15th floor

Tournament Tent: Magic Kingdom; in Fantasyland, near the Fantasyland Theater

Town Square Cafe: Magic Kingdom; east side of Town Square at the south end of Main Street

Trail's End Cafe: Fort Wilderness Campground; in Pioneer Hall

Trophy Room: Golf Resort; off the lobby

Troubadour Tavern: Magic Kingdom; in Fantasyland, west of Cinderella's Golden Carrousel next to Peter Pan's flight

Veranda Juice Bar: Magic Kingdom; in Adventureland, adjoining the Adventureland Veranda on the west

Verandah Restaurant: WDW Shopping Village

Village Lounge: WDW Shopping Village; next to the Village Restaurant

Village Pavilion Ice Cream Fountain: WDW Shopping Village; next to the Verandah Restaurant

Village Restaurant: WDW Shopping Village; on the shores of Buena Vista Lagoon

WHERE TO EAT, WHEREVER YOU ARE

You're at the Contemporary Resort, looking for a good meal. Or in the Magic Kingdom, and simply starved. Or you're at Walt Disney World Shopping Village, and you want to know where to get good fresh fish. The following pages are designed to help you zero in, wherever you are, on the nearest eating spot that will best suit your mood.

Even if you can't bring yourself to leave the Magic Kingdom for so much as an hour, you still have a fine choice of restaurants, each with a character all its own. Here we describe each one, land by land. The letters that conclude each restaurant entry are a key to the meals served there: breakfast (B), lunch (L), dinner (D), or snacks (S).

MAIN STREET

WAITRESS SERVICE

Town Square Cafe: This is one of the best bets for Magic Kingdom meals. The lunch and dinner menus offer simple baked chicken, beef stew, and chopped sirloin, plus a chef's salad and a variety of straightforward sandwiches, such as chicken or tuna salad, ham and cheese, and a delicious concoction known as a Monte Cristo—a batter-dipped, deep-fried turkey, ham, and Swiss cheese sandwich. For dessert: German chocolate cake or crepes angelica—pancakes filled with coconut cream and topped with vanilla ice cream, strawberry melba sauce, and shredded coconut. Patterned after a well-known New Orleans restaurant, the setting here is genteelly Victorian, with plenty of polished brass and curlicued, beautifully painted woodwork. The terrazzo-floored patio gives diners a fine view over the action in Town Square. A special children's menu is available.

Full breakfasts are also served: eggs, pancakes, waffles, cold cereals (with skim milk on request), biscuits, Danish pastry, and bacon, sausages, and smoked ham. B, L, D.

Plaza Restaurant: This airy, many-windowed establishment, around the corner from the Ice Cream Parlor, is done in mirrors with sinuously curved Art Nouveau frames. The menu offers lasagna, spaghetti, a turkey casserole, chef's salad, and thick sandwiches—plus milk shakes, floats, and the biggest, gooeyest sundaes in the Magic Kingdom. Café mocha, which combines chocolate and coffee, is another specialty. L, D, S.

CAFETERIA SERVICE

Crystal Palace: One of the Magic Kingdom's landmarks, and its only cafeteria. Modeled after a similar structure that once stood in New York State and after another that still graces San Francisco's Golden Gate Park, it serves standard cafeteria fare. There are stuffed peppers and fried fish, barbecued chicken dishes, assorted casseroles, and healthy-looking salads. Jell-O and cottage cheese and an assortment of tempting pies and cakes are also available.

This is civilized fare, and the fact that it's here at all is just more proof—as if any were needed—that the Magic Kingdom is not just for kids. The place is huge but not overwhelming, because the tables are well-spaced throughout a variety of nooks and crannies. Tables in the front look out onto flower beds and the passing throng beyond, while those at the east end have views into a secluded courtyard.

Not long ago, songbirds used to fly into the structure as guests came through the doors—and then became so lost they couldn't get out. Keen observers, looking carefully into the topmost reaches of the

tallest dome will see the remedy—an owl, still and brooding to all appearances, but actually a stuffed incarnation of the songbird's natural enemy. Its presence has far reduced the avian traffic through the dining area.

The Crystal Palace is also one of the few spots in the Magic Kingdom to serve full breakfasts—scrambled eggs and hashed brown potatoes, biscuits, sausage, bacon, ham, hotcakes, Danish pastry, and cold cereal. B, L, D, S.

FAST FOOD

Refreshment Corner: The small, round tables at this spacious, old-fashioned, red-and-white stop on the west side of Main Street (located near the Crystal Palace) spill out onto the sidewalk. Except when the weather is terrifically hot, it's a delightful spot for fast food—hot dogs (regular and jumbo sizes), brownies, and soft drinks. Old time Coca-Cola ads cover the walls, and during busy periods a pianist is on hand to plink away on the restaurant's white upright. L, D, S.

Plaza Pavilion: Just east of the Plaza Restaurant, this sleek pink-and-purple-and-orange spot on the edge of Tomorrowland serves hamburgers, hot dogs, fried chicken, and soft drinks. Everything comes with a side order of French fries and raisins. During the dinner hour in the summer, barbecued ribs are also available. Some particularly pleasant tables look past the graceful willow trees nearby, toward the Hub Waterways and an impressive topiary sea serpent. L, D, S.

SNACK SPOTS

Main Street Bakery: This genteel little tearoom, with its small, round tables and wire-backed ice-cream parlor chairs, is a good place for a light breakfast, a midmorning coffee break, or a mid-afternoon rest stop. Pound cake, pecan coffee cake, crumb cake, blueberry Danish, chocolate and strawberry cream layer cakes, cheesecake, and a variety of other Sara Lee–made sweets are the temptations. B, S.

Ice Cream Parlor: Ice cream freaks from all over the country converge on this corner of the Kingdom, which boasts the World's best variety of ice cream flavors—six in all: vanilla, peppermint, chocolate, strawberry, butter pecan, and orange sherbet. Containers of ice cream (to go) are available, in addition to cones by the scoop. Alas, no sugar cones.

Station Break: Located underneath the Main Street train station, this refreshment stand is especially good for grabbing coffee and a piece of Danish pastry in the morning on the way into the park—or for picking up a ham and cheese sandwich, potato chips, and a soft drink to munch on at nearby tables. The atmosphere is hardly noteworthy, but waiting time is nearly nil. B, L, D.

ADVENTURELAND

FAST FOOD

Adventureland Veranda: Bougainvillea cascades over the edges of a red tiled roof that looks as if it came straight out of the tropics. Tables are clustered outside on a small patio and inside under slowly rotating fans hung from mahogany ceilings. Off to the east end of this pretty, sprawling restaurant are a couple of open-air patios with views of Cinderella Castle. Screened from the gazes of passersby, these are among the most delightful meal sites in all the Magic Kingdom. The tropical fruit salads, served with mounds of cottage cheese, are just as successful. Also available are special Adventureland Veranda quarter-pound hamburgers, doused with teriyaki sauce, topped with a pineapple ring, and served with French fries and applesauce on the side. Chinese pepper steak and other Americanized versions of Oriental specialties also have their fans. Cornstarch is heavily used, and the chefs occasionally stir-fry the vegetables into sogginess. For dessert: Key lime and pecan pies, apple turnovers, and banana nut rolls.

Note that waiting lines here usually take about five minutes longer than those of similar length in other fast-food establishments, because of the greater number of choices. L, D, S.

SNACK SPOTS

Veranda Juice Bar: Adjoining the Adventureland Veranda (on the west), this refreshment stand sells corn dogs, brownies, potato chips, frozen bananas, ice-cream bars, and a fairly tasty piña-colada punch, among other offerings. B, L, D, S.

El Pirata Y el Perico: In English, the Spanish name of this snack stand, directly across from Pirates of the Caribbean (outside La Princesa de Cristal), means The Pirate and the Parrot. The offerings: ham and cheese submarine sandwiches, hot dogs, burritos, hot pretzels, brownies, and ice-cream bars. L, S.

The Oasis: Tucked away near the Jungle Cruise. Soft drinks and, in busy periods, light sandwiches. L, S.

Sunshine Tree Terrace: So close to the Tropical Serenade (Enchanted Tiki Birds) that you can hear the AudioAnimatronic parrot Jose squawking his spiel. Offerings here are some of the tastiest in the Kingdom: orange and grapefruit juices, orange slush, orange-Danish pastry, orange cheesecake and, in winter, hot citrus-flavored tea, not to mention the excellent citrus swirl—soft-serve ice cream swirled through with a not-too-sweet frozen-orange-juice concentrate. B, S.

FRONTIERLAND

WAITRESS SERVICE

Diamond Horseshoe: Several times daily, from about noon until early evening, a troupe of singers and dancers presents a sometimes corny, occasion- ally sidesplitting, always entertaining show in this Wild West dance-hall saloon. Waitresses serve pota- to and corn chips, freshly baked pie, fruit punch, and cold sandwiches before the show begins. Reserva- tions are required, and they're hard to come by. They must be made in person, and you can't count on getting them if you arrive much more than an hour after the Magic Kingdom opens. Those who miss the deadline can line up for possible cancellations, but with little hope of success except on days when the weather is so bad that some visitors depart early. L, S.

FAST FOOD

Pecos Bill's Cafe: This is not one of those Magic Kingdom eateries that is tucked away so that only those who look will find it. Sooner or later, almost every guest passing from Adventureland into Fron- tierland—ambling by the Frontierland depot of the Walt Disney World Railroad on the way to Big Thun- der or the Country Bear Jamboree—walks by Pecos Bill's. And, as a sidewalk cafe, this establishment— fitted out with leather-seated chairs, ceilings made of twigs, and red tile floors—has few peers. There are tables indoors (in cozy, air-conditioned rooms) and outdoors, under umbrellas and in an open-air court- yard. Hamburgers, cheeseburgers, and hot dogs are the staples. L, D, S.

The Mile Long Bar: The bar, a gleaming and intricately detailed beauty with a brass rail on which to lean and a set of antlers above, just goes on and on, or so it seems at first glance. Actually, it's the mirrors at either end that produce the effect that gives this relatively small refreshment stand its name. Three shaggy animal heads hang on the walls, in keeping with the Wild West theme. Guests who stand around long enough will see one animal turn to another and wink, for these are AudioAnima- tronic figures just like the ones on the walls at the Country Bear Jamboree. The fare, usually the same as at Pecos Bill's, which shares a kitchen and some eating space, is as basic as the decor is intriguing. Definitely worth a peek. B, L, D, S.

Aunt Polly's: The much-trumpeted sense of get- ting-away-from-it-all that islands always convey comes home once again out on Frontierland's Tom Sawyer Island. Though only a couple of minutes' ride across the Rivers of America via the Tom Sawyer Island Rafts, this landfall manages to seem remote even when there are dozens of youngsters clamoring through its caves, over its hills, and across its rickety barrel bridges. Therein lies the charm of Aunt Polly's. While the adults in a party get some well-needed R&R sipping lemonade in the shade of the old- fashioned porch and watching the gleaming white riverboats docking or chugging by, the kids can go out exploring and, at nearby Fort Sam Clemens, ping the toy rifles perched on the gunholes as if there were no tomorrow—an activity as delightful for youngsters as it is dispensable for grown-ups. It doesn't even matter that Aunt Polly's offers a selec- tion barely wider than the fare that that lady might have served her youthful nephew—shaved turkey, peanut-butter-and-jelly, and submarine sandwiches, Key lime and apple pies, cookies, iced tea, lemonade, and soda. An excellent choice for lunch. L, S.

SNACK SPOTS

Fort Sam Clemens: Also on Tom Sawyer Island. Brownies, soft-serve ice cream, orange and grape juices, and orange slush are available. S.

LIBERTY SQUARE

WAITRESS SERVICE

Liberty Tree Tavern: At this pillared and portico'd eatery opposite the riverboat landing, the floors are made of wide oak planks, the wallpaper looks as if it might have come from Williamsburg, the curtains hang from cloth loops, and the venetian blinds are made of wood. Pieces of pewter and Windsor and ladder-backed chairs are scattered throughout the premises, there's a spinning wheel and a hope chest in the waiting room, and an old-fashioned writing desk and a cradle, copper bowls, and tea kettles arranged near the wide fireplace. The window glass was made using eighteenth-century casting methods, and most of the tables and chairs were mass-produced (for sturdiness's sake). So the Liberty Tree Tavern's charm is not of a mismatched and random type.

At lunch, the staples are oversized salads and entrées such as pot roast, beef stew, and open-faced turkey sandwiches with cranberry relish; for dessert, there's apple cobbler, brown Betty, and pumpkin and pecan pies. The menu is similar, if a bit fancier, at dinnertime, when reservations are accepted. Walnut bread, Philadelphia pepper-pot soup, and New England clam chowder are served at both meals. L, D.

FAST FOOD

Columbia Harbour House: This is a fast-food fish house with some class. Though the fish has been frozen and is only served fried, good cornbread muffins and corn chowder are also available, and there are enough antiques and other knickknacks decking the halls to raise this place, located near the Liberty Square entrance to Fantasyland, above the ordinary. Model ships, copper measures, harpoons, and nautical instruments, and little tie-back curtains, small-print wallpaper, and low-beamed ceilings give the place a cozy air—despite its size. L, D, S.

SNACK SPOTS

Fife and Drum: Located in the peaceful nook behind the Silversmith Shop, this refreshment stand offers soft drinks, potato chips, soft-serve ice cream, Coke floats—and gooey sundaes topped with chocolate, pineapple, or strawberry sauce, plus plenty of whipped cream and walnuts. S.

Sleepy Hollow: Pretzels, Danish pastry, iced tea, soft drinks, Toll House chocolate-chip cookies, and a special Legendary Punch (fruity and not half bad) are for sale at this snack stand located opposite Olde World Antiques, near the Liberty Square bridge. In peak season, submarine and ham and cheese sandwiches are also served here. You can eat on a secluded brick patio outside. B, L, D, S.

FANTASYLAND

WAITRESS SERVICE

King Stefan's Banquet Hall: The hostesses at this establishment (named for Sleeping Beauty's father) wear thirteenth-century-style French headdresses and long medieval gowns with over-skirts. The hall itself is high-ceilinged and as majestic as the old mead hall it is supposed to represent. The delightful cold-vegetable salad and the casseroles on the noontime menu—seafood Newburg, fried chicken, and beef stew—make lunch here pleasant indeed. At dinner, there's roast beef, baked snapper, and chicken with broccoli in a Mornay sauce. However, the crepes offered for dessert (included with the meal) are not going to win any prizes. Spend your calories on a sundae at the Round Table instead. Children's portions are readily available for most entrées at reduced prices.

Reservations are required for both lunch and dinner. To make them, present yourself at the Castle door as soon after arriving in the Magic Kingdom as possible. L, D.

FAST FOOD

Pinocchio Village Haus: This is another of those Magic Kingdom restaurants that seems a lot smaller from the outside than it really is, thanks to a labyrinthine arrangement of a half dozen rooms decorated with antique cuckoo clocks, European tile-fronted ovens, oak peasant chairs, and murals depicting characters from Pinocchio's story—Figaro the Cat, Cleo the Goldfish, Monstra the Whale, and Gepetto, the puppet's creator. The menu offers a special hamburger topped with smoked ham and melted cheese (especially tasty with a bit of mayonnaise), plus fried chicken with French fries and raisins on the side, and plain hamburgers, cheeseburgers, and hot dogs. For dessert: apple turnovers and Key lime and pecan pies. Danish pastries are also available. B, L, D, S.

PIZZA

Lancer's Inn: This is the only place in the Magic Kingdom that serves pizza (although Tomorrowland Terrace has a pizza-like sandwich called Galactic Pizza); it can be ordered with pepperoni or plain cheese. Weight watchers and other light lunchers should note that a chef's salad is also available. For dessert, Key lime and apple pies are available, though the ice-cream specialties at the Tournament Tent and the Round Table (below) can be pretty irresistible. L, D, S.

SNACKS

Troubadour Tavern: Frozen-orange-juice bars, pink lemonade, a special sweet fruit concoction called Fantasyland Punch, and hot chocolate are available at this small refreshment stand west of Cinderella's Golden Carrousel. S.

The Round Table: Ice cream gets top billing here—soft-serve cones in chocolate, vanilla, and chocolate-vanilla swirl; sundaes topped with chocolate, strawberry, or blueberry sauce; floats in root beer or piled high atop rich, frosted brownies. S.

Tournament Tent: Hungry folk can buy ham and cheese subs, Fritos, lemon or strawberry slushes, fruit punch, and the strawberry swirl—soft-serve ice cream swirled through with sweet, strawberry-flavored slush. L, D, S.

TOMORROWLAND

FAST FOOD

Tomorrowland Terrace: The largest fast-food spot in the Magic Kingdom, where the menu is (for the most part) refreshingly familiar—hamburgers single and double, plain or with sauce and cheese, plus hot dogs and submarine sandwiches. The names of the specialties remind you that this sprawling establishment is in Tomorrowland—the Orbit Burger, the Gemini Burger, the Moon Burger. But like almost all the Disney eating spots, this one has something beside its burgers' names to set it apart from its fellows—that is, its Galactic Pizzas (thick slices of sourdough bread topped with pizza sauce, ground beef, pepperoni, and cheese); its chef's salads and fruit salads; and Michael Iceberg, a wizard of an entertainer who sits behind a battery of electronic musical instruments on a small stage (like a mad scientist) and plays music that is by turns tuneful and discordant, merry and mournful, sweetly melodic and outrageously pop, as he runs through a repertoire of facial expressions almost as varied. Since Iceberg performs several times daily, it's worthwhile to stop in. Inquire at City Hall, on the way into the park, for his performance times. L, D, S.

The Lunching Pad: This small spot between the Space Port and Mickey's Mart, near the Tomorrowland Information and Ticket Booth, serves some of the Magic Kingdom's best lunches—tuna-salad sandwiches, tuna- or egg-salad-stuffed tomatoes, and cheese platters. Its two lines seem to move slowly even when the people behind the counter are working at top speed, but the carob brownies, date-nut cookies, packs of almonds, raisins, and trail mix, apple and orange juice, diet sodas, frozen-yogurt cups, floats, and sundaes are well worth the extra wait. L, S.

SNACKS

WEDway Space Bar: Located at the base of the Star Jets in the center of Tomorrowland's vast concrete plaza, this small spot offers turkey and ham and Swiss cheese submarine sandwiches, plus apple turnovers, Key lime pie, and a variety of punches and soft drinks. No menu item stands out, and the place never seems too busy. S.

A WORD TO THE WISE

Ride Space Mountain *before* eating, not afterward. The trip can jostle even the strongest stomachs.

VENDORS

Throughout the Magic Kingdom, there are ice-cream wagons that sell ice-cream bars, ice-cream sandwiches, Mouse Bars, and three especially wonderful frozen treats—orange-juice bars, grape-juice bars, and frozen chocolate-covered bananas, invented by a Disney employee.

Popcorn wagons all over the park contribute their lovely aromas all day long.

MEALTIME TIPS

• The hours from 11 A.M. to 2 P.M., and again from about 5 to 7 P.M., are the mealtime rush hours in Magic Kingdom restaurants. Eat earlier or later whenever possible.

• When a restaurant has more than one food-service window, don't just amble into the nearest queue. Instead, inspect them all, because the one farthest from a doorway occasionally will be almost wait-free.

• Lines at the Adventureland Veranda don't move as quickly as those at most other fast-food eateries.

• Sit-down restaurants offering full-scale meals are usually less crowded at lunch than they are at dinner.

• To avoid queues, eat at a restaurant that offers reservations—King Stefan's at both lunch and dinner; the Diamond Horseshoe, a western-style saloon in Frontierland which serves cold sandwiches and presents an amusing show at lunchtime; and Liberty Square's Liberty Tree Tavern at dinnertime. Reservations are available in person on the day of the meal; book them as soon as you arrive in the Magic Kingdom.

WHERE TO STAY ON A DIET IN THE MAGIC KINGDOM

Dieters need not abandon all restraint for want of suitable foodstuffs in the Magic Kingdom. A number of restaurants offer foods that are suitable for a variety of diets. All are open for lunch and dinner.

Main Street: Crystal Palace, Town Square Cafe, Plaza Restaurant
Adventureland: Adventureland Veranda
Liberty Square: Liberty Tree Tavern
Fantasyland: King Stefan's
Tomorrowland: Lunching Pad, Tomorrowland Terrace

IN THE HOTELS

The letters following each restaurant's description indicate which meal may be enjoyed there: breakfast (B), lunch (L), dinner (D), or a snack (S).

CONTEMPORARY RESORT

Most of the hotel's restaurants are located on the Grand Canyon Concourse on the fourth floor, but there are also restaurants on the second and fifteenth floors, and snack spots by the marina and in the first-floor Fiesta Fun Center.

Terrace Buffeteria: On the Grand Canyon Concourse, this establishment opens at 7 A.M. and closes at midnight daily. Omelets and other egg dishes, grits and biscuits, cereal and French toast are served at breakfast, and fried chicken, baked fish, meat loaf, and assorted soups, salads, and sandwiches at lunch and dinner, when prime ribs are also available. B, L, D, S.

Terrace Cafe: On the Grand Canyon Concourse. Serves a bountiful, all-you-can-eat Italian buffet—one of the World's best buys—every evening. No reservations. B, D.

Pueblo Room: On the Grand Concourse, tucked away behind Coconino Cove, and quieter than other Grand Concourse eating spots. At breakfast, the roster of fairly standard offerings includes a fruit-and-cottage-cheese platter with Boston brown bread on the side and a low-cholesterol meal featuring cholesterol-free egg substitutes. At lunch, choose from salads, hearty sandwiches, and hamburgers with a choice of seven toppings. Dinners feature tossed greens and an assortment of fairly straightforward meat, chicken, and seafood dishes, among them prime ribs, veal cordon bleu, jumbo shrimp in garlic-lemon butter, red snapper, roast duckling with a Bing cherry sauce, and chicken Mornay. Children's portions are available at lunch, and there's a special children's menu at dinner. No reservations. B, L, D.

Outer Rim: On the Grand Canyon Concourse, opposite the Terrace Cafe, with a good view over Bay Lake. Dinner includes chicken cordon bleu, prime ribs, and shrimp in garlic-lemon butter and white wine. Children's portions are available for youngsters under twelve. No reservations. D.

Gulf Coast Room: One of the most elegant of Walt Disney World's continental restaurants, with a subdued, relaxed atmosphere that seems worlds away from the bustling Grand Canyon Concourse and the congestion of the elevator lobbies. Grilled lamp chops, New York strip steaks with herb butter, seafood en brochette, sautéed red snapper, and veal marsala are specialties of the house. There are delicious flambéed coffees for *après*. Carlos, the strolling guitarist, plays just about any song a guest may request. Children who don't delight in the leisurely pace of the service can be dispatched to the Fiesta Fun Center Snack Bar. Reservations are suggested; phone 824-1000, ext. 3684. D.

Top of the World: This view-filled room on the hotel's fifteenth floor offers bountiful, all-you-can-eat buffets for breakfast, lunch, and brunch on Sunday; dinner shows feature top-name entertainment at 6:30 and 9:45 P.M. nightly. The setting, with excellent views of the Magic Kingdom, is one of the best in the World. After dark, the golden spires of Cinderella Castle glitter under floodlights, and the white lights edging the rooflines of Main Street wink and twinkle like distant fireflies. Reservations are required for the dinner shows and Sunday brunch; phone the WDW Central Reservations Office at 824-8000. B, L, D.

Fiesta Fun Center Snack Bar: On the first floor, this snack bar serves light fare around the clock. B, L, D, S.

Dock Inn: Submarines, ham and cheese sandwiches, hot dogs, frozen-juice bars, frozen bananas, and ice-cream bars are the stock-in-trade at this stand at the marina behind the hotel. B, L, D, S.

THE POLYNESIAN VILLAGE

Some of WDW's more interesting eating spots are located here.

South Seas Dining Room: Dinner is served buffet style in this smallish room; roast beef and roast pork, Oriental-Polynesian dishes, vegetables, and salad fixings are standard offerings. D.

Papeete Bay Verandah: Serves sit-down dinners daily, breakfast and lunch buffets Monday through Saturday, and a copious brunch buffet on Sunday. The breakfast buffet features all sorts of fresh fruit, apple crepes, grits, and smoked fish. The hot-and-cold lunch buffet is a favorite; one highlight is the coconut-spiked rice pudding for dessert. The kabobs, prime ribs, and red snapper are the best choices for dinner, but more adventurous diners may be tempted by some of the Polynesian-style offerings. Among the appetizers are scallops marinated in coconut milk, with a touch of horseradish and sour cream; shrimp, kingfish, spinach, and cabbage steamed in ti leaves; and thin salted salmon fillets seasoned with lemon, scallions, and tomatoes. Main courses include Pua'a (pork loin seasoned and rolled in crushed peanuts and served with a fried banana), chicken pago-pago (a marinated chicken breast glazed with a honeyed sesame sauce and served in a pineapple half), almond duck tempura (a crispy boneless duck), or Laulua pig and prawns (pork fillet and prawns stuffed with cheddar cheese and crab meat, served with shrimp fried rice). The Papeete Lovo includes a selection of several of the more popular entrées. For dessert, the menu offers poached pear marinated in apricot brandy and served with a strawberry cream sauce; macadamia-nut pie with passion-fruit ice cream; rum-flavored banana-rice pudding served in a fresh coconut; and melon balls and lime sherbet doused with coconut milk. The room itself is large and open and offers fine views across the Seven Seas Lagoon all the way to Cinderella Castle. After dark, Polynesian dancers and a small combo entertain quietly. Reservations, available for all meals, are requested for dinner; phone 824-5494. B, L, D.

Coral Isle Cafe: On the second floor of the Great Ceremonial House, around the corner from Papeete Bay. This standard coffee shop with faintly South Seas decor serves the usual assortment of eggs every morning (including an interesting shrimp-and-cheese-stuffed omelet), plus granola and other cereals, and wonderful banana-stuffed French toast, one of the best of all Walt Disney World dishes. At lunch and dinner, the house does a booming business in big fruit salads, shrimp and crab-meat salads, chef's salads, and a variety of sandwiches. The assortment of hot entrées is expanded during the evening hours. Drinks, including the special Polynesian concoctions served at the Tambu Lounge, are available. A good choice when you want a no-fuss meal. B, L, D, S.

Tangaroa Terrace: This sprawling establishment, on the eastern edge of the property near the Oahu longhouse, has never been as heavily patronized as some of the other Polynesian Village restaurants because of its somewhat remote location. Increas-ingly, however, the word is spreading about its star breakfast offering, banana-stuffed French toast made with sourdough bread (eggs and other more usual breakfast selections also are available), and its dinners of prime ribs, steak, snapper, fried chicken, and a variety of more exotic entrées in an Oriental mode—sautéed pork fillets topped with mushrooms and pea pods, teriyaki steak, stir-fried shrimp and vegetables, and macadamia-nut duckling. Reservations are a good idea at dinner; phone 824-2000. B, D.

Barefoot Snack Bar: A good spot for Continental breakfasts, hamburgers, hot dogs, ham and cheese sandwiches, fruit salads, and snacks; beer in cans is also available. The most unusual specialty: coconut hot dogs. L, D, S.

Tangaroa Snack Isle: Most guests discover this snack bar on their way to Tangaroa Terrace, the game room, or the East Pool, to which it is extremely convenient. Hamburgers and hot dogs, a variety of submarine sandwiches, chef's and fruit salads, and light snacks like yogurt and ice-cream cones are all available. Canned beer is sold here, as well. L, D, S.

THE GOLF RESORT

The sleek, contemporarily styled **Trophy Room**, the hotel's single full-service restaurant, also ranks among the most pleasant spots in the World for a meal. Many Disney executives come here for lunch because even when there are lines at the Polynesian Village and the Contemporary Resort, the Trophy Room is fairly quiet. Also, the food is quite good. At breakfast and lunch, there are immense all-you-can-eat buffets; in season, the noontime spread features oysters on the half shell. At dinner, crab claws and shrimp cocktail are among the appetizers, as well as a platter piled with French-fried artichoke hearts, mushrooms, and cheddar cheese. Entrées include steaks, prime ribs, duck in a peach-brandy sauce, chicken breast, pork tenderloin, seafood platters, and red snapper. French-fried ice cream, served on a peach half with a vanilla sauce, is offered both at lunch (on the à la carte menu) and at dinner; it's truly scrumptious. At the Sunday brunch buffets you can choose, as an eye-opener, a Bloody Mary or a glass of champagne. Reservations are suggested; phone 824-2200, ext. 1484. B, L, D, S.

For snacks, there's the **Sand Trap** poolside. L, D, S.

FORT WILDERNESS CAMPGROUND

Most people cook their own meals; supplies are available at the Meadow and Settlement Trading Posts (open from 8 A.M. to 10 P.M. in winter, to 11 P.M. in summer). Deli-style sandwiches can be concocted there for carrying-out; you can eat them at your own campsite, on the beach, or at tables just outside River Country.

Trail's End Cafe: This informal, log-walled, beam-ceilinged cafeteria offers standard breakfasts (plus grits, biscuits and gravy, and bread pudding) every morning; and, during the rest of the day, hearty lunches and dinners featuring barbecued chicken, fish, chicken pot pie, turkey à la King, franks and beans, spare ribs, steaks, lasagna, and more. Carved entrées such as prime ribs, glazed ham, and roast turkey are also available. Specially priced children's portions are available. Pizza is served every night from 9 P.M. until 12:30 A.M. Beer and sangría are available by the glass or by the pitcher. B, L, D, S.

Campfire Snack Bar: Hot dogs, chili dogs, hamburgers and cheeseburgers, French fries, chili and beans, soft drinks, lemonade, beer, and sangría are among the offerings. L, D, S.

Beach Shack: Located near the Bay Lake beach. Ham and cheese subs, potato chips and Fritos, ice-cream bars and sandwiches, grape- and orange-juice bars, and frozen bananas are available. Among the potables are sarsaparilla to sip and beer to tipple. L, D, S.

WDW VILLAGE

Some of the World's best restaurants are located in this enclave on the southeastern edge of the property—in the Lake Buena Vista Club, which has its own restaurant and a snack bar, and many more in the Shopping Village scattered among the boutiques, and nearby aboard the gleaming *Empress Lilly* riverboat restaurant. It's worth noting that while the restaurants hereabouts really hop at dinnertime, none is terribly crowded at lunch, except on Saturdays and Sundays when Orlando and Kissimmee residents make the trip to WDW Village for a day of shopping. And these restaurants have the added advantage of being just a couple of hundred yards' dash from the marina; so that kids can go off and hire a pedal boat or a Water Sprite (at least during lunchtime and in late afternoon) while parents linger over coffee or drinks. The letters following the restaurant descriptions indicate the meals served: breakfasts (B), lunches (L), dinners (D), or snacks (S).

Verandah Restaurant: This airy, gardenlike establishment serves three meals a day. There's the usual range of egg dishes at breakfast, and oversized sandwiches and salads, barbecued pork, oysters en brochette, patty melts, burgers, omelets with bean sprouts, chicken, ham, and similar fare at lunch. Prime ribs, beef Wellington, seafood platters, and veal Parmesan are staples at dinnertime. The list of ice-cream specialties is so varied that a separate menu is devoted solely to them; if all that's wanted is something simple, you can drop into the Cone Shop next door for a scoop to lick as you're window-shopping your way through the village—or back to your car. B, L, D, S.

Cap'n Jack's Oyster Bar: The menu at this waterside spot is so full of good things—seafood marinara, stuffed clams, ceviche (marinated raw fish), crab claws, clams and oysters on the half shell, and delicious smoked kingfish with guacamole—that it's as terrific for a light lunch or dinner as it is for a snack, even though the place is nominally a bar. Cap'n Jack's is a terrific place to be, especially in late afternoon, as the sun streams through the narrow-slatted blinds and glints on the polished tables and the copper above the bar. And the house's special frozen strawberry margaritas—made with fresh fruit, strawberry tequila, and a couple of other potent ingredients—are as tasty as they are beautiful. They're served in big balloon-shaped goblets, with a slice of lime astraddle the rim: tart, slightly fruity, and altogether delightful. L, D, S.

Heidelberger's Deli: This is the best sandwich spot in the World, though it's not likely to fully satisfy delicatessen devotees from Los Angeles or New York. Four different kinds of breads and five types of rolls are offered, not to mention a whole case of meats, cheeses, and other fillings. Every sandwich comes with a choice of potato salad, cole slaw, baked beans, sauerkraut, applesauce, cottage cheese, or cucumber salad, and imported and domestic beers (as well as soft drinks) are available. But the food doesn't quite measure up to the setting—a large, lofty-ceilinged room with a terra-cotta tile floor and a delightful outdoor terrace framed in crinkly-blossomed crepe myrtle trees. Though the Florida weather is a bit too hot to make al fresco dining very much fun in summer, the terrace is a real pleasure in other seasons. L, D, S.

Lite Bite: This is the shopping area's fast-food spot, serving hamburgers, hot dogs, and assorted soft drinks to eat inside or out. L, D, S.

Village Restaurant: This unassuming dining room is one of the most pleasant restaurants in Walt Disney World. Not pretentious in any way, it never disappoints, and it's well worth the wait that is usually necessary because it doesn't take reservations. There are fine views over Buena Vista Lagoon, and the sunshine that streams through the windows keeps a whole garden's worth of house plants robust and green all year. Fresh fish is usually available here, even when you can't get it elsewhere in the World. At lunch, the menu offers shellfish salads, eggs Benedict, quiche, and an interesting omelet stuffed with crab and artichoke hearts, as well as a selection of terrific sandwiches and soups. Adjoining the Village Restaurant is the living room–like Village Lounge. Fitted out with comfortable low sofas and club chairs, it presents the kind of top-name jazz performers who don't usually venture far away from big cities. Music students from nearby colleges used to come in droves before a modest minimum per-set charge (about $2.50) was levied not long ago. A great spot for after-dinner drinks. Valet parking is available near the restaurant. L, D.

Lake Buena Vista Club: The menu at this coolly elegant, country club–like establishment is ambitious, even at breakfast, when it offers blueberry crepes with vanilla sauce, omelets, and eggs Florentine (drenched in Hollandaise sauce and served on a bed of spinach atop an English muffin). Interesting fruit and vegetable salads and sandwiches, and entrées featuring pastry shells, crepes, and rich sauces, are available at noon, along with the house's special Gold Brick sundae—vanilla ice cream doused in a scrumptious, crunchy, milk-chocolatey sauce. Both at lunch and dinner, the menu offers onion soup des Halles, a thick, rich Parmesan- and Swiss-cheese-topped broth for which the chef is locally famous. Things are even fancier at dinner, and the Club's Sunday brunch is one of the World's most popular. Reservations are necessary for dinner and brunch; phone 828-3735.

Worth looking into is the special evening package known as *A Night of Wine and Roses*, which features a wine tasting, dinner at the Lake Buena Vista Club, with a bottle of the wine chosen at the tasting, and a cruise on the Buena Vista Lagoon. The cost is $50 per couple; offered Mondays through Thursdays from 6 to 9:30 P.M.; for reservations, which are required, phone 828-3735. B, L, D.

Lake Buena Vista Club Snack Bar: The only breakfast fare is coffee and pastries; otherwise hot dogs, subs, and other snacks are available. L, D, S.

ABOARD THE EMPRESS LILLY

Named after Walt Disney's wife, this 220-foot-long Disney version of the stern-wheelers that plied the rivers of America during the nineteenth century rises gleaming and white at the west edge of the Buena Vista Lagoon, ornate as a Victorian ball gown, looking perpetually ready to sail off into the sunset. She really isn't, of course: Permanently moored, she's stacked from bottom to top with restaurants and lounges, and always bursting at the seams with diners and merrymakers having a very good time indeed.

In some very interesting ways, the *Empress* is authentic, however. Like early riverboats, she has tall stacks like those that once allowed the sparks vented from the boiler's fire to cool off before hitting the all-wood deck or the often-flammable cargo. She also has "hog chains" strung between the two slanted poles that extend from the hull through the third deck. (Steamboats were flat-bottomed, with a superstructure light enough to allow them to draw only a few feet of water; the hog chains kept the boat from sagging in the middle from the weight of its cargo, and from "warping" or sinking at the stern from the weight of the heavy engine, boiler, and paddle wheel.) Since the *Empress* represents a cross between an excursion boat and a showboat, she has her share of jigsaw-cut gingerbread trimming, not only on the second story, or Promenade Deck, but also on the first level, the Main Deck. The railings on both decks are elaborate; the posts are turned and then bracketed to create an archway effect.

The hallways and public rooms are full of polished Honduras mahogany, Victorian-style flowered carpets, old-fashioned prints and brass fixtures, and tufted Victorian love seats with damask and velvet upholstery; the curtains are swagged or sheer, each of the restaurants and lounges is a little different. Note that after 11 A.M., "dressy casual" attire (a jacket for men) is required on board. Valet parking is available near the boat.

Fisherman's Deck: This seafood spot on the Forward Promenade Deck has a huge curved expanse of window—180 degrees' worth—and in the afternoon, the sunlight that washes the pale cream-colored tongue-in-groove paneled walls and the blue tufted Victorian side chairs is as remarkable as the food. At lunch, the chefs offer first-class poached salmon; smoked whitefish and salmon; crab meat, shrimp, and avocado salads; sandwiches made with grilled crab meat, cheddar, tomato, and bacon; and fresh snapper. The fried-oyster-and-bacon-stuffed omelet is one of several dishes on the menu that might have been served in nineteenth-century riverboating days. At dinner, shrimp cocktail, oysters en brochette, stone-crab claws with avocado-mustard sauce, snapper, prawns en brochette, and fresh Maine lobster are the specialties; the Empress Delight includes a bit of everything—pompano, oyster and bacon en brochette, and crab meat-stuffed lobster. At both lunch and dinner, there are also limited offerings for meateaters. No reservations are accepted; give your name to the hostess and then wait over drinks in the Promenade Lounge on the starboard Promenade Deck, or the always-lively Baton Rouge Lounge, on the forward Main Deck. Note that Central Florida is big on "fresh frozen" fish; if you prefer yours fresh-fresh, be sure to check the precise chill on that day's offerings before ordering. L, D.

Steerman's Quarters: This ornate Main Deck salon, full of heavy red upholstery and turned mahogany spindles and paneling, is named for the steering gear that would have occupied this area in one of the original stern-wheelers. Meat is the big deal—cold prime ribs with minced horseradish, ground steak in puff pastry, strip steak, beef tenderloin—though oysters on the half shell and shrimp cocktail are available, along with specialty crepes stuffed with seafood in white-wine sauce, or diced chicken in Mornay sauce. At dinner, prime ribs and a half-dozen grilled meats are orderable. While you're waiting for your food, you can sit by a big glass window that seems only inches away from the paddle wheel's gleaming white arms and watch the turning wheel throw off sprays of water. No reservations are accepted; give your name to the hostess and wait in the Promenade Lounge or in the Baton Rouge Lounge. L, D.

The Empress Room: The most amazing thing about this restaurant (located amidship on the Promenade Deck) is not its food (though the menu is Walt Disney World's most ambitious), but the service, the atmosphere, and the Louis XV surroundings—light-painted paneling, damask wallpaper, a shallow-domed ceiling with an Italian brass chandelier glittering with crystal droplets, and, between the tables-for-four along the wall, dividers fitted out with paneling and etched glass. Parts of the elaborate moldings are covered with enough real gold leaf (worth $8,000 when the *Empress* was constructed in 1977) to form a cube measuring 1¾ inches on a side.

The culinary offerings include hot and curried spinach and oyster soup or chilled avocado soup, Bibb lettuce and fresh mushroom salads, country pâté, smoked duck with creamed horseradish, crab meat sautéed in butter with brandy, Dover sole stuffed with salmon mousse and mushrooms and doused with a Vermouth sauce, whole young chicken in a cream-and-cider sauce, and more. The quality of the food preparation is often erratic, and a bit less garlic (and seasonings in general) would keep the cuisine more haute. But this is the most elegant eating place in the World, and its eminence is suggested by the fact that the Empress Room is the only place in WDW where the pats of butter are not embossed with the WDW logo. Not all the fish here is fresh; if this matters to you, be sure to get a status report before ordering. Jackets are required for men, and reservations are a must; they are available to all up to 30 days in advance (828-3900). D.

138

WDW VILLAGE HOTEL PLAZA

At the Dutch Inn: This gleaming white high-rise has two eating spots: the Tulip Cafe, which serves standard cafeteria-style coffee-shop fare around the clock; and The Flying Dutchman, a somewhat fancier and more expensive eating spot that offers an all-you-can-eat buffet at breakfast time, sandwiches and hot entrées at lunch, and Florida and Maine lobsters, steak, veal specialties, and some of the rare fresh fish served in WDW at dinner. B, L, D, S.

At the Howard Johnson's: The restaurant and the adjacent coffee shop here offer the standard HoJo menu in standard HoJo style—food that is reassuringly predictable, if not overwhelmingly tasty, at a speed that brings to mind the old phrase about molasses in winter. The ice cream (the best on the WDW property, and some of the best in Orlando), is worth the wait, however, and it's served 24 hours a day. B, L, D, S.

At the Hotel Royal Plaza: This sprawling resort boats a pleasant (but unremarkable) coffee shop, The Knight's Table, which is open from 7 A.M. until midnight daily—serving pizza from early evening until closing. B, L, D, S.

The ambitious El Cid, decorated in somber reds with plenty of pewter and dark wood (carved in Mediterranean style), offers steak Diane, chateaubriand, rack of lamb, and fresh Maine lobster.

At the TraveLodge: This hotel's family-style restaurant, the Coral Grotto, offers a buffet at both breakfast and lunch, and at dinner gets just a little fancier with prime ribs and crab legs. B, L, D.

Next to the restaurant, Sleepy Bear's Ice Cream Parlor serves sodas, shakes, scoops, and sundaes from late afternoon until midnight. Pizza and hot dogs are also available here. L, D, S.

MEAL BY MEAL

When you're looking for something special in the way of a meal, and you're willing to go a bit out of your way to find it, the descriptions below should provide sufficient suggestions to sate your appetite. What follows are the highlights of WDW breakfasts, lunches, and dinners, as well as some suggestions for avoiding mealtime crowds at the eatery of your choice. This is a selective, not a comprehensive, list; for complete information see the preceding listings under *Where To Eat, Wherever You Are.*

BREAKFAST

WHAT'S SPECIAL

Most people opt for eggs and bacon or something similar at their own hotel. But those who decide to go farther afield will be amazed at the choices available. For instance, the French toast served at the Polynesian Village Resort's **Coral Isle Cafe** and **Tangaroa Terrace**—made with thick slices of real sourdough bread, stuffed with bananas, deep fried, and then rolled in cinnamon and sugar—is one of the best breakfast concoctions ever—even without real maple syrup.

Except during the busiest periods, restaurants in the Magic Kingdom are good choices for quick morning meals. Most fast-food spots serve coffee and Danish pastry from park opening until about 11 A.M.

MISSING THE MASSES

At most breakfast spots in the hotels, there are likely to be lines between 8 and 10 A.M., the morning rush hour. So allow yourself plenty of time at these hours—or eat earlier or later, or stop at a snack shop for something light to stave off hunger until time for a lineless breakfast (or an early lunch). It's also possible to use the long card you'll find hanging from the doorknob of any WDW guest room to order breakfast from Room Service the night before. Be forewarned: ordering from Room Service on the same morning occasionally can mean waiting up to two hours for your food; in any event, don't count on your toast being piping hot.

LUNCH

WHAT'S SPECIAL

Breaking up a day in the Magic Kingdom with lunch at one of the resorts can provide the energy to keep going until closing time. A few of the eating spots do get crowded around midday, but the **Pueblo Room** at the Contemporary Resort and the **Trophy Room** at the Golf Resort are usually particularly peaceful. At the latter, there are usually oysters on the half shell (in season) on the noontime buffet; the house special dessert—French-fried marzipan–coated ice cream,

BREAKFAST WITH DISNEY CHARACTERS

Food takes second place to Donald Duck, Minnie Mouse, Goofy, and the rest of the Disney gang, who take turns making special appearances at these especially delightful breakfast-time affairs. Breakfast à la Disney on the *Empress Lilly* riverboat restaurant at Walt Disney World Village takes place at 9 A.M. daily; the scrambled eggs-and-bacon meal is served banquet style. (To reserve, phone Central Reservations at 824-8000.) The other character breakfast which takes place on Sundays from 8 to 11 A.M. (daily during peak periods) at the **Terrace Cafe** in the Contemporary Resort, features a buffet of eggs and roast beef hash, biscuits and gravy, raisin bread and bread pudding, blueberry muffins, fresh fruit and cheeses, and more. No reservations are necessary. There is also a character breakfast that's part of the Eastern Airlines packages. The Eastern character breakfast is held at the Village Restaurant in Walt Disney World Shopping Village.

SUNDAY BRUNCHES

These grand spreads take over the **Lake Buena Vista Club** (9:30 A.M. to 1:30 P.M.), the Golf Resort's **Trophy Room** (10 A.M. to 3 P.M.), and the **Top of the World** at the Contemporary Resort and the **Papeete Bay Verandah** at the Polynesian Village (both 9 A.M. to 2:30 P.M.) every Sunday. All feature hot dishes along with traditional breakfast fare, fruit, pastries, and complimentary bloody marys and/or champagne. The especially varied Trophy Room buffet often includes oysters on the half shell, seafood Newburg, and quiche Lorraine. Prices range from about $7 to $9 (less for children under 12 and juniors aged 12 to 18). Reserve in advance by calling the individual restaurants: Top of the World (824-1000), Papeete Bay (824-2000), Trophy Room (824-2200, ext. 1484), and the Lake Buena Vista Club (828-3735).

served on a peach half and drizzled with vanilla sauce—is well worth ordering, even though it costs extra. The buffets at **Papeete Bay** in the Polynesian Village and at the **Top of the World** in the Contemporary Resort are also worth a detour. Lunch highlights in Walt Disney World Shopping Village are **Heidelberger's Deli** and **Cap'n Jack's Oyster Bar**. If you can't tear yourself away from the Magic Kingdom for even an hour to go elsewhere for lunch, there's still no lack of selection. Hamburgers and French fries are for sale at practically every turn, and

then there are the Monte Cristos (batter-dipped, deep-fried turkey, ham, and Swiss cheese sandwiches) served at the **Town Square Cafe**, or the vegetable and fruit salads available at the **Crystal Palace**, both on Main Street; the Philadelphia pepper pot soup, clam chowder, and black walnut bread served at the **Liberty Tree Tavern** in Liberty Square; the teriyaki-sauced hamburgers topped with pineapple rings, and fruit salads at the **Adventureland Veranda**; peanut butter and jelly sandwiches at **Aunt Polly's** on Tom Sawyer Island in Frontierland; pizza at **Lancer's Inn** in Fantasyland; and chocolate crepes at **King Stefan's** in Cinderella Castle; and health food at the **Lunching Pad** in Tomorrowland.

MISSING THE MASSES

As at breakfast, crowds can be a problem; the three hours between eleven and two are the busiest. To avoid the rush, eat a light breakfast and a big early lunch—or have a late breakfast and a late lunch. If necessary, snatch a midmorning snack to tide you over until things get less hectic.

Another option (especially during the summer and holiday periods), is to leave the Magic Kingdom altogether for lunch at Walt Disney World Shopping Village or at one of the resort hotels, which are less crowded than the Magic Kingdom at noon.

Except on Saturdays and Sundays, when local residents usually come out to shop, none of the Walt Disney World Shopping Village restaurants are ever horribly crowded at lunchtime.

The hours between 11 A.M. and 2 P.M. in the Magic Kingdom are very busy, however, even though the lines usually move fairly quickly. It's usually far swifter to eat earlier or later. When there are several food service windows operating, evaluate them all before wandering into the nearest queue: Occasionally, the one farthest from the doorway will be almost

A SHIPBOARD LUNCH

Discovery Island is a wonderful diversion and a fine place to escape the Magic Kingdom's often fatiguing afternoon crowds. It's especially pleasant to take a midday sailing of the narrated World Cruise (aboard an authentic side-wheeler). Departures are scheduled on the hour from 10 A.M. to 4 P.M. daily; fare is about $4.

(if not entirely) wait-free. Note that the lines at the **Adventureland Veranda** generally move more slowly than those at other fast-food establishments because of the greater variety of offerings. Also, while the sit-down restaurants offering full dinners—such as Cinderella Castle's **King Stefan's** and Liberty Square's **Liberty Tree Tavern**—are crowded at lunch, they're busier still at dinnertime.

DINNER

WHAT'S SPECIAL

There's an awesome choice, from the humblest snack center to the *Empress Lilly*'s ambitious **Em-**press Room. Walt Disney World is not exactly a bastion of haute cuisine, but that doesn't mean that dinner experiences are anything less than pleasant. Service is almost unfailingly good (slipping just slightly during the busiest seasons), and the best of Walt Disney World's dinners are just fine. For a night on the World, some good choices are the **Steerman's Quarters**, **Fisherman's Deck**, and the **Empress Room**, all on the *Empress Lilly*; the **Village Restaurant** on the shores of Lake Buena Vista in Walt Disney World Shopping Village; the **Lake Buena Vista Club**; the **Gulf Coast Room** in the Contemporary Resort; and the **Papeete Bay Verandah** in the Polynesian Village.

For Family Fare: Children are welcome at every WDW restaurant, but the leisurely pace of service at

SCOOPS, SUNDAES, AND SOFT SERVE

Absolutely the worst thing about Walt Disney World is the total absence of sugar cones. Yet there's something about a hot, humid summer afternoon that makes even the snootiest food critic join the queues for refreshing sustenance.

BY THE SCOOP

IN THE HOTELS: Pueblo Room and **Fiesta Fun Center Snack Bar** at the Contemporary Resort. Peach brandy ice cream is also served at the **Outer Rim** in the Contemporary Resort.

South Seas Buffet and **Coral Isle Cafe** at the Polynesian Village Resort, passionfruit ice cream at **Papeete Bay Verandah** at the Polynesian Village.

IN THE MAGIC KINGDOM: Liberty Tree Tavern, Liberty Square; and **Town Square Cafe**, Main Street.

WALT DISNEY WORLD VILLAGE: Lake Buena Vista Club restaurant and snack bar, and **Village Restaurant**.

CONES

Cone Shop, Main Street, Magic Kingdom; and the **Village Pavilion Ice Cream Fountain**, Walt Disney World Shopping Village. Six flavors each. **Tangaroa Snack Isle**, Polynesian Village.

SOFT SERVE

IN THE MAGIC KINGDOM: Round Table (with strawberry or blueberry melba sauce, chocolate sauce, or over brownies) and **Tournament Tent** (swirled through with sweet, strawberry-flavored slush), Fantasyland; **Fort Sam Clemens**, Frontierland; **Sunshine Tree Tavern** (with a tangy frozen orange juice ripple), Adventureland;

Fife and Drum (strawberry, pineapple, chocolate sundaes), Liberty Square.

ASSORTED SUPER SUNDAES

IN THE HOTELS: Gulf Coast Room (doused with Grand Marnier or with flambéed hot fudge) and **Pueblo Room** and **Top of the World**, at the Contemporary Resort.

Papeete Bay Verandah (with flambéed pineapple bits, served in a pineapple half), **Tangaroa Snack Isle**, **Tangaroa Terrace**, and **Coral Isle Cafe**, at the Polynesian Village.

Trophy Room, at the Golf Resort.

IN THE MAGIC KINGDOM: Ice Cream Parlour, Main Street.

WALT DISNEY WORLD VILLAGE: Fisherman's Deck and **Steerman's Quarters**, *Empress Lilly* (topped with stewed berries or chocolate sauce and nuts); **Verandah Restaurant** (for particularly mammoth confections), Walt Disney World Village.

Lake Buena Vista Club (with a special chunky Gold Brick chocolate sauce at lunchtime, and atop bananas Foster and cherries Jubilee at dinner).

FRENCH-FRIED ICE CREAM

Trophy Room, Golf Resort.

LEMON SHERBET PUNCH

IN THE MAGIC KINGDOM: Liberty Tree Tavern, Liberty Square.

A TIP FOR THE FINICKY: Soft serve tastes better than the scooped stuff. Frozen yogurt, served at Tomorrowland's **Lunching Pad**, in the Magic Kingdom, has the most flavor of all (try the honey nut sundae).

some places makes some kids fidget. But there are plenty of choices that are particularly well suited to dining en famille. In the Contemporary Resort, for example. a special family buffet is usually served in the banquet rooms on the second floor (contact Guest Services for details). Other restaurants in that resort especially good for families are the **Terrace Buffeteria** and the **Terrace Cafe**, which offers a large (and economical) Italian buffet and salad bar every night.

MISSING THE MASSES

The decision about where to dine may ultimately depend on the plan for the rest of the day. Especially in slack periods, the familiar long lines at the most popular attractions in the Magic Kingdom are practically nonexistent from about 6 P.M. onward, and even in the busiest times, the queues ease up a bit as the afternoon wanes. So it's a wise visitor who takes advantage of this phenomenon by having a late lunch or a 4 P.M. snack—then dines after 9 P.M. (This plan also allows time to catch the second, less-crowded run-through of the Main Street Electrical Parade, staged every night that the park stays open until midnight.)

WDW restaurants are busiest in the evening between 7 and 9 P.M.

ABOUT DINNER RESERVATIONS

In most WDW restaurants, it's first come, first served. The lines that result can be avoided by eating early or late—or by choosing one of the handful of restaurants that accept dinner reservations:

CONTEMPORARY RESORT: Gulf Coast Room (824-1000, ext. 2684).

POLYNESIAN VILLAGE: Papeete Bay Verandah and **Tangaroa Terrace** (824-2000 for both).

GOLF RESORT: Trophy Room (824-2200, ext. 1484)

MAGIC KINGDOM: King Stefan's in Cinderella Castle and the **Liberty Tree Tavern** in Liberty Square. Reservations must be made in person at the restaurant on the day of the meal; go first thing after arrival in the Magic Kingdom.

WALT DISNEY WORLD VILLAGE: Empress Room aboard the *Empress Lilly* (828-3900); and **Lake Buena Vista Club** in the villa area (828-3735).

Or plan to take in the dinner show at the **Top of the World** in the Contemporary Resort, the **Luau** at the Polynesian, or the **Hoop-Dee-Doo Musical Revue** at Pioneer Hall—but note that *reservations for these activities must be made well in advance; some seatings sell out a year ahead!* No deposits are required, so there's no reason not to reserve early enough to avoid disappointment. (Call the Central Reservations Office at 824-8000 for all dinner-show reservations.)

DINNER SHOWS

The fact that the Disney organization is the king of family entertainment is nowhere more strongly apparent than amid the whooping and hollering troop of singers and dancers who race toward the velvet-curtained stage at **Fort Wilderness Campground's Pioneer Hall**. As you plough through barbecued ribs, fried chicken, corn on the cob, and strawberry shortcake, those enthusiastic performers sing, dance, and joke up a storm until your mouth is as sore from laughing as your stomach is from ingesting all the food. This is the **Hoop-Dee-Doo Musical Revue**, presented daily at 5, 7:30, and 10:00 P.M. and it is the most fun of the three dinner shows presented regularly at Walt Disney World. Cost is about $16 per adult, $13 for juniors (12 to 17), and $9 for children (3 to 11); reservations can be made through Central Reservations (824-8000), and are required well in advance.

The **Polynesian Revue at the Polynesian Village** (aka the Luau and available on Eastern Airlines packages), is presented nightly at 5 and 8 P.M. (and, from the end of March through late August, at 10:30 P.M. as well), and has its moments. The performers' dancing is some of the most authentic this side of Hawaii's well-respected Polynesian Cultural Center—where many of the WDW dancers have studied. The full Polynesian-style meal served at the first two shows is not one of the Disney chefs' better efforts; unless you have young children along, you may prefer to catch the last show (in season), where platters of fruit and cheese provide showtime sustenance. The late show costs about $10, about $6 less than the earlier shows.

The **Top of the World at the Contemporary Resort** hosts true nightclub-type entertainment, featuring top-name performers or the Top of the World orchestra and their big-band music—plus a view over the Magic Kingdom that will dazzle you when the music doesn't. As for the food, prime ribs are an especially good choice (entrees about $10 to $13). Seating is at 6:30 and 9:45 P.M. for the 8:15 and 11:30 P.M. shows; the entertainment charge is about $8 for adults.

Whichever site or show you choose, plan to arrive 15 minutes or so before starting time, and allow enough time for transportation and parking.

For dinner shows and supper seatings alike, you can book a table as soon as you get your confirmed reservation number if you're staying at WDW resorts; 45 days ahead if you're lodging at one of the Walt Disney World Village Hotel Plaza Establishments and 30 days if you're putting up outside Walt Disney World. Empress Room reservations may be made 30 days in advance, no matter where you're staying, and Top of the World reservations aren't available to anyone until 21 days before the dining date. In the case of dinner shows, if you can't get a place for an early performance, try for a later one (usually less heavily booked).

LOUNGES

No one ever said that the Magic Kingdom's no-liquor policy means that all of the World is a teetotaller. Actually, some of WDW's tastiest offerings are liquid (and decidedly alcoholic), and some of its most entertaining places are its bars and lounges.

DINNER WITH THE DISNEY CHARACTERS

A prime rib, chicken, or grouper dinner that is served family style in the Trophy Room at the Golf Resort features a visit by a handful of the Walt Disney characters—larger than life and always appealing. And each youngster takes home a special Disney trinket. Cost is about $11, and reservations are required. Call 824-5029.

CRUISE AND DINE

For a special evening out on the World, sign up for **A Night of Wine and Roses**, which features an elegant dinner at the Lake Buena Vista Club, followed by a cruise on the Buena Vista Lagoon. The $50-per-couple tab includes a wine tasting, then a full dinner with the wine of your choice. Offered Mondays through Thursdays from 6 to 9:30 P.M. Reservations required; call 828-3735.

LATE-NIGHT PIZZA

The thin-crusted variety is available from 9 P.M. to 12:30 A.M. in **Pioneer Hall**, while silent movies and sing-alongs entertain. In the Golf Resort, Room Service offers this classic, plus a thick-crusted, deep-dish Sicilian version from 10:30 P.M. until midnight.

CONTEMPORARY RESORT

Monorail Club Car: Near the elevators on the Grand Canyon Concourse, this long, skinny bar overlooking Bay Lake is a cozy, companionable sort of place for serious drinking. No entertainment but the company you bring.

Coconino Cove: On the Grand Canyon Concourse, just outside the Pueblo Room. Guests waiting to be seated can have drinks and Mexican snacks here, and watch the monorail glide in and out of the hotel. There's entertainment nightly.

Top of the World Lounge: Adjoining the Top of the World restaurant, this spacious room offers superb views over the Magic Kingdom. This is a good spot to watch the sunset and, when the park is open until midnight, the fireworks. Dash out onto the more easterly of the two observation decks nearby at 10:05 to see the Electrical Water Pageant blipping, bleeping, and glittering on Bay Lake below.

POLYNESIAN VILLAGE

The resort's Polynesian theme has inspired a whole raft of deceptively potent potables like the Blue Lagoon (creme de banana and blue curaçao), Seven Seas (fruit juice, grenadine, orange curaçao, and rum), Chi Chis (a standard piña colada made with vodka instead of rum), and WDW piña coladas (which include orange juice in addition to rum, pineapple, and coconut cream). There's even a special Polynesian Village nonalcoholic treat—the pink Lei-Lani, a delicious orange juice and strawberry mixture.

These drinks are specialties at Polynesian Village lounges, listed below.

Barefoot Bar: Adjoining the swimming pool lagoon, serving soda, draft beer, piña coladas, frozen daiquiris, mai tais, and various other mixed drinks. Open from 11 A.M. until 10:30 P.M. in summer (to 5 P.M. in winter).

Tambu Lounge: Cozy and clublike, this lounge adjoining the Papeete Bay Verandah is open daily beginning at 11 A.M., and offers low-key entertainment nightly. A good spot for a quiet conversation. Open from 11 A.M. until 2 A.M. year round.

Captain Cook's Hideaway: Off the lobby of the Great Ceremonial House, this small, dark nook also has entertainment nightly. Open from 6:30 P.M. to 2 A.M. daily.

GOLF RESORT

The **Players' Gallery**, adjoining the Trophy Room, with a view over the Palm golf course, serves an assortment of specialty drinks and cocktails—Double Eagles (Kahlua on the bottom and a tequila sour floating on the top), Banana Bogeys (light rum, fresh bananas, cream, and vanilla), Unplayable Lies (champagne doused with Southern Comfort served over a whole frozen apricot), and Lateral Hazards (light rum and curaçao blended with orange and lime nectar). Beer is available at the Sand Trap, poolside.

FORT WILDERNESS CAMPGROUND

Beer and sangría are served in Pioneer Hall. For

something stronger, take a blue-flagged watercraft to the Contemporary Resort or a gold-flagged watercraft to the Polynesian Village. Be sure to check the operating hours before boarding so that you don't miss the last trip back. Or, if you have a car, make the short drive to Walt Disney World Village.

WALT DISNEY WORLD VILLAGE

Cap'n Jack's Oyster Bar: Agleam with copper, right on the water, this bar serves delicious strawberry margaritas, made with strawberry tequila and real strawberries. The nibbles of smoked kingfish, oysters, and seafood marinara are good enough for an entire meal.

Village Lounge: This boîte, comfortable as a living room, hosts top jazz musicians and is one of the World's best-kept secrets. You can enjoy an entire evening for the price of a single drink.

ABOARD THE EMPRESS LILLY

Baton Rouge Lounge: This spacious Main Deck Lounge is one of the liveliest spots in WDW, thanks to the quick, barbed tongue of comedian-banjoist Denny Zavett, who appears with the Riverboat Rascals, who play Dixieland and bluegrass between Zavett's sets. Specialty drinks are sold by the pitcher—things like Mississippi River Water, concocted of white creme de cacao, fruit juices, and blue curaçao; Huckleberry's Cooler, made with blackberry brandy, blue curaçao, and grape and citrus juices; and Scarlett O'Haras—Southern Comfort, cranberry juice, and a splash of lemon-lime flavoring. The Bayou chips—crunchy homemade potato chips sold by the basket—are delicious enough to make it easy to abandon dinner plans altogether. Open from 11 A.M.

The Empress Lounge: Almost as elegant as the Empress Room, whose guests this mahogany-paneled bar is meant to pamper before and after a meal. The Empress Lounge features a harpist who happens to look like Snow White.

Starboard Lounge: On the starboard Main Deck, this room offers an assortment of appetizers—chicken-liver pâté, sautéed crab meat, oysters and cherrystone clams on the half shell—along with assorted sweet after-dinner drinks (Buena Vista Coffee, for instance, is laced with Amaretto and brandy and topped with whipped cream; Starboard Coffee includes Drambuie, brandy, Tia Maria, Grand Marnier, and a dollop of whipped cream).

Promenade Lounge: On the starboard Promenade Deck above the Starboard Lounge, this sitting area—with its old-fashioned wallpaper and paneled wainscoting—seems more like a Victorian parlor than a bar.

MORE SPECIAL NIGHTTIME FUN

IN THE MAGIC KINGDOM: The Magic Kingdom, open late during several busy periods of the year, takes on additional dazzle after dark. In peak seasons, there's the Main Street Electrical Parade, a procession so spectacular that it alone is worth the trip to WDW—even though it's necessary to visit during a busy period in order to see it.

FIREWORKS: During summers and holidays when the Magic Kingdom is open late, there are fireworks at 10 P.M. nightly. The show lasts just five minutes, but packs as much dazzle as those many times its length.

ELECTRICAL WATER PAGEANT: Best seen from the nearest beach, this sparkling show is composed of a 1,000-foot-long string of illuminated floating creatures. Guest Services or City Hall can tell you when and where the Electrical Water Pageant can be seen—usually at 9:05 P.M. from the Polynesian, 9:45 P.M. from Fort Wilderness, 10:00 P.M. from the Contemporary Resort, and, during the hours that the Magic Kingdom is open late, at 9:35 P.M. from River Country and 10:20 P.M. from the park itself.

MOONLIGHT CRUISE: An authentically styled sidewheeler floating through Bay Lake and the Seven Seas Lagoon is a pleasant place for evening cocktails or after-dinner drinks. These cruises, which last just over an hour, leave the Contemporary Resort dock twice nightly (once only in January and February), and both trips take in the Electrical Water Pageant en route. The fare is about $2. Reservations are requested; phone 824-1000.

MARSHMALLOW MARSH EXCURSION: This entertainment consists of a trip by canoe through the winding Fort Wilderness waterways, a hike along a footpath (for a few hundred feet) to a well-hidden campfire spot on the lakeshore, a merry sing-along, a story-telling fest, and a marshmallow roast. Cost is about $3, and reservations are required; to make them, appear in person on the day of the trip at the Pioneer Hall ticket booth, or call 828-2788.

RIVER COUNTRY: This archetypical, all-American swimming hole is open until 10 P.M.—under the lights—during the summer, and crowds are minimal. River Country admission costs $1 less after 6 P.M.

CAMPFIRE PROGRAM: This event at Fort Wilderness, held nightly near the Meadow Trading Post at the center of the campground, features a sing-along, Disney movies, and cartoons. Chip and Dale usually put in an appearance.

DISNEY MOVIES: A good choice when feet refuse to take even one more step. Full-length Walt Disney feature films are shown nightly at the Contemporary Resort for WDW guests, in the theater near the Fiesta Fun Center—usually at 4:30, 7, and 9 P.M. Movies are also shown at the Fort Wilderness Campground every evening at the campfire.

TENNIS: The courts at the Contemporary Resort, the Golf Resort, and the Lake Buena Vista Club are open until 10 P.M. year round. (See *Sports*.)

MEETINGS AND CONVENTIONS

Among Walt Disney World's 15,000 employees, there are photographers and videotape experts, printers and computer wizards, carpenters and sign painters, specialty merchandise and floral designers and pyrotechnics specialists, even singers and dancers—and all of their talents and expertise are at the disposal of meeting planners. Just a single WDW account representative works with each individual meeting client to map out an overall conference plan; then the full corps of support forces is mobilized to make these ideas become reality. Only a single phone call is required when questions arise, no matter how many diverse areas may be involved.

The fact that the readers of *Meetings and Conventions* magazine have rated Walt Disney World among the nation's top meeting centers for three years in a row suggests the quality of the meetings that this system can produce. While other meeting centers may outstrip Walt Disney World in some single area, the total meetings package—accommodations, food, service, amusements, and meeting facilities—has few equals. Between the **Contemporary Resort Hotel** and the **Walt Disney World Conference Center** at Walt Disney World Village—where the bulk of meetings are held at WDW—there are facilities to handle television broadcasts, major press conferences, and virtually any other complex technical undertaking, including the sorts of multimedia shows that usually have to be contracted to outside firms at other meeting sites.

Sophisticated audio systems can be installed: When one meeting of chief executive officers required an individually controlled mike for each of its 65 attendees, the Disney sound men designed and executed an elaborate control grid just for that event. When another group requested a single-slab conference table to seat 30, Disney carpenters built one—

right on the property—with only three days' notice. For delegates' leisure time, WDW offers an attraction that some 14 million people travel from around the world to see—the **Magic Kingdom.** Banquet entertainment is developed by the same creative staff that puts together the SRO shows at the **Pioneer Hall** and **Diamond Horseshoe** theaters. All of this puts WDW at the forefront of site choices for meetings or seminars requiring extensive support facilities and first-class frills.

WDW meetings are not for everyone, however. Groups who want to convene all day every day might do just as well to take their conventions to a site where participants won't be so sorely tempted by the beaches, the golf courses, and the Magic Kingdom. And while both entertainment and banquet prices at WDW are at least comparable to (and occasionally less than) those elsewhere, the overall package may be too costly for some economy-minded groups, since no discounts are given on room rates.

World Conference Center floor plan.

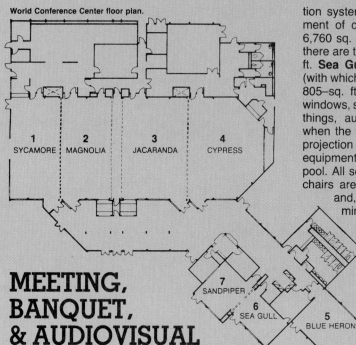

| 1 SYCAMORE | 2 MAGNOLIA | 3 JACARANDA | 4 CYPRESS |
| 7 SANDPIPER | 6 SEA GULL | 5 BLUE HERON | |

MEETING, BANQUET, & AUDIOVISUAL FACILITIES

Rooms for meetings and banquets are scattered all over the property, with the bulk concentrated at the **Contemporary Resort Hotel** (used mainly for large groups) and the **Walt Disney World Conference Center** (designed with small- and middle-sized meetings in mind). There are extensive audiovisual facilities at both sites.

CONTEMPORARY RESORT HOTEL: Most meeting facilities are located on the second floor of the Tower. The 11,968–sq. ft. **Ballroom of the Americas,** at the north end of the hotel, is the largest single facility, accommodating up to about 1,400 seated theater-style, or about 1,000 for a banquet. It can be divided into two smaller rooms, each with a capacity of about half the above numbers. The 8,777–sq. ft. **Grand Republic Ballroom** holds slightly fewer people; it can be split into three rooms ranging in size from 2,080 to 4,290 sq. ft. In addition, there are five other rooms nearby of 800 to 1,160 sq. ft. each; and on the 15th floor there are two others measuring 697 sq. ft. and 1,247 sq. ft. Both have wonderful panoramic views over the rest of the World.

CONFERENCE CENTER: This sleek cedar creation is located on the banks of Club Lake at Walt Disney World Village. It was designed expressly with small- and medium-size meetings and seminars in mind, and may be one of the most innovative structures of its type in existence. Four large rooms, each with its own light, sound, and projec-

tion systems, can be combined in a wide assortment of configurations, the largest comprised of 6,760 sq. ft., to seat 355 theater-style. In addition, there are three smaller meeting rooms, the 400–sq. ft. **Sea Gull,** the adjacent 460–sq. ft. **Sandpiper** (with which the Sea Gull can be combined), and the 805–sq. ft. **Blue Heron**—each with big lakeview windows, sophisticated lighting (which, among other things, automatically turns up the room's lights when the sun goes behind a cloud), and rearview projection screens that can be supplemented by AV equipment rented from Disney's own equipment pool. All seven rooms are extremely attractive; the chairs are comfortable enough for all-day sitting; and, despite the fact that you're just a 15-minute drive from the Magic Kingdom, the whole facility has a relaxed, away-from-it-all atmosphere.

OTHER BANQUET AND MEETING SPACE:

A smallish meeting could be arranged at the quiet, but centrally located, **Golf Resort Hotel,** using the 1,024–sq. ft. Tournament Room for meetings, and individual hotel suites for cocktail receptions. Another option is the third deck of the **Empress Lilly** riverboat restaurant at Walt Disney World Village; dinner for as many as six dozen can be set up in the airy room known as the Skipper's Table,

cocktails can be served at the polished bar of the adjacent Texas Lounge, and receptions for as many as 250 can be staged in both rooms and on the promenade decks outside. Larger quarters are available at the **Lake Buena Vista Club** across the lagoon. Conceivably, drinks could be served aboard the Empress Lilly, then meeting attendees might cruise across the lagoon in canopied Flote Botes for dinner in the Lake Buena Vista Club's 2,275–sq. ft. Vista Room. **Luau Cove, Pioneer Hall,** and the **Kingdom Queen** ferryboat also can be used to provide entertainment and dining space.

Still larger conventions will be possible in Orlando—albeit outside Walt Disney World—beginning in October 1982, when Phase I of the new **Orange County Civic and Convention Center** opens, with 150,000 sq. ft. of exhibit and meeting space. Details: Orlando–Orange County Convention Bureau; 5750 Major Blvd., Suite 501; Orlando, FL 32805; 305-351-7047.

AUDIOVISUAL EQUIPMENT: Lecterns, microphones, projectors, viewers, screens, special lenses, tape recorders, videotape equipment, record players, lights, and sound equipment of virtually any type can be rented on a daily or per-use basis. In addition, technicians are available to record meetings, set up sound and lighting systems, and edit and splice film and tape.

LODGINGS

Large meetings use the rooms and suites at the **Contemporary Resort Hotel,** with overflow lodged at the **Polynesian Village Resort** and the **Golf Resort Hotel.** Smaller groups use the **Club Lake Villas,** the **Fairway Villas,** the **Vacation Villas,** or the **Treehouses,** just a couple of minutes' electric cart ride away from the Conference Center. The L-shaped rooms at the Club Lake Villas each have a patio and a wet bar, and a sitting area separate from the sleeping area. In the Fairway Villas' six Conference Units, two of the apartments have adjoining cathedral-ceilinged living rooms, whose dividing wall can be opened to provide an exceptionally handsome setting for meetings.

All meeting-related and personal charges can be handled by individual invoices or on a single master bill, or billed to individual MasterCard and American Express credit cards. Note that the Disney organization requires all reservations to be confirmed thirty days in advance. And attendees who want to remain after the conclusion of a convention should book stayovers as soon as meeting plans are finalized, or risk finding no room at the inn. Some of these arrangements must be concluded as much as a year in advance. For more basic information about the WDW lodgings, consult *Transportation and Accommodations.*

AFTER HOURS

One of the main attractions of Walt Disney World as a meeting site is the availability of ample banquet and entertainment space, plus post-meeting pastimes of a sort that just are not found in many other spots on earth. And where else in the world can your banquet table's floral centerpiece be surrounded by a ring of Mouseketeer hats that can be worn when a meeting gets a bit too serious?

ENTERTAINMENT: Normally, meeting planners choose one of several popular WDW theme parties: **Speakeasy Scandals,** a Roaring Twenties–type party that ends with a Keystone Cops–like raid on the ballroom; **Bourbon Street,** which features banjo-strumming and Dixieland and honky-tonk piano music from the banquet's beginning, and a closing half-hour-long show that concludes with a rousing "When the Saints Go Marching In"; **Taste of Americana,** showcasing the best of American music; **Musical World,** an extravaganza of melodies from many lands; **Good Ole Days,** which revives the music of the 1950s; the folksy, down-home **Country-and-Western Show;** and **America Is,** at which WDW's own singing group, the Kids of the Kingdom, performs a medley of the best U.S. popular songs. For large groups, it's also possible to stage a sort of moveable feast—a different party in each of several rooms, each festivity featuring the appropriate food (served buffet style) and entertainment.

Anyone with a penchant for playing impresario (and the funds to pay the piper) can concoct a special affair-of-a-lifetime just by marshalling the resources of the Walt Disney World talent pool. One company, for instance, ended a clambake on the beach with a pyrotechnical display set off from a barge out on the lake—the company logo emblazoned in fireworks. Similarly, WDW chefs can be called upon to produce far more sophisticated menus than those normally offered. WDW is, above all, a special paradise for the creative meeting planner.

Children attending a meeting with their parents can be entertained by Disney movies; magicians, mimes, and caricature artists; rock bands; and hot-dogs-and-corn-on-the-cob banquets of their own. Or you can just use the Magic Kingdom as a nonpareil babysitter.

Disney liaison people can fill you in on all your choices and provide specific guidance.

AFTER-MEETING DIVERSIONS: Arrangements can be made for meeting guests to take advantage of just about everything in the WDW vacation inventory—**River Country,** the **Magic Kingdom, Discovery Island,** horseback rides at **Fort Wilderness,** the three **golf courses** (and the Walt Disney World Golf Studio instructors), the **tennis courts,** and more—often at group rates. Account representatives can even set up golf and tennis tournaments.

FOR MORE INFORMATION: Contact Walt Disney World Sales; Box 40; Lake Buena Vista, FL 32830; 305-828-3200.

ORLANDO

The city of Orlando has become so closely identified with Walt Disney World that it's easy to forget that it's an important city in its own right, with its share of assets and problems just like any other sizable community in the country. Now boasting a population of nearly 130,000, it began as a campground for soldiers during the mid-nineteenth-century Seminole War; it is said to have been named for a sentry who sent out an alarm of an Indian attack, then died of wounds he sustained in the ensuing battle.

Later, a Philadelphian brought sugar cane to the area, but the agricultural venture failed, and cattlemen took over—the area is still one of the country's

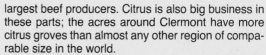

largest beef producers. Citrus is also big business in these parts; the acres around Clermont have more citrus groves than almost any other region of comparable size in the world.

The city of Orlando is surrounded by small towns—among them Ocoee, Maitland, Windermere, Kissimmee, Fern Park, and Winter Park (home of that sinkhole that made headlines when it swallowed up a few Porsches and part of a swimming pool, among other things, during the worst of the 1981 drought; the gaping hole, which looks a bit like a construction site in its initial stages, can be seen off Fairbanks Avenue).

The boom that all of these towns have enjoyed since the coming of Walt Disney World has left them crisscrossed by wide, treeless highways, and bordered by fast-food restaurants, used car lots, and other unbeautiful legacies of the modern commercial age. Many Orlandoans live in look-alike housing developments or apartment complexes, but on the other hand, around Winter Park in particular, there are neighborhoods where the lawns are large and green and dotted with palms or huge old live oaks, thickly veiled by Spanish moss. There the houses of gleaming white stucco are sprawling, with roofs of red-orange ceramic tile in the Spanish style. Just to go for a drive through this area can be a visual treat.

Orlando, Kissimmee, and the other communities are also home to many attractions other than those contained inside Walt Disney World, and many restaurants in these surrounding towns are well worth investigating. This chapter will steer you to many of them. (Unless otherwise noted, all phone numbers are in the area code 305.)

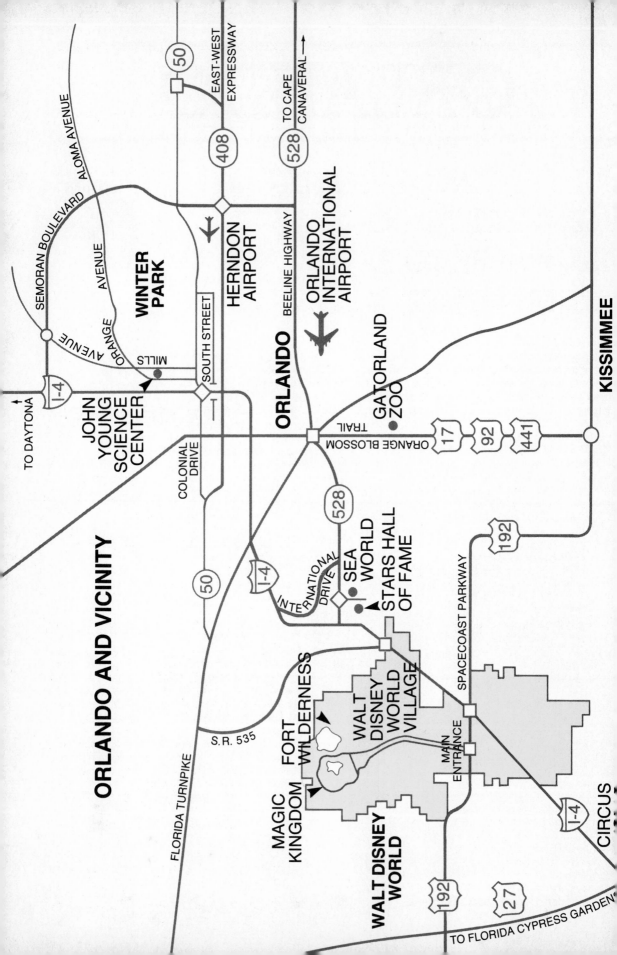

GETTING AROUND

Unless you spend all your time in Walt Disney World, it's most convenient to have a car. (For a description of Orlando geography and the interlocking surrounding roads, see "Orlando-area Highways" in *Transportation and Accommodations*.)

CAR RENTALS: Those who don't bring the family car can rent one at any one of some 60 car-rental agencies—Orlando has the greatest number of fleet vehicles of any city in the nation—and the rates (most on an unlimited mileage basis) are relatively modest. When shopping around for the best car rental deal, be sure to include the cost of collision damage insurance in your calculations, for it can vary enough from agency to agency to make a substantial difference in the cost of a rental lasting a week or more. (Note that most vacation packages that include a rental car do not include collision damage insurance; if you opt not to take it, the agency will require a large deposit—either in cash or by credit card.) Many firms allow you to drop a rental car elsewhere in Florida at no extra charge; if that matters to you, be sure to ask. Eastern Airlines' "Super 7" packages include a rental car, and National Car Rental Co.—the "official" car rental firm of WDW—offers special deals.

The larger Orlando-area car rental firms include Alamo (toll-free 800-327-9633; or, from Florida, 800-432-0657); Avis (toll-free 800-331-1212; from Oklahoma, check directories for numbers); Budget (toll-free 800-527-0700; from Texas, 800-442-0700; or, in Dallas, 214-988-0700); Hertz (toll-free 800-654-3131; or, from Oklahoma City, 405-755-4424); General Rent-A-Car (toll-free 800-327-7607); and National (toll-free 800-328-4567; or, from Minnesota, 800-862-6064).

Classic Motor Cars, Ltd., Inc., based at the TraveLodge at the Walt Disney World Village Hotel Plaza at I-4 and S.R.-535, rents reproductions of 1929 Model A's, complete with quail radiator ornaments, spoked wheels, and horns that make a strange *ah-ooo-gah* sound. The body is of fiberglass, the drive train is strictly up-to-date, and there's an AM/FM radio; they come with automatic transmission or stick shift. Rates are about $10 an hour, $50 for eight hours, $90 for a full day, $225 for four days, and $350 for a week (with unlimited mileage).

BUS TRANSPORTATION: City buses are not nearly adequate for vacationers' purposes, but a number of firms provide transportation from hotels all over the city to the major attractions—not only WDW, but also Circus World, Cypress Gardens, Church Street Station, Stars Hall of Fame, Sea World, the Altamonte Mall, and the like. You don't have to worry about park-

ing, and frequent service is provided. At about $4 a person per ride, however, fares are high enough that those who plan to do much traveling around will find it less expensive to rent a car. Gray Line and Rabbit are among the big tour operators; hotel desks can provide up-to-the-minute details.

TAXIS: Several firms provide service, among them the City Cab Company (422-4561), Yellow Cab Company (423-5566), and Rainbow Taxi (896-3645). The normal price of a cab ride from the Orlando International Airport to Walt Disney World is $26 to $28.

WHAT TO DO

Though it has no beaches, the Orlando area is so full of natural attractions it would be easy to spend a whole vacation here, even if there were not a single man-made attraction in sight. Meandering streams, like Reedy and Shingle Creeks, in the few remaining still-wild areas make for fine flat-water canoeing; big lakes like Tohopekaliga, the state's third-largest, are known Florida-wide for their bass fishing action, and many largemouth fishing tournaments have been staged here. And the sugary-sand beaches and the placid surf of the Gulf Coast are only about 80 miles away, while the hard, wide beaches and the pounding waves of the Atlantic, only about 60 miles distant, can be reached by car in just an hour.

Add to that an assortment of golf courses, tennis courts, and all manner of other man-made attractions—not to mention Walt Disney World itself—and it can become fairly difficult not to hit upon a plan of action that satisfies every visitor's vacation desires.

BALLOON TRIPS: The ride is the smoothest imaginable as you float above the flat central Florida pinewoods and farmlands, and it's absolutely soundless—like nothing you've ever experienced before. Phineas Phogg's—one of the four establishments at Church Street Station (described below in the "Nightlife" section of this chapter)—stages ascensions daily, weather permitting, beginning early in the morning before the ground breezes begin to stir. Passengers leave Church Street Station for the balloon field at 6:30 A.M., and return 3½ hours later. The fee (about $84 per person) includes a picnic of cheese, bread, and fruit, as well as assorted trinkets. Wear trousers and comfortable shoes; a certain amount of scrambling into and out of the basket is required, and because of its small size, you will have to stand for the entire duration of the ride. Reservations, which are required, can be made at the Church Street Station gift shop, or by phone at 422-2434.

CATTLE AUCTIONS: Before Kissimmee took to calling itself the Gateway Community to Walt Disney World, its main claim to fame was as the "Cow Capital of the South," because of the extensive cattle industry in the surrounding area. That business is still flourishing, as any Sunday drive along the narrow streets and county highways around Kissimmee will demonstrate. The live cattle auctions that take place at 1 P.M. every Wednesday at the Kissimmee Livestock Market (on S.R.-527 north) are as full of Stetsons and cowboy boots as ever—and quite as colorful, as fast-paced, and as exciting as always. It's worth a visit. Details: Kissimmee–St. Cloud Convention & Visitors Bureau; Box 2007; Kissimmee, FL 32741; toll-free 800-327-9159, or, from Florida, 800-432-9199.

CIRCUS WORLD: The full extent of the Disney achievement in the Magic Kingdom becomes immediately apparent when you visit this multimillion-dollar theme park on 850 acres southwest of Orlando at I-4 and U.S.-27. By comparison, the landscaping here is far less lush, the unrelieved expanses of concrete are far greater, and the attention to detail is far less complete. After you've seen the Magic Kingdom, you may be disappointed; and if you have only a short time to spend around Orlando, you may want to skip this attraction entirely. Nonetheless, Circus World boasts features that even Disney World doesn't: there's the Cinema Circus, which uses a you-are-there system called IMAX and a six-story-high movie screen to show how it feels to perform on a high wire, somersault through the air on a flying trapeze, work with the big cats, or put elephants through their paces. There's a wonderful display of miniature circus models and circus memorabilia, worthy of a museum (Chicago's celebrated Museum of Science and Industry mounted a special exhibition for just such a collection only a few years ago). Kids can have their faces made up as clowns, complete with whiteface and red noses. You can ride elephants and feed and play with baby animals. Every few hours, high divers stage a fabulous show that involves a plunge into a 16-foot-deep pool from the top of a 100-foot-high platform, a point higher than the tops of the fabled cliffs of Acapulco. The circus spectacular features performing elephants and several first-rate acts, and the Be-A-Star Circus (perhaps most fun of all) gives audience volunteers (strapped into safety harnesses) the chance to fly on a trapeze and walk the high wire.

Not to mention the midway, where you can compete in games of chance, and where you can get jostled and jolted until your knees turn to jelly on an array of thrill rides. The Flying Daredevil—a new-style roller coaster that lurches into a 50-foot drop, zooms through a 360-degree loop, climbs to a 50-foot-high platform, pauses, and then zooms backward through the loop and back to the starting point—leaves even dedicated thrill-ride lovers a bit jangled. For tamer sport, there's an old-fashioned wooden roller coaster billed as the largest in the Southeast. Shops, a few other shows, an innovative children's play area, several all-American fast-food stands, a lovely turn-of-the-century carousel, and an assortment of other rides round out the show. Count on spending a full day if you go.

At press time, admission was $9.50 for adults ($7.95 for children under 12; under 3, free), and hours were 9 A.M. to 10 P.M. from June through September, to 6 P.M. the rest of the year. Details: Circus World; Box 800; Orlando, FL 32801; 422-0643 or 813-424-2421.

FISHING: Bass anglers make a big deal about Florida's third-largest lake, Tohopekaliga—which is full of the kind of shoreline weed beds, reeds, grass, cattails, and other vegetation that make fine feeding grounds for lunkers; the record catch stands at 16 pounds, 8 ounces. There are several fishing camps where boats can be rented and bait purchased; the Kissimmee–St. Cloud Convention and Visitors Bureau (Box 2007; Kissimmee, FL 32741; 847-5000) can send a list.

FLORIDA FESTIVAL: This multipeaked tent full of shops and eateries is a good place to visit in combination with Sea World (its parent operation just across the narrow road), either for lunch or for dinner after a day of watching sea creatures and water-skiers. The boutiques stock merchandise that tends toward the trinkety, but the food stands offer Cuban, Italian, and various popular and indigenous Floridian dishes like fried plantains; black beans and rice; fried chicken; tacos and burritos; conch chowder; fried catfish; spareribs; oysters on the half shell; alligator; hearts of palm (aka swamp cabbage); and more. This place ranks high on any list of the more eclectic Orlando-area eating spots. Stay around afterward for drinks and live entertainment (the same group of banjo players, guitarists, and singers that keeps things moving at the Sea World water-ski show), and you have one of Orlando's more amusing evenings. Open from 11:30 A.M. to 11:30 P.M. daily. No admission charge. Details: Florida Festival; 7007 Sea World Dr.; Orlando, FL 32809; 351-3600.

FLORIDA CYPRESS GARDENS: It's said that a traveler would have to visit 70 countries at different times of year to see all the plants and flowers that can be viewed in a single day at this 228-acre attraction, developed in the mid-1930s. The Original Gardens, with their elaborate plantings of some 8,000 species (including 27 varieties of palm)—best seen on foot along meandering pathways or on electric-motored boat rides for which there's a slight additional charge—are as lush and lovely as ever. The Gardens' water-ski shows are also thrilling, with athletes skiing barefoot and backward, performing graceful water ballets and assorted stunts, and swooping high above the crowd in hang gliders. In 1980, after 44 years of operation, two new areas were added: the Living Forest (where there are displays of various exotic animal species, live shows featuring birds and alligators, a walk through a large aviary, and areas where youngsters can cuddle the llama, pat the bunny, and hitch a ride on a 300-pound tortoise) and Southern Crossroads, an assortment of shops, restaurants, and theaters (for magic shows and a you-are-there sort of movie). You may be shopped out by the time you get here from WDW, but Cypress Gardens, lovely as it is, is well worth a day's visit. Be sure to call ahead to find out about any special events that may be coming up here at the time of your visit; hang-gliding competitions, car meets, water-ski championships, and various other events frequently scheduled here are often worth a detour. At press time, operating hours were 8 A.M. to 5:30 P.M. daily, and admission fee was $6.95 ($3.95 for children under 12; under 6, free). Details: Florida Cypress Gardens; Box 1; Cypress Gardens, FL 33880; 351-6606 or 813-324-2111.

GATORLAND ZOO: Good for a couple of hours and an eyeful of literally thousands of alligators ranging in length from about six inches (the newborns) to fifteen feet (the three-quarters-of-a-ton elders of the clan). An assortment of snakes is also on view. Some of the alligators can be fed, and some of the snakes can be handled. Located between Kissimmee and Orlando on U.S.-17-92-441, about 20 minutes from the WDW main gates. At press time, operating hours were 8:30 A.M. to 7 P.M. daily in summer (to 6 P.M. in winter), and admission was $3.60 ($2.60 for children under 12; under 3, free). Details: Gatorland Zoo; U.S.-17-92-441; N. Kissimmee, FL 32741; 855-5496.

LOCHAVEN ARTS CENTER: Orlando's art museum has permanent displays of paintings and sculpture, as well as frequent special exhibits. The John Young Science Center (described below) is nearby. At press time, hours were from 10 A.M. to 5 P.M. Tuesday through Friday, from noon on Saturday, and from 2 P.M. on Sunday. Free. Details: Lochaven Arts Center; 2460 N. Mills Ave.; Orlando, FL 32803; 896-4231.

MYSTERY FUN HOUSE: Wavy mirrors, a mirror-maze, crazy ladders, and more—all fine for a couple of hours on a rainy day when youngsters are really stir crazy. Located near the Court of Flags and the Sheraton Towers in the Florida Center area, eight miles from the WDW main gates. At press time, admission was $3.95 ($2.95 for children 4 through 12; under 4, free); hours were 10 A.M. to 10 P.M. daily. Details: Mystery Fun House; 5767 Major Blvd.; Orlando, FL 32805; 351-3359.

SEA WORLD: Imagine a fine big-city aquarium. Then add plenty of greenery and some water-skiers, whales, dolphins, sea lions, and sea otters (all performing to hopelessly corny scripts)—and you have a fair idea of what Sea World is all about. The *This is Shamu!* show reveals the 8,000-lb. black-and-white killer whale in balletic leaps and rolls, in the company of a pair of sprightly dolphins. The new Shark Encounter exhibit, which begins with an amazing film that includes a sequence depicting a savage sharks' feeding frenzy, gives you the opportunity to go into the midst of a collection of lemon, nurse, brown, tiger, bull, and bonnethead sharks, all housed in a 60,000-gallon aquarium; a nine-foot-high tunnel walled in clear acrylic cuts through the bottom of the big tank. Best of all, perhaps, are the feeding pools, where you can toss fish to sea lions and sea otters. Large and small aquariums displaying undersea life from around the world, and exhibits that tell you about tide-pool life, North American river otters, and walruses, are also on view. There are several refreshment spots on the property, but it's more fun to amble (or bus) across the road to the Florida Festival, a multipeaked tent full of small boutiques and kiosks where you can buy foods indirectly indigenous to Florida—Cuban, Spanish, Italian, and Florida "cracker" specialties (such as alligator, which tastes a bit like a cross between chicken and fish). Al E. Gator's, the only full-service restaurant on the property, serves gator, conch, snapper, and such. At press time, park admission was $9.50 ($8.50 for children under 12; no charge for those under 3), and operating hours were 9 A.M. to 7 P.M. daily in fall, winter, and spring (with extended hours during peak holiday seasons), 8:30 A.M. to 8 P.M. in summer. Gates close daily two hours before the park itself. Guided tours are available at a slight additional charge. The park is located at the intersection of I-4 and the Bee Line Expressway, 12 miles southwest of Orlando and a few minutes north of Walt Disney World. More information: Sea World of Florida; 7007 Sea World Dr.; Orlando, FL 32809; 351-3600.

STARS HALL OF FAME: The world's largest wax museum, located opposite Sea World in a 61,000–sq.-ft. building east of I-4, maintains billboards all along the highway; and thousands of visitors come to see the more than 100 elaborate "sets" that show off stars at memorable moments in their careers—Shirley Temple in a scene from the 1934 film *Bright Eyes*; Lionel, Ethel, and John Barrymore in the 1932 *Rasputin and the Empress*; Mary Pickford and Douglas Fairbanks in the 1929 *Taming of the Shrew*; and Greta Garbo and John Gilbert in *Queen Christina* (1933), to name a few. Mae West, Rudolph Valentino, Wallace Beery, W. C. Fields, Fred Astaire and Ginger Rogers, Clark Gable and Vivien Leigh, Edward G. Robinson, Hedy Lamarr, Boris Karloff, Omar Sharif, Ali McGraw, Brigitte Bardot, Elizabeth Taylor, and many more are all immortalized in wax here, looking fairly true to life (some more so than others, though great art it's not). A multi-media show, a cafeteria, a games area, gift shops, and snack bars provide other diversions—usually enough to fill up a couple of hours. Strollers and wheelchairs are available; parking is free; and bilingual information is available. At press time, operating hours were 10 A.M. to 10 P.M. daily (box office closes at 8:30 P.M.), and admission was $6.75 ($4.15 for children under 12; those under 4, free). Details: Six Flags' Stars Hall of Fame; 6825 Starway Dr.; Orlando, FL 32809; 351-1120.

WET 'N WILD: Walt Disney World's River Country may be the archetypal all-American swimming hole, all trees and clean-and-clear lake water. But this latter-day version of the chlorinated, concrete-paved, and shadeless municipal swimming pool may seem more familiar to many visitors, and among connoisseurs of water slides, Wet 'N Wild gets top marks. This is the place to explore the water slide in all its manifestations. There's the Kamikazi, an undulating, 300-foot-long slide that sends you into the water at cruising speed; the white-water slideways, four 200-foot-long plumes; the twisting and turning 60-foot-high Corkscrew, which ends by shooting you into a pitch-black tunnel; the Banzai Boggan, a gut-wrenching water roller coaster. A huge surf lagoon where you can ride the big waves on air mattresses, a simple swimming pool, a shallow area where you can splash around in a fountain and sit underneath a waterfall, a bubble machine that makes the water feel like whipped cream, a beach, and a lakeside marina where sailboats and speedboats are available for rent, round out the aquatic offerings. The place is jammed most afternoons in summer, and there are lines for all the slides. So unless you're going to sunbathe, you may enjoy yourself more in the evening. Special low rates are available. Towels are available for rent on the spot, but it's best to bring your own. Hours vary from season to season; admission fee at press time was $6.95 ($4.95 for children under 13; under 3, free). Located on International Drive. Details: Wet 'N Wild; 6200 International Dr.; Orlando, FL 32809; 351-3200.

WINGS AND WHEELS: The movie *To Fly*, first presented at the Smithsonian's National Air and Space Museum, is now a major drawing card at this attraction housed in a gigantic former airplane hangar alongside the Orlando airport. The fine display of classic airplanes and automobiles from 1890 to 1940 draws applause from history-of-transportation buffs, who make it a point to plan a couple of hours here on the way into or out of Orlando. At press time, operating hours were 9:30 A.M. to 5 P.M. daily, and admission was $5.50 ($2.75 for children under 13; under 6, free). Details: Wings and Wheels; 8989 Florida Rd. S.; Orlando, FL 32809; 859-9600.

WINTER PARK: This upper-crust community about a half-hour's drive north of Walt Disney World is full of one-of-a-kind restaurants (described in "Where to Eat," below) where expensive trinkets are the stock in trade. The Langford Resort Hotel offers a handsome and informative little walking-tour guide, available at the hotel for the asking. It includes stops at a number of the small museums here that you might want to visit on your own, among them the following:

Morse Gallery of Art: Houses a remarkable collection of the work of the stained glass artist Louis Comfort Tiffany—windows, lampshades and vases, drinking glasses, desk sets, dishes, and windows, many of them from Laurelton Hall (Tiffany's Oyster Bay, Long Island, summer home, which burned to the ground in 1957). The works of John LaFarge, Frank Lloyd Wright, Rene Lalique, Emile Gallé, and Victor Durand, a few of Tiffany's contemporaries, are also on display. At press time, hours were Tuesday through Saturday, from 9:30 A.M. to 4 P.M., Sunday from 1 P.M. to 4 P.M. (closed Mondays, Christmas, New Year's, Thanksgiving, and July 4); and admission was $1.50 ($1 for children and students). Details: Morse Gallery of Art; 151 E. Welbourne Ave.; Winter Park, FL 32789; 645-5311.

Beal Maltbie Museum: Some 100,000 species of shells—nearly 2,000,000 shells in all, assembled between 1888 and 1945, and added to since then by Cocoa Beach resident Dr. James H. Beal—are displayed in this red-tile-roofed building on the pretty Rollins College campus. At press time, hours were from 10 A.M. to 5 P.M. Monday to Friday, and admission fee was $1 (50¢ for children under 13; under 6, free). Details: Beal Maltbie Museum; Rollins College; Winter Park, FL 32789; 646-2364.

JOHN YOUNG SCIENCE CENTER: Located near the Lochaven Arts Center and named for astronaut John Young, an Orlando resident, this institution has special science exhibits, a Discovery Room for youngsters, and a planetarium that stages not only star shows (in the afternoons), but also elaborate light shows that are big favorites of the teenage set. At press time, hours were from 9 A.M. to 5 P.M. Monday through Thursday, 9 A.M. to 9 P.M. on Friday, noon to 9 P.M. on Saturday, and noon to 5 P.M. on Sunday; admission was $1.75 ($1.25 for children under 18 and senior citizens over 55; those under 5, free). Details: John Young Science Center; 810 E. Rollins St.; Orlando, FL 32803; 896-7151.

SHOPPING: If Walt Disney World Shopping Village doesn't wear out your wallet, the Orlando area has three major shopping malls that will be happy to finish the job. The Altamonte Mall (½ mile east of I-4 on S.R.-536 in Altamonte Springs) is a vast shopping complex featuring four major department stores— Jordan Marsh, Burdine's, Sears, and Robinson's. Fashion Square (3201 East Colonial Drive in Orlando) has Sears, Robinson's, and Burdine's, among many other shops. Colonial Plaza Mall (East Colonial Drive at Bumby Street) houses about a hundred stores, including a Woolworth's and a branch of Jordan Marsh.

Factory outlets: Among the several in the Orlando area are the Danskin Factory Outlet at the Interstate Mall in Altamonte Springs, which stocks leotards, tights, skirts, tops, and more in women's and children's sizes (339-3840); just north of there, at Casselberry Square, in Casselberry, there's the Polly Flinders Outlet, which features savings of up to 60% on the kind of high-quality hand-smocked dresses that make little girls look like little girls (830-1310); and there's the Dansk Factory Outlet at 7000 International Drive in Orlando (351-2425).

WHERE TO EAT

Orlando is not, like New Orleans or New York, a city that gets especially high marks for food. As recently as ten years ago, Central Florida was almost entirely rural; away from downtown Orlando, much of the area still is. That means that steak houses are still among the fanciest places to celebrate a birthday or an anniversary; that the French and Continental restaurants that do exist offer the kind of buttery, creamy, complicated concoctions that the lighter, more contemporary French cooking known as *nouvelle cuisine* made passé in more cosmopolitan centers; and that the differences between fish fresh out of the sea and fish that has been frozen is not as widely appreciated as might be expected in a town so close to both the Gulf of Mexico and the Atlantic Ocean.

Nonetheless, the growth of the city has brought chefs here from all over the world, and the variety and the quality of Orlando restaurant meals have improved considerably during the last decade, so that now—while there's little of the kind of subtly sophisticated cooking available in the world's gastronomic centers—just plain good food is abundant, and first-class mealtime experiences, ones that derive their enjoyment as much from atmosphere as from food, are more than easy to find. A selection of the best spots follows.

As an indication of what you should expect to spend for a meal, we've classified restaurants as **expensive** (lunches over $8, dinners over $30), **moderate** (lunches from about $6 to $8, dinners from $15 to $30), and **inexpensive** (lunches under $6, dinners under $15). These prices are for an average meal for two, not including drinks, taxes, or tips. Operating hours were correct at press time; but it's advisable to call in advance just to make sure that the restaurant will be open when you arrive. Acceptance of credit cards is signaled after each listing with AX = American Express; CB = Carte Blanche; DC = Diners Club; MC = MasterCard; and V = Visa.

CAFE ON THE PARK: Done up (by a New York designer) in luscious shades of peach, with mirrors aplenty, this eatery in downtown Orlando's Harley Hotel overlooks Lake Eola, and the fountain at its center is the kind of gorgeous place that most people pick for an Occasion To Remember. Tableside cooking (steak Diane, flambéed crepes, bananas Foster) adds an elegant note. Veal, live lobster, crab, and jumbo shrimp are also available. On Sunday, there is an all-you-can-eat brunch featuring wine or champagne cocktails, soups, breads, and a main luncheon course or breakfast items, plus desserts ($8.95). On other days, lunch is served buffet-style. Breakfasts are nothing out of the ordinary, though the decor certainly lends an illusion to the contrary. Open from 11 A.M. to 5 P.M. for lunch (with the buffet served only until 2 P.M., Monday through Saturday, and the brunch on Sunday offered until 3 P.M.), and for dinner from 6 to 10 P.M. daily (to 11 P.M. on Friday and Saturday). Reservations accepted. AX, CB, DC, MC, V. In the Harley Hotel, at 151 E. Washington, Orlando; 841-3220. Expensive.

LIMEY JIM'S: A favorite of many Orlando residents for a special night on the town. Roast duckling, sirloin steaks in sherry mushroom sauce, roast rack of lamb, veal Oscar, prime ribs, stuffed broiled pork chops, and chicken Sicilian (with olive oil, garlic, shallots, diced potatoes, and herbs) are the specialties. Open from 5:45 to 10:30 P.M. daily for dinner. Reservations accepted. AX, CB, DC, MC, V. At the Orlando Hyatt, at 6375 W. Spacecoast Pkwy., Kissimmee; 846-4100 from Kissimmee, or 422-3106 from Orlando. Expensive.

MAISON & JARDIN: Locally nicknamed the "Mason Jar," this is an elegant place with high ceilings and white arches, widely spaced tables, and vast windows that take in the formal gardens that surround the mansion building in which meals are served. Appetizers include mushrooms thermidor (stuffed with sautéed crab meat and baked in a creamy sauce), escargots in garlic butter, and oysters Florentine au gratin. The many meat, fish, and fowl entrees are equally ambitious. Steaks are available with or without sauces (though this is definitely not a steak house). All dinners include vegetables and potato or blended wild rice, and crackers with homemade cheese spread. Open for dinner Tuesday through Saturday from 6:30 to 10:30 P.M. and on Sunday from 5:30 to 9 P.M., and for brunch on Sunday from 11 A.M. to 2 P.M. Reservations accepted. AX, CB, DC, MC, V. 430 S. Wymore Rd., Altamonte Springs; 862-4410. Expensive.

PARK PLAZA GARDENS: With gardenlike awnings, skylights, and lush greenery, this is one of the two prettiest eating spots in Winter Park (the other is La Belle Verriere, which has a collection of stained glass as spectacular as its food is disappointing). Park Plaza Gardens offers consistently rich concoctions of seafood, fowl, and meat, liberally sauced with cream, butter, and herbs. Open for lunch from 11:30 A.M. to 3 P.M. from Monday through Saturday, and for dinner from 6 to 10 P.M. Sunday through Thursday and to 11 P.M. on Friday and Saturday. Reservations accepted. AX, CB, DC, MC, V. 319 Park Ave. S., Winter Park; 645-2475. Expensive.

LE CORDON BLEU: Almost every Orlando food fancier has his favorite Winter Park dining spot, and this one—installed in an ordinary storefront that looks like it ought to house a Chinese restaurant—gets a good share of votes for its renditions of locally popular specialties like artichoke bottoms filled with crab meat and glazed with Mornay sauce; snails in garlic butter; beef Wellington; chicken in wine sauce; and duck à l'orange. The decor tends toward the gaudy with its red-flocked wallpaper, etc., but there's something warm and homey about this place that is absent in many others arranged with a more sophisticated hand. A platter of fresh vegetables is listed among the house specialties for vegetarians. Open from 11:30 A.M. to 2:30 P.M. Monday through Friday, and from 5:30 to 10:30 Monday through Saturday. Reservations accepted. AX, CB, DC, MC, V. 537 W. Fairbanks, Winter Park; 647-7575. Expensive to moderate.

AL E. GATOR'S: This full-service restaurant in the Florida Festival, opposite Sea World, features foods popular throughout Florida, and the menu lists such dishes as cracked conch, Gulf snapper, deep-fried zucchini, crab quiche, and mango muffins. Reuben sandwiches are fixed with swamp cabbage (aka hearts of palm), and alligator meat—which tastes a bit like chicken and a bit like fish—is on the menu in about as many different styles as you can name. The deep-fried potato skins alone are worth a trip. Open from 11:30 A.M. to 10 P.M. Sunday through Thursday, to 11 P.M. on Friday and Saturday. No reservations. AX, CB, DC, MC, V. 7001 Sea World Blvd., Orlando; 351-3326. Moderate.

BARNEY'S STEAKHOUSE: The salad bar has 30 entrees, but the big sellers are steaks, prime ribs, and seafood. Voted Orlando citizens' favorite steak house in an annual Orlando *Sentinel* reader survey. Open for lunch from 11:30 A.M. to 3 P.M. Monday to Friday, from 5 to 11 P.M. daily (until midnight on weekends). Reservations accepted only for eight or more. AX, CB, DC, MC, V. 1615 E. Colonial Dr., Orlando; 896-6865. Moderate.

CASA D'ANTONIO'S: An unprepossessing, dimly lit restaurant done in varying shades of red. The food is hearty southern Italian (lasagna, spaghetti, stuffed shells, baked ziti, and such), with good red sauce. There are daily specials. This is the stereotypical Italian restaurant according to most of America. Open from 5 to 10 P.M. daily except Sunday. Reservations accepted. MC, V. 1336 Orange Ave., Winter Park; 629-1139. Moderate.

CHI CHI'S: Though a franchise operation, this always-packed restaurant serves some of the best Mexican food in Orlando, and the menu is incredibly varied. Open from 11 A.M. to midnight daily. No reservations. AX, DC, MC, V. 655 Maguire Blvd., Orlando; 894-0655. Moderate.

FREDDIE'S STEAK HOUSE: This clubby, very masculine eating spot north of Winter Park (in Fern Park) attracts more than its share of male conventioneers and other big meat eaters for its selection of steaks and prime ribs. But the seafood, particularly the fresh pompano and grouper, has it's local fans as well, and Orlando residents often drive here to celebrate something special. A good relish bowl, a crock of cheddar and crackers, a rather ordinary green salad, and a good baked potato are all included in the price of the main dish. Open for dinner only, daily except Sundays from 4:30 P.M. until 1:30 A.M. Reservations accepted. AX, CB, DC, MC, V. U.S.-17-92, Fern Park; 339-3265. Moderate.

LA CANTINA: The decor is fairly nondescript, but the steaks are huge and usually good, and there are Italian specialties as well—eggplant and veal parmigiana, lasagna, and spaghetti. Many of the Disney executives from California make a beeline for the place when they get to town. Locals also keep it jammed, and the wait for a table sometimes stretches to as long as an hour—except in the early evening. Good for families. Open Tuesday through Thursday from 5 to 10:30 P.M., to 11:45 on Friday and Saturday (closed on Sunday and Monday). No reservations accepted. AX, CB, DC, MC, V. 4721 E. Colonial Dr., Orlando; 894-4491. Moderate.

LILI MARLENE'S AVIATORS' RESTAURANT: The single eating spot in the Church Street Station complex, Lili Marlene's is less notable for its food (though the nutty, earthy flavor of the crisply French-fried baked-potato skins offered among the appetizers will haunt you for weeks afterward) than for the decor—high paneled and beamed ceilings, lovely stained-and-leaded glass windows, ceiling fans, stunning chandeliers, oak pews and round and square oak tables, wide-planked wooden floors, and a scattering of props and model airplanes throughout. The long, polished, and mirrored bar is more splendid still. Fish, steaks, chicken, and hamburgers are available. Open for lunch from 11 A.M. to 4 P.M. daily, and from 5:30 P.M. to midnight daily for dinner. No reservations accepted. AX, MC, V. 129 W. Church St., in Church Street Station, Orlando; 422-2434. Moderate.

TWO FLIGHTS UP: Hefty and unusual sandwiches, unusual entrees (chicken, fish, beef, vegetables), terrific meal-sized salads. Liza Minelli loved the place when she was in town; the high noise level, the fanciful food, and the high-tech decor make it about as New York–trendy as the Orlando area gets. Open Monday through Saturday from 11:30 A.M. to 2 A.M. Reservations accepted for parties of eight or more. AX, MC, V. 329 Park Ave. S., Winter Park; 644-9868. Moderate.

VALENTYNE'S: Oysters, crepes, salads, and quiches are on the lunch menu; and oysters, steaks, quiches, shrimp, and stuffed pork can be ordered at dinner. But the plants, bricks, wood, and antiques that decorate the place (in an eclectic quasi–New Orleans style) are what draws the big crowd of young professionals—and keeps them coming back. On Monday night, there's bluegrass entertainment; Tuesday through Saturday, a jazz group performs. Open Monday through Friday from 11:30 A.M. to 3:30 P.M. for lunch, 5:30 P.M. to 1 A.M. Monday through Saturday for dinner. AX, MC, V. 54 N. Orange Ave., Orlando; 849-0862. Moderate to inexpensive.

BEE LINE RESTAURANT: Doctors and lawyers, construction workers and tourists, all manage to find their way to this casual, hard-to-find Tex-Mex cafe, a real old-time hole-in-the-wall. The tacos are the best in town, and the guacamole is great. Since the place only seats about sixty, there's usually a wait after 7 P.M. Open from 5 to 10 P.M. Tuesday through Saturday. No reservations, no credit cards. U.S.-15, Orlando; 277-9829. Inexpensive.

BENNIGAN'S: One of the more interesting of the several chain restaurants on International Drive, this one gets its atmosphere from a jungle of hanging plants (75 different species), and the antique memo-

platoon of lush, oversized tropical plants, this is certainly one of the prettiest places for light meals in Orlando. Waffles, bagels, cereal, Danish pastry, and eggs in more imaginative combinations than usual are offered at breakfast, while big deli-style sandwiches appear for lunch and dinner. But the star of the show is the ice cream produced daily on the premises in out-of-the-ordinary flavors, then sauced (if you choose) with walnuts in syrup, hot fudge, butterscotch, marshmallow, or other toppings. Cheesecakes, layer cakes, pies and strudels, and an assortment of fresh pastries are also available. A real treat. Open from 8 A.M. to midnight Monday through Thursday, to 1 A.M. on Friday and Saturday, and from 10 A.M. to midnight on Sunday. No reservations or credit cards accepted. 327 Park Ave. S., Winter Park; 638-2305. Inexpensive.

GARY'S DUCK INN: The theme at this big restaurant—which has nothing at all to do with duck—is nautical; the menu offers plenty of seafood—shrimp, lobster, scallops, and various seafood platters. And the portions are large, so this is a fine spot for families. Open for lunch from 11:30 A.M. until 3 P.M. Monday through Friday and to 4 P.M. on Sunday (no lunch served on Saturday); dinner menus are available from opening until 10 P.M. Sunday through Thursday, and to 11 P.M. on Friday and Saturday. No reservations accepted. AX, MC, V. 3974 S. Orange Blossom Trail, Orlando; 843-0270. Inexpensive.

LEE AND RICK'S OYSTER BAR AND SEAFOOD HOUSE: Lee and Rick broke up over this restaurant (or so the help will tell you), but the institution they began lives on. And though the decor is basic—linoleum floors, formica-topped tables, and plywood-paneled walls—you can't beat the food: oysters on the half shell raw or steamed (by the bucket if you ask), rock shrimp by the dozen, scallops, snapper, flounder, snow crab, smoked mullet, and combination platters thereof. Beer is available by pitcher or glass; sangría and chablis by the glass or carafe. Open for lunch from 11:30 A.M. to 4 P.M. Monday through Saturday, and for dinner daily from 4 to 11 P.M. Reservations accepted. AX, MC, V. 5621 Old Winter Garden Rd., Orlando; 293-3587. Inexpensive.

ORIENT IV: Orlando's best for Szechuan and Hunan-style Chinese cooking. Tung-Ting shrimp, Tai-Chin chicken, and dry sautéed beef are the bestsellers. Open for lunch from 11:30 A.M. to 3 P.M. Monday through Saturday, and for dinner from 3 to 10:30 P.M. Monday through Thursday, until 11 P.M. on Friday and Saturday, and from 1 to 9:30 P.M. on Sunday. Reservations accepted. AX, CB, DC, MC, V. 104 Altamonte Ave., Altamonte Springs; 830-4444. Inexpensive.

ROSSI'S: A funky, family-owned pizza house—a welcome change from the chains. The double-crusted pizzas stand out. Assorted other Italian specialties also are available. Open for lunch from 11 A.M. to 3 P.M. Monday through Friday, for dinner from 3 to midnight Monday through Thursday, to 1 A.M. on Friday and Saturday, and from 4:30 to 11 P.M. on Sunday. Reservations accepted. DC, MC, V. 5919 S. Orange Blossom Trail, Orlando; 855-5755. Inexpensive.

rabilia strewn around the room—golf clubs and bags, impedimenta from old railroad stations, and more. Quiches and appetizer platters made up of fried mushrooms, fried artichoke hearts, fried zucchini, and fried mozzarella cheese are the specialties, and sirloin and strip steaks are popular. The French fried baked potato skins are terrific. Open from about 11 A.M. until 2 A.M. weekdays, with brunches served from 10 A.M. to 3 P.M. on weekends. The happy hours, from 11 A.M. to 7 P.M. and from midnight to 2 A.M. daily, give you two drinks for the price of one. Reservations accepted. AX, MC, V. 6324 International Dr., Orlando; 351-4436. Inexpensive.

CHESAPEAKE CRAB HOUSE: This single, red-painted, cinderblock building, not much bigger than a Dairy Queen built in the early 1960s, is usually jammed at mealtimes with enthusiastic, hammer-wielding eaters whanging away at bright-red stone crabs, picking over the shells, and piling up the empties in the center of brown-paper covered tables—hardly big enough to contain all the mounds, let alone pitchers (and mugs) of beer and soft drinks (the only libations served here). Informal, to say the least, and fairly inexpensive (though not so dirt cheap as the decor might lead you to believe). Open from 5:30 to 10 P.M. Monday through Thursday, an hour later on Friday and Saturday (closed Sunday). No reservations or credit cards accepted. 1700 N. Orlando Ave., Maitland; 831-0442. Inexpensive.

EAST INDIA ICE CREAM COMPANY: With small round tables that crowd together inside under one of those impossibly ornate pressed-tin ceilings, and reappear outside on a covered terrace among a

NIGHTLIFE

Walt Disney World boasts some of the Orlando area's best after-dark entertainment, but not all of it.

DINNER THEATERS: There are three—**Once Upon A Stage**, at which a buffet meal is followed by a Broadway musical with a professional cast (3376 Edgewater Dr., Orlando; 422-3191); and the **Musicana Dinner Theater**, where an evening's entertainment is made up of a thematic medley of favorite old songs (665 N. Orlando Ave., Winter Park; 628-8700). Expect to pay about $28 to $32 for two at the former, about $30 at the latter, not including drinks. **Theatre on Park** (401 Park Ave. N., Winter Park; 645-5757) presents Broadway classics like *Grease* and *The Wiz* nightly except Monday; submarine sandwiches, hot soup, cheese platters, pastries, and beer and wine are available beforehand at moderate fees (under $4), and tickets sell for $8.25 ($9.50 on Friday and Saturday nights).

THEATER: In summer, the **Annie Russell Summer Theatre** at Winter Park's Rollins College, which presents student productions during the school year, does a repertory season of musicals and drama with professional casts (ticket prices vary from production to production; phone 646-2145 for details). The drama department here is excellent; Tony Perkins is one of the better-known alumni.

NIGHT SPOTS: All the larger hotels have lounges of varying degrees of attractiveness, and many feature live entertainment. For young people, a favorite hangout is **Harrigan's**, a low-key and very informal tavern affair, which offers up a diet of bluegrass and jazz, spiced by an occasional comedian (310 Park Ave. S., Winter Park; 628-1651); **Uncle Waldo's**, in the alley behind Harrigan's, is also popular (325 Moody Way, Winter Park; 645-5214). **Harper's**, the bar at the Cordon Bleu restaurant (537 Fairbanks, Winter Park; 647-7858) attracts a slightly younger crowd, mainly students from nearby Rollins College. There's live entertainment Tuesday through Saturday. **Valentyne's** draws a chic group of young professionals (54 N. Orange Ave., Orlando; 849-0862), and **Bennigan's** (6324 International Dr., Orlando; 351-4435) is jammed at happy hours. **Park Avenue** (4315 N. Orange Blossom Trail, Orlando; 295-3750) has lovely decor, a great sound system, and a big dance floor; when the hubbub gets to you, you can sit outside on the lakeview terrace. **Dallas**, a trendy country-and-western club modeled after *Gilley's* (the Pasadena, Texas, bar where *Urban Cowboy* was filmed), has C&W music on records, as well as its own mechanical bull. **Sullivan's Trailway Lounge** (1108 S. Orange Blossom Trail, Orlando; 843-2934) draws Orlando citizens of all ages; it's the kind of place where you're apt to see a couple in their fifties in his-and-hers outfits out for a night on the town with a daughter and son-in-law, and some of the clogging that can be viewed on the dance floor is as lightning-fast as any you'll see anywhere.

Florida Festival, opposite Sea World, is also a terrific place to while away an evening; in addition to the many food stands, there are drinks and excellent live entertainment at **Al E. Gator's Bar** (7001 Sea World Blvd., Orlando; 351-3326).

Daisy's Basement (18 S. Gertrude's Walk; 425-9991), by the railroad tracks a block and a half north of Church Street Station, features sing-alongs, peanut-throwing contests, silent movies, and a corny old-fashioned melodrama Monday through Saturday. Beer, wine, peanuts, and light sandwiches are served. Admission is $4.75; food costs extra.

Special events: Programs of dance, music, and theater are often presented at the **Mayor Bob Carr Performing Arts Centre** (401 W. Livingston St., Orlando; 849-2363). Check the local papers or call for details.

AFTER DARK AT
CHURCH STREET STATION

If you leave Walt Disney World for only one other Orlando-area attraction, make it this one. Once a pair of decaying hotels in a depressed section of none-too-lively downtown Orlando, the complex known as Church Street Station has few peers elsewhere in the U.S. Orlando residents come here for a lively night on the town; tourists come by the busload; and nobody grumbles too much—especially on the way home—about the cover charge (about $4.25), which admits you to the disco, the restaurant, and two lounges where the management passes out hats and balloons and waiters twirl trays like frisbees and occasionally don the costumes of Stan Laurel, Oliver Hardy, and Charlie Chaplin.

Rosie O'Grady's Goodtime Emporium, a vast wood-floored room with ceiling fans and chandeliers overhead and with railroad-station-waiting-room pews providing the downstairs seating, is the best known of the lounges; the members of the band providing the Dixieland music that keeps the place so lively enter by sliding down a shiny brass firepole onto the small stage. The adjacent **Apple Annie's Courtyard**, decorated with brick floors and plenty of wicker, plants, and fountains, has country-and-western music. **Phineas Phogg's Balloon Works** is the local disco; the rock 'n' roll exhibitions are worth a look even if you don't dance yourself.

Lili Marlene's, described in the "Where to Eat" section of this chapter, is the fourth of the Church Street Station quartet; those who go just for a meal can have their cover charge refunded or applied to the cost of a drink on the way out. (Insider's tip: Pay the cover on the way in, do your drinking at Apple Annie's or Rosie's before dinner, and then have your meal at Lili Marlene's, stopping on the way out immediately afterward for your refund. This way you enjoy the entertainment for next to nothing.) Also note that the cost of many of the specialty drinks includes a charge for the glass itself; if you don't want it, you may turn it in at the gift shop for a $1 refund.

Children are welcome—and a common sight—at all the operations in the complex, except Phineas Phogg's.

FOR MORE INFORMATION

The tabloid-size *Florida Tourist News* (free at stores and hotels) provides good information about things for visitors to see and do around Orlando. *Orlando Magazine*, the top city magazine, has a what-to-do pullout center section, "The Guide," which covers real estate, food, and local goings-on. And the *Orlando Sentinel* publishes what's-doing sections on Fridays ("After Hours") and on Sundays ("Go Guide," published in Spanish and English).

The Kissimmee–St. Cloud Convention and Visitors Bureau (Box 2007; Kissimmee, FL 32741; 847-5000) can send you a wealth of information about where to play golf and tennis outside WDW, and can put you in touch with local canoe liveries and fishing camps. The Orlando Convention and Visitors Bureau (Box 1234; Orlando, FL 32802; 425-1234) can tell you about man-made attractions, local eating spots, and the like.

WELCOME TO
WALT DISNEY's
MAGIC KINGDOM CLUB ®

WELCOME TO Walt Disney's Magic Kingdom Club. For over 20 years, the Magic Kingdom Club has provided the unique Disney leisure-time benefits and programs for millions of employees in thousands of participating organizations. The Magic Kingdom Club offers Club families the most complete, most value-packed ways to visit Walt Disney World Vacation Kingdom in Florida. Your membership card, which has been provided free by your company or organization, is the key to these benefits—and they are available *only* to Club members.

It is important to remember that Club benefits are available year round, and that your Club membership card may be used by any member of your family. To qualify for any Club benefits, however, a valid Club membership card always must be presented at the time of purchase or registration. Company identification, authorizing letters and such, cannot be accepted as proof of Club membership.

Complete, up-to-date price listings may be found in the Club Price Guide, available through your Club Director, or in *Disney News* magazine, the official Magic Kingdom Club magazine.

CHECK THE BLUE PAGES LAST

Information on all the prices and services available at Walt Disney World is listed throughout the preceding pages of this special copy of the Official Guide to Walt Disney World. But as a Club member, many special prices and vacation plans are available to you that are *not* available to the general public, and these are detailed on the pages of this special blue Club insert. Consequently, some of the following information supersedes that noted elsewhere in the Guide. When prices or services are mentioned in the preceding pages of this guide, always check this special section for specific Club rates and information.

Most of the material contained in this guide applies to anyone visiting Walt Disney World. This special blue section will assist you in fully understanding all of the unique Club benefits and special programs available only to Club members.

For additional details or information, contact your Club Director or write the Magic Kingdom Club Travel Center (see the last page of this insert). We sincerely hope you have a memorable visit at Walt Disney World—the Vacation Kingdom of the world.

$$SPECIAL

MAGIC KINGDOM

As a Magic Kingdom Club member, you and your family will always receive the best prices available for tickets at Walt Disney World—and you will always pay less than the general public. Club members receive one dollar discount per day, per person, on all Passport (unlimited-use) tickets. Example: a Club family of four pays $8.00 less than the general public when it purchases 4 Two-Day Passports. To purchase tickets at the special Club price, just present a valid Club membership card at any Main Entrance ticket booth. Current Club prices are:

	One-Day Passport	Two-Day Passport
Adult	$12.00	$20.50
Junior (12 through 17)	11.00	18.50
Child (3 through 11)	10.00	16.50

CLUB PRICES$$

GOLF

Walt Disney World features three of the finest golf courses in Florida—or the entire country, for that matter: the Palm and Magnolia courses at the Golf Resort, and the Lake Buena Vista Club course at Walt Disney World Village. As a Magic Kingdom Club member, you always receive a substantially reduced rate for golf play. The current Club price is $21.00 (versus $26.00 for the general public), which includes greens fee *and* electric cart. Advance reservations are always recommended; just call the Master Starter at 305-824-3625. (For more information on golf at Walt Disney World, see the *Sports* chapter on the preceding pages.)

RIVER COUNTRY

Club members always receive a reduced admission price when purchasing tickets for exciting River Country, located in the Fort Wilderness Campground resort area. A valid Club membership card must be presented upon purchase. Please keep in mind that River Country occasionally is closed for refurbishing during certain periods of the year. (For more information on River Country, see the preceding *Everything Else In The World* chapter.) Current Club prices for admission to River Country are:

	General Public	Club Members
Adult	$6.50	$5.75
Child	$4.25	$3.50

TENNIS

Tennis facilities in Walt Disney World are located at the Contemporary Resort, the Golf Resort, and the Lake Buena Vista Club. As a Magic Kingdom Club member, you receive a special reduced rate for court time. Reservations are recommended. *Contemporary Resort:* 305-824-1000, ext. 3578; *Golf Resort:* 305-824-2200; *Lake Buena Vista Club:* 305-828-3741. (For further details on tennis, see the preceding *Sports* chapter.) Current Club prices are:

	General Public	Club Members
Singles	$4.00/hour	$3.00/hour
Doubles	$6.00/hour	$5.00/hour

EXCLUSIVE CLUB

The best way to visit Walt Disney World is by using one of the exclusive Magic Kingdom Club Vacation Plans, truly the ultimate way to enjoy a Disney vacation in Florida. Each year, thousands of Club families take advantage of these specially designed plans for Club members. All components and features have been tested for years to assure maximum value and acceptance, and are fine-tuned to deliver the ideal vacation—with neither too little nor too much to do. And all Club Vacation Plans are "individual"—you are never regimented or grouped with other visitors. Your selection of a specific plan will depend primarily on your own choice of accommodations, length of stay, and the number of special features you desire. And you can be assured that no matter which plan you choose, Magic Kingdom Club Vacation Plans offer the finest, most value-packed Walt Disney World experience available today.

1982 MAGIC KINGDOM CLUB VACATION PLANS AT WALT DISNEY WORLD

Here is a summary of Club Vacation Plans for 1982. Complete details and rates appear in the 1982 Membership Guide, available from your Club Director or by writing to the Magic Kingdom Club Travel Center (see the last page of this insert for address). Junior and children's rates also are available for all plans.

VACATION PLANS

WORLD VACATION

This is the ultimate vacation experience, with unlimited access to the Magic Kingdom, dining, and recreational facilities in Walt Disney World.

- Five nights/six days.
- Accommodations in the Contemporary Resort Hotel Tower or the Walt Disney World Resort Villas.
- Admission and unlimited use of all attractions in the Magic Kingdom (except the Shootin' Gallery).
- Unlimited use of all Walt Disney World recreational activities and facilities.
- Breakfast, lunch, and dinner at any Walt Disney World restaurant or dinner show (excludes Magic Kingdom fast-food locations and room service).
- Unlimited use of the transportation system in the Walt Disney World Vacation Kingdom.

Priced from $568 per adult, double occupancy.

VACATION KINGDOM HOLIDAY

The most popular family vacation plan in the Walt Disney World Resort Complex, featuring accommodations in the Disney hotels.

- Four nights/five days.
- Accommodations at the Contemporary Resort Hotel, Polynesian Village Resort Hotel, or Golf Resort Hotel.
- Admission and unlimited use of all attractions in the Magic Kingdom (except the Shootin' Gallery).
- A variety of dining and recreational activities.
- Unlimited use of the transportation system in the Walt Disney World Vacation Kingdom.

Priced from $346 per adult, double occupancy.

CAMPING JAMBOREE

At the Fort Wilderness Campground, you'll find a heap of outdoor fun and recreation, plus fully equipped campsites.

- Four nights/five days.
- Accommodations in the Fort Wilderness Campground (campsite only, or with a Fleetwood Travel Trailer).
- Admission and unlimited use of all attractions in the Magic Kingdom (except the Shootin' Gallery).
- A variety of dining and recreational activities.
- Unlimited use of the transportation system in the Walt Disney World Vacation Kingdom.

Priced from $151 per adult, double occupancy.

VILLA HIDEAWAY ADVENTURE

For a perfect home away from home, choose a luxurious Walt Disney World Resort Villa for your vacation.

- Four nights/five days.
- Accommodations in a fully equipped two-bedroom Walt Disney World Resort Villa.
- Admission and unlimited use of all attractions in the Magic Kingdom (except the Shootin' Gallery).
- A variety of dining and recreational activities.
- Unlimited use of the transportation system in the Walt Disney World Vacation Kingdom.

Priced from $415 per adult, double occupancy.

VILLAGE HOLIDAYS

Enjoy family-sized accommodations at one of four high-rise hotels in the Walt Disney World Village Hotel Plaza.

- Three, four, or five nights.
- Accommodations in the Walt Disney World Village Hotel Plaza.
- Admission and unlimited use of all attractions in the Magic Kingdom (except the Shootin' Gallery).
- Additional dining and recreational activities.

Priced from $165 per adult, double occupancy.

FAMILY GETAWAY

Budget-priced accommodations in nearby hotels make this an ideal vacation solution.

- Three nights/four days.
- Accommodations at one of several nearby quality hotels.
- Admission and unlimited use of all attractions in the Magic Kingdom (except the Shootin' Gallery).

Priced from $97 per adult, double occupancy.

ADDITIONAL BENEFITS

Magic Kingdom Club members also are entitled to a variety of other special benefits in the Walt Disney World Resort/Central Florida area.

WALT DISNEY WORLD VILLAGE HOTEL PLAZA

Club families not taking advantage of a Magic Kingdom Club Vacation Plan are eligible for a 10 percent discount on accommodations only, for each night spent at the *Dutch Resort Hotel*, *Travelodge Tower*, *Hotel Royal Plaza*, and *Howard Johnson's Motor Lodge* in the Walt Disney World Village Hotel Plaza. (This applies only to reservations you make directly through the hotel or the Club Travel Center, at regular rates, and not using a travel agent.) A valid Club membership card must be presented upon registration.

FLORIDA CYPRESS GARDENS

Beautiful Cypress Gardens, located approximately 45 minutes from Walt Disney World, is one of Florida's most delightful attractions. Plan to spend a half day or more enjoying the world-famous Water Ski Show, elegant landscaping, and the new Southern Crossroads and Living Forest areas. Magic Kingdom Club members receive $1.00 off the regular admission price upon presentation of a valid Club membership card.

HOWARD JOHNSON'S MOTOR LODGES

As the Official Host of the Magic Kingdom Club, over 400 participating Howard Johnson's Motor Lodges offer Club members a 10 percent discount on double-occupied rooms, *nationwide*. There are twelve Howard Johnson's in the Orlando area alone, and many others throughout Florida; most participate in this program. Advance reservations must be made by calling Howard Johnson's toll-free reservation number (800-654-2000), and a valid membership card must be presented upon registration.

NATIONAL CAR RENTAL

National Car Rental is the Official Car Rental Company of the Magic Kingdom Club and offers Club members a 9 percent discount on all unlimited-mileage rentals in Florida (except on Class "A" economy cars). This can add up to a real savings over several days of vacation driving. Discounts also are available to Club members nationwide and throughout the world. Reservations are recommended, and may be made by calling toll-free 800-328-4567.

NORWEGIAN CARIBBEAN LINES CRUISES

While vacationing in Florida, you also may want to take advantage of a relaxing ocean cruise. In conjunction with Norwegian Caribbean Lines, the Magic Kingdom Club offers members a choice of exciting Caribbean and Bahamas cruises at special year-round reduced rates. Choose from 3-day, 4-day, or 7-day cruises to the most exciting islands in the Caribbean.

For complete information, please write the Magic Kingdom Club Travel Center (see below).

RESERVATIONS AND INFORMATION

The Magic Kingdom Club Travel Center provides an exclusive information and reservation service for all Club members and their families. Our Travel Center staff is specially trained to serve all your needs as a Club member. Because accommodation availability at Walt Disney World is always changing, we suggest that you write for information, but *call* for reservations. We also recommend that in order to be sure of getting the dates you want, be sure to make reservations at least six months to one year in advance of your desired arrival date. The Travel Center maintains a special air/car reservation service so that we also can handle your flight and auto rental needs when you book your vacation. Please ask for assistance from our friendly and knowledgeable Travel Center personnel.

For reservations or further information, please call or write:

Walt Disney's Magic Kingdom Club
Travel Center
P.O. Box 600, Lake Buena Vista, Florida 32830
305-824-2600
Always include your Chapter number.
Business hours: 8:30 A.M.-8 P.M., Monday through Friday ● 9 A.M.-7 P.M. Saturday and Sunday
(Eastern Standard Time)

All prices, ticket media, and benefits subject to change without notice.